Other Ways to
Win

Third Edition

KENNETH C. GRAY   EDWIN L. HERR

Other Ways to

Creating Alternatives for High School Graduates

Third Edition

CORWIN PRESS
A SAGE Publications Company
Thousand Oaks, California

For information:

Corwin Press
A Sage Publications Company
2455 Teller Road
Thousand Oaks, California 91320
www.corwinpress.com

Sage Publications Ltd.
1 Oliver's Yard
55 City Road
London EC1Y 1SP
United Kingdom

Sage Publications India Pvt. Ltd.
B-42, Panchsheel Enclave
Post Box 4109
New Delhi 110 017 India

Printed in the United States of America

Library of Congress Cataloging-in-Publication Data

Gray, Kenneth C.
Other ways to win: Creating alternatives for high school graduates/Kenneth C. Gray and Edwin L. Herr.—3rd ed.
    p. cm.
Includes bibliographical references and index.
ISBN 978-1-4129-1780-3 (cloth)—ISBN 978-1-4129-1781-0 (pbk.)
    1. Career education—United States. 2. High school students—Vocational guidance—United States. 3. High school graduates—Employment—United States. 4. Postsecondary education—United States. 5. High school graduates—United States-Social conditions. I. Herr, Edwin L. II. Title.
LC1037.5.G73 2006
370.11′3′0973—dc22   2005022992

This book is printed on acid-free paper.

            09   10   9   8   7   6   5   4

Acquisitions Editor:	Elizabeth Brenkus
Editorial Assistant:	Desirée Enayati
Production Editor:	Beth A. Bernstein
Copy Editor:	Jennifer E. Withers
Typesetter:	C&M Digitals (P) Ltd.
Proofreader:	Caryne Brown
Indexer:	Karen Mckenzie
Cover Designer:	Michael Dubowe
Graphic Designer:	Scott Van Atta

Contents

Preface to the Third Edition

I t has been 10 years since the first edition of *Other Ways to Win* was published. Much has happened in 10 years: some good, some not so good. One thing has not changed. The "one way to win" mentality—the idea that the only chance of winning economically is to get at least a 4-year college degree—is still very much with us. In fact, it could be argued that the federal No Child Left Behind legislation, with its stated goal of preparing every child for college, has institutionalized the paradigm. Unfortunately, the negative effects of the "one way to win" mentality on young Americans and the nation's economy also have not changed. Factors such as globalization and state-mandated high stakes testing have made matters worse, not better. Presently, 1 out of every 10 ninth graders in the United States graduates from a 4-year college and finds commensurate employment. We wish after 10 years this were not the case; we wish a third edition of *Other Ways to Win* were not necessary. But because the success rate for teens in the academic middle has not improved, we write this third edition. We have updated the figures and charts with more recent data, and we have rewritten much of book to take into account the new realties this generation of teens now faces.

Fortunately, there are still "other ways to win" for teens from the academic middle. Our goals remain the same, namely to point out the negative effects of the "one way to win" mentality on those in the academic middle and to identify other ways for this group to pursue careers that are both rewarding and lucrative, many of which require college but at the 1- and 2-year pre-baccalaureate level.

—Ken Gray
—Edwin Herr

Preface to the Second Edition

This second edition of *Other Ways to Win* was prompted by the many requests from readers of the original. They wondered in particular if there were more recent statistics regarding other ways for teens—in the academic middle—to win. Thus, new data have replaced old where necessary and possible. We have also modified some of our observations and recommendations as a result of both changing times and discussions with educators across the nation.

Alas, we had wished that the plight of the academic middle would be greatly improved and a second edition of *Other Ways to Win* would not be necessary. But, although progress has been made, the need to spread the other ways to win message still exists. Teens from the academic middle still need a lot of help; all too many are still heading off to college, thinking it is the only way to win, and the success rate among those who do is still one in four. But there are other, better, alternatives. . . . If you don't believe it, read on!

Preface to the First Edition

Having worked earlier in our careers as both high school teachers and counselors, we enjoy being in high schools, particularly at the beginning or end of any high school day, as students file in and out of the building. It is always fascinating to see the diversity, fashions, and interpersonal dramas that are played out. It always leaves us with a feeling of wellness, that the future is in good hands. Well, at least it used to.

During the past 10 years, we have found ourselves worrying more and more about high school–aged adolescents as they approach graduation. Not all of them, of course; in particular, not the top 25% or 30%, the academically blessed, who seem to have everything going for them. We are concerned about the fate of the rest, particularly those from the academic middle. We worry because these adolescents face a difficult and uncertain labor market. We worry because they have been told there is only one way to win, namely, to prepare for the professional ranks by going to a 4-year college. Unfortunately, although this career advice is realistic for some high school students, it is clearly unrealistic for many of them. Particularly for many of those from the academic middle, this advice is totally out of sync both with their high school academic records and with the labor market they will face if they actually graduate with a 4-year college degree. Tragically, for these students, the only certainty is that the majority will accumulate significant student loan debt in the process.

Thus, we wrote this book for those in the academic middle of our high school classes, their parents, and their teachers—to alert them to an important fact: There are other ways to win in today's labor market. Our intent is not necessarily to dissuade students from attempting a 4-year college program; rather, it is to point out alternatives that carry, for many, a higher probability of success, as well as lower tuition costs. We argue that the key to future economic security is not education per se, but rather obtaining the occupational skills that lead to high skill/high wage work. Whereas some of these skills are typically learned in 4-year colleges or graduate schools, others can be learned at 1- or 2-year postsecondary technical institutions, and still others can be learned in work-based programs sponsored by employers and employee groups.

This book is divided into three parts. In Part I, the one way to win belief is explored in detail. In Part II, the secondary and postsecondary experiences of those in the academic middle are analyzed in order to document the frequent failure of those who attempt a 4-year college degree program to either complete a degree or attain a professional job. In Part III, we outline three major steps and various strategies that high school educators can take to modify the high school program in order to create other ways to win for those in the academic middle. We hope, ultimately, to create advocates for the academically average and to bring them into the mainstream of educational reform debates.

ACKNOWLEDGMENTS

Many individuals have made this book possible, beginning with Alice Foster, formerly of Corwin Press, who urged the consideration of the project in the first place, 10 years ago. We wish to acknowledge in particular the contribution of Sang Hoon Bae, our research assistant, who did much of the new data research for the third edition, and to all those, too numerous to name, whose encouragement regarding the importance of the topic kept the project moving along. Our thanks to you all.

Corwin Press gratefully acknowledges the contributions of the following reviewers:

John Casper
Supervisor of Secondary
   Instruction
Nelson County Public Schools
Bardstown, KY

Craig Spiers
Principal
Joliet Township High
   School
Joliet, IL

Robert Todd
Principal
Theodore Roosevelt High
   School
San Antonio, TX

Paul Martin
Principal
Kenwood High School
Baltimore, MD

Joseph Cronin
Professor
Boston University
Boston, MA

About the Authors

Kenneth C. Gray is Professor of Education in the Workforce Education and Development Program at Pennsylvania State University, Main Campus. He holds a BA in Economics from Colby College, an MA in Counseling Psychology from Syracuse University, and a doctorate in Technical Education from Virginia Tech. Prior to joining the faculty at Penn State, he was Superintendent of the Vocational Technical High School System in Connecticut and has been a high school English teacher, guidance counselor, and administrator. He has published widely and is frequently quoted in the national press. He is coauthor with Edwin Herr of the text *Workforce Education: The Basics*. His last book, *Getting Real: Helping Teens Find Their Future*, addressed the importance of helping teenagers develop career direction as a prerequisite to postsecondary success.

Edwin L. Herr is Distinguished Professor Emeritus of Education (Counselor Education and Counseling Psychology) and Emeritus Associate Dean, College of Education, Pennsylvania State University. He received his BS degree in Business Education from Shippensburg State Teachers College (Now Shippensburg University), and an MA and EdD in Counseling and Student Personnel Administration from Teachers College, Columbia University, where he was an Alumni Fellow. A former business teacher, school counselor, and director of guidance, he previously served as Assistant and Associate Professor of Counselor Education at the State University of New York at Buffalo (1963–1966) and as the First Director of the Bureau of Guidance Services and the Bureau of Pupil Personnel Services, Pennsylvania Department of Education (1966–1968). The author or coauthor of more than 300 articles and 32 books and monographs, he is Past President of the American Counseling Association, Past President of the National Vocational Guidance Association, and Past President of the Association for Counselor Education and Supervision. He has been elected a Fellow of the American Counseling Association, the American Psychological Association, the American Psychological Society, the American Association for Applied and Preventive Psychology, and the National Career Development Association. Among the many awards he has received are the Eminent Career Award of the National Career Development Association, the Extended Research Award from the American Counseling Association, and the Counseling Innovation and Vision Award of the Association for Counselor Education and Supervision.

PART I

The One Way to Win Myth

CHAPTER ONE

The One Way to Win Myth

How beautiful is youth! how bright it gleams
With its illusions, aspirations, dreams.

—*Longfellow (1807–1882)*,
"Morituri Salutamus"

Each year, almost three million teens graduate from high school, and most do the same thing. They heed the ubiquitous "one way to win" message and head off to college, mostly 4-year colleges, and then a large percentage fail. Of those who go to 4-year colleges, or to 2-year colleges with the intent to transfer, about half at best will graduate, and of those who do, about half will end up in jobs they could probably have gotten right out of high school. But this is only half the story, because not all teens graduate from high school (one-third drop out and do not graduate), and among those who do graduate, 30% go to work. In either case, these teens are viewed by their teachers, their peers, and society in general as "losers"—failures because they failed to heed the one way to win message, they did not do what everyone else did, they did not go to college.

As will be documented shortly, if the only acceptable goal we have for all teens is a 4-year college degree and finding commensurate employment thereafter, the present success rate in the United States is 10%. That's right, *ten percent*. Not very impressive, is it? One wonders if we could not do a little better—by creating and

3

valuing other ways to win for some teens, particularly the majority from the academic middle.

THE ACADEMIC MIDDLE

The focus of this book is on today's high school–age youth, though not necessarily all of them. Not the 10% who are already winning: the academically blessed, the kids who take advanced placement or honors courses. These teens are doing just fine; if anything, they already are getting more attention than they deserve. This book is about most of the rest, the largely silent and neglected academic middle: the students who fall in the second and third quartiles of their high school class, those who make up the invisible middle. Sometimes they are referred to as the "unspecial," neither being academically blessed nor fitting into special education categories— those whose academic record and college entrance tests predict a questionable future in baccalaureate education (see Chapter 4).

One way to picture those who make up the academic middle is to think back to the last high school graduation you remember: the long line of graduates in caps and gowns, some jubilant, some crying, most just silent and pensive. There were those whose names everyone knew, the so-called "future leaders," the National Honor Society members, those who were heading off to those name brand colleges that are the hope of every parent. But what about all the rest? What about the academically average kids, whose names even their teachers have a hard time remembering? These are the teens who make up the silent middle of their high school class. They exist in every high school, no matter how wealthy or poor, or how urban or rural the district.

Given the present prevalence of the one way to win message that everyone should be preparing to go to college, the tack taken here is to define the middle in terms of how well they are prepared academically for college (see Table 4.3). Using the criteria of the 4-year high school grade point average, courses completed in high school, and College Board tests, and using the most liberal definition of academically prepared, research suggests that at least 60% of high school students who graduate are neither academically prepared for college nor special education students with significant learning disabilities.

Some (30%) of these teens go to work full time, though few will have been prepared to do so by their high school. And the rest? They go to college not really knowing why, except that they do not know what else to do, and despite being somewhat unprepared to handle college-level academic studies. And, of course, most fail with mathematically predictable certainty.

This book is about these teens from the academic middle. They are the real challenge for education reform. Their post–high school plans are largely inconsistent with reality; they are floundering, and ultimately, many end up failing. The objective of this book is to help all those who would—teachers, parents, and policy makers—do a better job by creating and valuing "other ways" for these teens to win.

There are, of course, many reasons why teens in the academic middle lose out in high school, starting with the Taylorist idea that they are somehow less important than the academically blessed (see Gray, 1993). This is not, however, the central problem. The core issue is that virtually everyone has come to believe in the "one way to win" paradigm.

SECTION I

The One Way to Win Paradigm

The "one way to win" mentality is best explained by expressed views of teens themselves. Such insights can be gained from the annual national survey of college freshmen (American Council on Education, 2004), as well as survey and other data from the National Center for Education Statistics (NCES). The one way to win paradigm preaches a three-part doctrine (what teens should do when they graduate from high school, why they should pursue this course, and where in the labor force they will find their reward) regarding the path all teens should follow because it is the best chance of leading to future economic success.

The One Way to Win Paradigm Defined

The one way to win proponents have a three-part message for teens.

1.   All teens should pursue a 4-year college degree.

Within two years of graduating from high school, 72% of graduates have enrolled in higher education. Ninety-eight percent of college freshmen in the 2003–2004 American Freshman Survey, for example, were 18 or 19 years old and had just graduated from high school that same year. One might expect that at least half would be pursuing 1- or 2-year associate degrees. Not so! Eighty percent indicated that they expect to earn bachelor's degrees. Only 2% indicated that they planned to study at the pre-baccalaureate 1- and 2-year level in technical fields such health care, information technology, or manufacturing; only 1% of women so indicated.

2.   Why? Because it is the only sure way to get a high-paying job.

Most young adults are in college in hopes that it will lead to future economic gain—economists call it "labor market advantage." Table 1.1 reports the results of asking 2003 college freshmen what were important reasons for matriculating. Arguably, four of the top five are economic reasons. In an earlier survey, a somewhat startling 72% of freshmen reported that they already foresaw the need to go to graduate school.

3.   Where? In the professional ranks.

When asked what job they would like to have by the time they are 30, high school students overwhelmingly pick professional occupations (see Table 1.2). About half of all young men and more than two-thirds of all young women surveyed as high school seniors pick

Table 1.1   Reasons Noted as Very Important in Deciding to Go to College: 2003 College Freshmen

	Total (%)	Men (%)	Women (%)
To learn about things that interest me	73	73	80
To get a better job	70	70	70
To get training for a specific career	70	66	73
To make more money	70	73	66
Parents wanted me to go	40	37	41

Plan to go to graduate school: 72%.

Source: Compiled from American Council on Education, 2004.

Table 1.2   Percentage of High School Seniors Who Expected
to Be Employed in Various Occupations, by Gender

Occupation	All seniors		Males		Females	
	1972	1992	1972	1992	1972	1992
Clerical	14.2	3.5	1.9	1.2	25.5	5.7
Craftsman/trade	7.5	2.8	15.1	5.3	0.5	0.3
Farming	1.6	1.0	2.7	1.6	0.6	0.4
Homemaker	3.1	1.2	0.0	0.1	5.9	2.2
Laborer	2.5	0.8	4.9	1.4	0.3	0.1
Manager	3.1	6.0	5.1	6.6	1.3	5.4
Military	2.4	3.2	4.1	5.6	0.8	0.8
Operative	2.3	1.2	3.9	2.1	0.8	0.2
Professional	45.4	59.0	41.8	49.3	48.8	68.8
Proprietor	1.8	6.7	3.2	8.7	0.5	4.8
Protective services	2.2	4.1	4.2	6.9	0.4	1.4
Sales	3.0	1.9	2.7	2.3	3.3	1.5
Service	4.2	2.6	1.6	0.6	6.7	4.6
Technical	6.6	6.0	8.8	8.4	4.6	3.7
Total	**100.0**	**100.0**	**100.0**	**100.0**	**100.0**	**100.0**

Sources: Compiled from *National Longitudinal Study, 1972 (base year),* by the National Center for Educational Statistics, 1972, Washington, DC: U.S. Department of Education; and *National Educational Longitudinal Study of 1988, 1992 Second Follow-Up,* by the National Center for Educational Statistics, 1992, Washington, DC: U.S. Department of Education.

Note: Percentages may not add to 100 due to rounding.

professional occupations. Only 8.4% of males and 3.7% of females indicate aspirations in technical occupations. In a period of significant and growing skill shortages in skilled blue/gold-collar occupations, it is noteworthy that only 5% of males and virtually no females (0.3%) expected to be employed in the highly lucrative and in-demand skilled craft careers. As a result, many industries are experiencing skill shortages, which can only be solved by importing non-native-born workers or transferring the work overseas.

With this final piece of information about high school graduates' career plans, the "operational definition" of the one way to win paradigm is complete.

The one way to win paradigm is the belief that the only hope for future economic security for today's youth is to earn at least a 4-year college degree because it will lead to a good-paying job in the professions.

The extent to which all high school graduates appear to be internalizing the one way to win paradigm, or at least the get a baccalaureate degree part, is truly astonishing. The most recent Department of Labor Projections predict a steady decline in the percentages of recent high school graduates who pursue anything but a 4-year degree. In a 2003–2004 survey of entering college freshmen, 98% indicated that they planned to get at least a bachelor's degree; 74% were already planning on graduate study.

Equally intriguing, if not depressing, is to realize that it is the one way to win message that is at the heart of present educational reform efforts and the federal No Child Left Behind legislation. Preparing everyone for college is the goal of this legislation (*Vocational Training News,* 2004). While the title may suggest each child deserves individual attention, the legislation in truth suggests a one way to win fix for all.

Merriam-Webster's Collegiate Dictionary (2004) defines *mania* as "excessive or unreasonable enthusiasm." The current enthusiasm for a 4-year college degree is excessive and unreasonable; thus it does not seem unjust to suggest it is manic in nature. It is excessive because it is expressed without any consideration of the reality that not all teens are blessed with the academic talent to do college-level work or mature enough to pursue college at age 18, or that many just plain do not like school.

Furthermore, the one way to win mantra and the legislation that flows from it ignore the reality that while most teens indicate that they want to go to college to get a good-paying job, very few have taken the time to think about the details of such a goal and to consider in particular the reality that the economy will not generate enough jobs that pay them a college-level wage even if they were successful in completing a baccalaureate degree. Most teens aspire to the professional ranks, but only 21% of all jobs in the United States require a 4-year degree or higher; in fact, only 12% require just a 4-year degree. Meanwhile, less than 2% of teens aspire to preprofessional technical careers, which are among the fastest-growing and largest sources of high skills employment in the economy.

But the teens themselves are not necessarily to blame for such restrictive and unrealistic views regarding future career opportunity. Adults share much of the fault. It is the adults who preach the one way to win message to all and who are unwilling to accept alternative education and career choices. The fact is that many teens go to college because they have no idea what they want to do or what options are available other than attending a 4-year baccalaureate degree program. It is what their parents want, so they apply, and with few exceptions, getting admitted somewhere is all but guaranteed. Higher education, particularly at the university level, has become the default decision for today's youths and their parents as well. Not knowing what else to do, they head off to college with about the same level of commitment as if they were going from middle school to high school. And then most, particularly those from the academic middle, end up failing.

Section II

The Human, Financial, and Economic Development

So what? you may ask. Who cares if the majority of teens from the academic middle of American high schools go to college, despite being academically unprepared and lacking even the most rudimentary career motives? After all, it's a free country; it is their and their parents' decision to make, isn't it? And it is true that this would not be a cause for general concern—or none of our business, for that matter—were it not for the facts that (1) students are mostly subsidized with public money, not just spending their or even their parents' money, and the majority of higher education costs are borne by the taxpayers, many of whom never have kids in college; (2) most teens from the academic middle who try the one way to win route are not academically qualified in the first place and thus fail; and (3) the whole situation has led to the country's having to rely on non-native-born immigrants to fill many of the most critical jobs in the economy, thus creating potential for serious long-run negative impacts on the nation's economic health. While public opinion pollsters report that the public generally agrees that "all students who are capable should go to college" and are willing to support this with tax dollars, few understand that probably at least half who go to college are not qualified and/or have no idea why they are going, except that they do not know what else to do. One doubts that the public would be so generous with its tax dollars were this reality widely known.

COSTS OF THE ONE WAY TO WIN PARADIGM

For the academically blessed (the top 20%—those who attend a so-called medallion or prestigious college or at least a college employers may have heard of), the one way to win paradigm makes sense. The rest would be wise to at least consider other alternatives, and the nation would be wise to provide, promote, and value those who pursue these alternatives.

Wise because there are human costs, financial dollars and cents costs, and economic development costs associated with the one way to win mentality. Wise because the one way to win paradigm is not benign for many students. It is not like trying out for the senior play or some athletic team in high school where, in the long run, the stakes, win or lose, are not a big deal. But pursuing the one way to win paradigm without adequate academic qualifications or at least tentative career motives has long-run consequences, and they are a big deal. The resulting costs accrue to the students, their parents, and society.

And let us not forget the more than half of all teens who either drop out of high school or do not go to college. The one way to win philosophy, as will be pointed out below, hurts them as well, even though they never see a college dorm.

THE HUMAN COST OF THE ONE WAY TO WIN PARADIGM

There is a fundamental problem with the one way to win philosophy. If the only way to win is to get a 4-year college degree in hopes that it will lead to a high-paying job in the professional ranks, then at best, only 1 in 10 high school graduates will win.

To illustrate this problem, let us imagine a typical ninth grade classroom of 20 teenagers and, using national data, project how many, under present educational policy, will win the one way to win game.

As illustrated in Figure 1.1, the first reality is that the national dropout rate in the United States is now 33%. The dropout rate has increased in all but seven states since the beginning of the 1990s. Six of the original teens will not graduate from high school. Importantly, the dropout rate has risen at the very time states have added more

Figure 1.1   Human Cost of the One Way to Win Paradigm

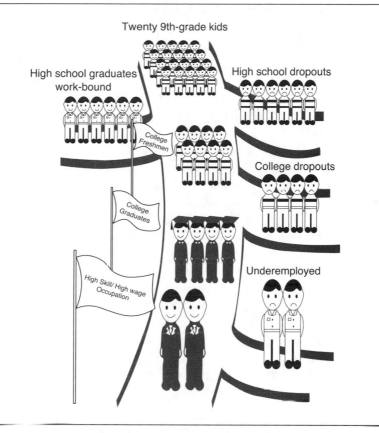

Note: Illustration by Kee Ho Choi.

graduation and testing requirements and de-emphasized alternatives such as career and technical education (CTE). As a result, it is difficult not to conclude that there is a cause-and-effect relationship and to conclude that public policy based on the one way to win mentality makes some kids liabilities; they leave school and no one much cares.

The second reality is that even during the economic boom years of the 1990s, a persistent 30% of high school graduates went directly to work, and this statistic is not likely to change soon. Thus, of the 14 from the original 20 that do graduate from high school, 30% will go to work directly after high school.

We have now accounted for one half of all entering ninth graders. Half of all teens who start the ninth grade in public high school either drop out or go to work, not college, when they graduate.

It is hard to see how the one way to win philosophy will lead to education programs that will help them. In fact, if anything, this philosophy and the educational policies it spawns, such as No Child Left Behind legislation, seem mostly to ignore these kids or even to justify their neglect and the elimination of programs—such as high school CTE—that could serve them by providing occupational skills that pay well and are in demand.

The third reality is that the national combined dropout rate from 4-year colleges and 2-year transfer programs at community college is at best 50%. By one estimate, only 18% of entering high school ninth graders will earn a 4-year college degree. Thus, of the 10 teens in the original ninth grade class who went to college, 5% or 25% of the original group of 20 will graduate from college. Was the college experience of benefit to the 5 who did not graduate? Probably not. The research is clear that the labor market benefits from college go only to those who graduate. One thing that is clear, however, is that the experience was not free. The majority of students who drop out of college do so with student loan debt and statistically are the most likely to default on their student loans.

The final reality is that while we might suppose that the 5 young adults who earn a university degree are the winners, the well-kept secret is that there are not enough 4-year college-level jobs to go around; in fact, there are almost twice as many 4-year college graduates as there are job openings that require this level of education. The most recent studies suggest that 43% of today's 4-year college graduates end up in jobs that do not require this level of education or have career potential. Colleges love to report how many graduates find jobs; what they do not report is what kinds of jobs the graduates end up in. Do the jobs pay a wage that justifies the expense of college, or could students probably have gotten the jobs directly out of high school?

This leaves 2 of the original 20 ninth graders who win. Just 2. Losers in the world dominated by the one way to win message outnumber winners 9 to 1. Such a waste! And while among the 18 losers, some will, in fact, do just fine economically, but they are nonetheless often stereotyped as inferior and looked down upon, and they know it.

The Rope Climbing Allegory

A less publicized but more insidious and cruel human cost that results from the one way to win mentality is the resulting pejorative attitude toward all who do not pursue and earn a 4-year college degree or who get one but end up in low skill/low wage employment. To illustrate the human cost of the one way to win paradigm when preached to all kids of all ages, let us recall an experience some of us may have had in elementary school—an experience where most of us were losers and many of us had no hope of ever succeeding—and remember how that situation felt. Some kids must also feel the same way in high schools that value only one way to win.

If you attended an elementary school that had a gym, chances are that unless it was a new one, it was equipped with what was then standard physical education equipment, namely, a set of exercise ropes that hung from the ceiling. Their use was quite limited (once or twice a year) and, in today's litigious times, a bit alarming. Specifically, the ropes were used to test fifth and sixth graders' rope climbing skills by seeing if they could shinny up the rope to the gym ceiling.

Once or twice a year, students were marched down to the gym, the PE teacher would fiddle with some little rope on the wall, and down would come the big ropes from the ceiling. Of course, safety equipment was provided. It took the form of gray, dusty mats that were at most two inches thick and, even to an elementary school kid, not very reassuring.

To this day, it is not clear exactly what the point of this experience was. We never practiced rope climbing, we never did math problems related to rope climbing, and we did not read about famous people who climbed ropes.

The important point, though, of this allegory is that there was only one way to win or to pass the rope climbing test: climb to the top of the rope. Getting just a little off the ground or even partway up did not count. Nothing else was valued except total success in climbing all the way up to the ceiling of the gym. The way this rope climbing in gym class was conducted is similar to the way society values only the one way to win goal of pursuing a 4-year degree and nothing else.

Of course, some kids, not many but a few, approached the ropes with confidence and proceeded to shinny to the top. It was, to the rest of us, something close to mystical; we were awestruck. Looking back on it today, it would seem some kids were just blessed with rope climbing intelligence: they did not practice rope climbing, it was not something they worked at, they could just do it. And, of course, because it was the only way to win, these kids got much praise for their achievement. It reminds one of what must be the experience of high school students who are academically blessed at birth. Many of these students do not have to study much at all in high school, but they do very well and become the stars of every graduating class.

But what about the rest of the student population, those who were not born blessed with rope climbing intelligence? We got a chance to fail in front of everyone else. We were certified failures in rope climbing. For those of us who could hardly get off the ground, the rope climbing test was not a very motivating experience.

The problem was that to those of us who were weak or fat, there was, in our eyes, no hope that we would ever be able to climb the ropes. For many of us, the only effect of the experience was to confirm that we hated gym, and similarly, many teens who find academics difficult learn to hate school as well. Clearly this was a scene we were never going to be a part of, so why bother? In fact, if we had a choice, we would not have gone to the gym at all; we would have in effect dropped out of the whole experience. The point is that this is how many kids in the academic middle view high school. What we want them to do, they view as impossible; in turn, what they want to do (go to work, go to technical schools, etc.) and what they can do are not valued, so they either stop coming to school or they come and go through the motions. Educators label them as unmotivated, but in fact, their attitude is the same as those of us who knew we could never pass the rope climbing test nor would we want to if we could; to some of us, climbing to the top of the gym on a rope was terrifying even if we could have done it. Likewise, teens in today's high schools who do not buy the one way to win idea are alienated, left out, unmotivated, and looked down upon. It is not right!

THE DOLLARS AND CENTS COST
TO STUDENTS AND THEIR PARENTS

The one way to win mentality that has gripped the nation might not be a concern—or at least as much of a concern—if students and parents were spending just their own money and they found it affordable. In reality, however, and despite efforts by higher education to debunk the truth, college is costly; college costs continue to increase at rates higher than inflation. Between 1986 and 1996, tuition, room, and board increased 20% at public institutions and 31% at private. According to the College Board Annual Survey (2004), college costs rose 14% in 2003–2004 and another 10% in 2004–2005. More important is the ability of families to pay. To paraphrase research by the NCES (1998), after a period of decline in the 1960s and 1970s, tuition, room, and board rose to 15% of family income at public institutions and 42% at private. For a family at the 10th percentile of family income, it amounts to 32% of income at public and 88% of income at private colleges.

A second reality of higher education costs is that now, the majority of all full-time students need financial aid. According to the NCES (1998), 76% of all full-time undergraduate students in 2003– 2004 received financial aid. More important, financial aid is today just a code word for debt. In the 1970s and even the early 1980s, only a small part of a student financial aid package was loans, whereas now, it is closer to two-thirds. Of the full-time students receiving financial aid in 2003–2004, 62% of the aid was student loans that must be paid back. The States Higher Education Research Project (Gross, 2004) reports that based on normal public sector lenders' standards, 39% of students who graduate do so with "unmanageable" student loan debt and thus will have poor credit ratings the day they graduate. Forty percent of graduates leave with a debt equal to or greater than $20,000.

Figure 1.2   Grants and Loans as a Percentage of Total Aid, 1994–2004

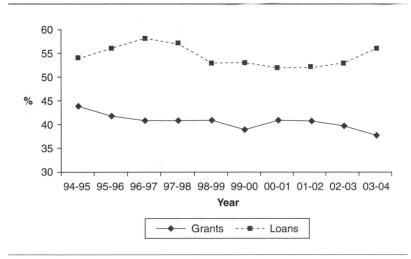

College Board (2004). Trends in Student Aid 2004. Princeton, NJ. Author.

THE DOLLARS AND CENTS COST TO THE PUBLIC

Although the rising cost of higher education for students and parents is well publicized, the cost to the taxpaying public through direct government aid to institutions and financial aid to students is not. At public institutions, state and federal governments pay the largest part of the costs. Federal and state appropriations/grants and contracts account for 62% of revenues at public universities and 65% at public 4-year colleges. This does not include financial aid to students; the federal government alone allocates billions for financial assistance and guaranteed loans to students in higher education. These expenditures have, for a long time, gone unquestioned. No longer! Facing a $4 billion shortfall in 2005, the U.S. Office of Education changed the funding guidelines to save money, making an estimated 89,000 students no longer eligible for financial assistance from the federal government.

Particularly at the state level, elected officials are beginning to ask what they are getting for their multibillion-dollar investment in higher education and student financial aid. If the goal is to provide opportunities for graduates, how much opportunity is being created as indicated by job placement? If the goal is to stimulate economic growth, are the degrees awarded consistent with the labor market needs of the state? These are increasingly issues of accountability directed to officers of higher education institutions.

When state officials charged with oversight of higher education examine the outcomes of the public investment in higher education, they typically find all the predicted results of the one way to win mania. Specifically, they find that (a) the vast majority of enrollment is in 4-year degree programs or 2-year general studies transfer programs, (b) graduation rates are 50% or lower, (c) students take longer and longer to graduate, (d) growing percentages of graduates are underemployed, (e) the degrees awarded are out of sync with the economic development needs of the state, and (f) many graduates leave the state. As a result, a few states are implementing performance funding (Schmidt, 1999), which is based on graduation rates, employment rates, and successful certificate exams passed.

THE ECONOMIC DEVELOPMENT COST

While the primary casualties of the one way to win philosophy are teens and the most visible costs are best defined in dollars and cents terms, there is a final, less noticeable problem. Because the one way to win message itself is contrary to labor economic demands for 4-year college graduates, it results in a surplus of young adults with degrees in nontechnical majors and in low demand and a shortage of adults with skills that are needed to grow the economy.

Technical Skill Shortages

By the mid-1990s, a quiet national dilemma had developed in the United States. There is now an unprecedented shortage of skilled technicians, traditionally trained in high school CTE programs or post-secondary certificate, diploma, or associate degree programs. At the same time, there is a growing percentage of underemployed 4-year college graduates. Be it information technology, precision manufac-turing, electronics production, building construction, or health care, virtually all industries that employ technical workers—workers who use mathematics and science principles to make decisions on the job—are dealing with shortages of technician-level workers. The Hudson Institute, as far back as 1997, predicted that unless this skills gap was closed, the gross domestic product could be negatively affected by as much as 5%.

At the state and local levels, it is now apparent to policy makers that economic growth in general and plant expansion and relocation in particular depend as much on the availability of a suitable labor force as on tax breaks and transportation systems. In most labor mar-kets, companies locating to a new geographic area can usually find unskilled or semiskilled individuals who could be trained on the job in a matter of weeks, and they either bring their professional engineers with them or recruit nationally. They prefer, however, to be able to recruit technicians from the local labor market and thus choose to locate or expand where this is possible. To quote a study conducted by the Pennsylvania Economy League (1996), "A region that does not have a growing percentage of its 'non-professional' workforce trained at the postsecondary pre-baccalaureate level will face increasing difficulty attracting and keeping high valued added employment" (p. i).

The reality of such predictions is confirmed by a study of the impact of labor shortages on economic development (Passmore, Wall, & Harvey, 1996). For example, the inability of one firm to hire 30 precision machinists required it to curtail expansion plans. This curtailment, in turn, led to a direct and indirect countywide loss of

$20 million in economic output and $3 million in tax revenue. One can find similar news reports from virtually anywhere in the country today, indicating economic losses related to the lack of workers with technician-level skills, while the nation's colleges turn out graduates with few skills in demand, forcing firms to seek workers from abroad.

Foreign Workers, 9/11, and Exporting of Jobs

Unable to fill technician-level vacancies in the 1990s, employers increasingly turned to recruiting foreign-born workers and relied on the Congress to increase the number of H-1B immigration/work visas. Between 1996 and 2000, foreign-born workers made up almost half of the entire labor force growth in the United States. Of new additional jobs created by the economy during this period, foreign-born workers filled 31% of technician and 49% of precision production and craft vacancies (Mosisa, 2002). Presently, there are over a million foreign-born workers in the United States working under temporary H-1B visas. It is important to note that these workers did not take these jobs away from native-born young adults; our kids simply did not have the skills needed. Many had degrees, and few had skills.

The reliance on foreign-born workers became increasingly problematic after the terrorist attacks on September 11, 2001. The Congress is now much less willing to grant H-1B visas, and foreign-born workers are less willing to come to the United States. Importantly, employers faced with technician-level labor shortages in the domestic labor market firms have three choices: turn work away, try to get a special visa to enable them to recruit non-native-born workers, or move operations overseas where a trained and willing labor force exists. The reality is that if firms cannot find skilled technicians in the domestic labor market and are no longer able to rely on foreign-born workers coming to the United States, they will likely move operations abroad.

Predictably, the schools, both high schools and colleges, are the first to be blamed for this situation. A common charge is that skilled-labor shortages are somehow related to insufficient math and science course-taking and achievement in the U.S. high schools. But data suggest that the average high school student takes more math and science than ever before, and most high schools now offer math and science courses that were previously available only in college.

We would suggest a little different explanation for technical-skill shortages. The problem is not that students are not taking enough math and science; the problem is the one way to win message. The shortage of technicians may be ascribed to the simple reality that, among those with the necessary talent, few are interested, or they are discouraged by the one way to win message from pursuing pre-baccalaureate technical occupations. Statistics regarding college enrollment patterns and intended majors of incoming freshmen confirm this view; less than 2% indicate any interest in technician-level occupations.

The shortage of technicians trained at the pre-baccalaureate level will not disappear until the nation's youths choose to pursue careers in areas of high technical demand. In the United States, the government has neither the power nor the will to mandate these decisions. It is up to the individual. The only hope is that teens will make better choices when they are better informed, when the myth of the one way to win mentality is exposed, and when technical education becomes valued by adults they look to for advice and by their nation's leaders. The purpose of this book is to assist those who would take on such a task.

Section III

The Argument for Creating Other Ways to Win

From experience (this is the third edition of this book), it seems wise to summarize the other ways to win theme lest there be some confusion about what is being argued and not argued. This is not an anti–higher education or college-bashing book; the intent is to document that there are alternatives to baccalaureate education, alternatives that make a lot more sense for some teens. The following five points summarize this argument.

1. The one way to win paradigm, the message that the best hope for future economic security lies in getting a 4-year college degree that guarantees a high-paying career in the professional ranks, is not just false; it is destructive to many kids, particularly those in the academic middle of their high school class. Those who preach the one way to win mantra may have good intentions, but they set the majority of teens

up for failure. Most teens either fail to graduate or, if they do, fail to find commensurate employment and end up in jobs they themselves report have limited prospects and do not require a baccalaureate degree.

2. There are other ways to win—ways that do not require a 4-year college degree, ways that result in salaries comparable to those earned by university graduates, and ways that actually provide more net opportunity, particularly for those in the academic middle.

3. All students should go on to some form of post–high school education or training but only (a) when and (b) if they can benefit from the experience. Postsecondary training includes 4-year baccalaureate education but also pre-baccalaureate technical education at the certificate, diploma, and associate degree level, as well as other occupational training opportunities such as formal apprenticeship programs and the military. The "go-to-college" message here is a qualified one. First, many teens are not ready right after high school to leave home and go to college, and many are not adequately prepared or occupationally focused to succeed. Second, some teens simply are not intellectually or emotionally equipped to do legitimate college-level academic work at the baccalaureate or any other level and never will be. Present educational policy seems to deny they exist. Yet we all know that not only do they exist, but they also exist in significant numbers, and they deserve some attention from their school and their country.

4. High schools have as much responsibility to teens who are at risk of dropping out of high school and those who want to go to immediately to work after graduation as they do to those who are bound for 4-year college. Those who have a pejorative attitude toward teens who do something other than pursue a 4-year college degree should rethink this prejudice; it is just plain wrong, it is unethical, and it is destructive. These kids (a) are the majority and (b) are just as deserving as the academically blessed.

5. The traditional academic program of study alone is not likely to serve well those in the academic middle who, after

graduation, go to work, pre-baccalaureate technical education, or some other form of postsecondary occupational education. If anything, academic courses alone will increase the dropout rate in most schools. Leaving no child behind in today's high schools requires alternatives for teens with different ambitions and talents, and alternative transitional pathways to prepare teens for other ways to win.

These are the five points that are the basis for what follows. We have argued in this chapter that many of today's graduating high school seniors, particularly those from the academic middle, are seriously adrift. They have been led to believe that a baccalaureate degree will lead to a career in the professions and is the only way to ensure future economic security and status. This mentality, in turn, has fueled baccalaureate mania: the unfounded faith in that the economic return from a 4-year degree is guaranteed. This one way to win paradigm is a myth, but it is not benign: it has significant costs to the country and to its youths. Most devastating, it has caused many youths to give up hope. This one way to win mantra is blight on the nation. Like any affliction, its pathology must be understood before a cure can be developed. This analysis is the purpose of Chapter 2.

However, should there still be any doubt about the problems caused by the one way to win mantra, this chapter ends by relating a true story of one young man and the one way to win doctrine.

A CASE STUDY

Keith and the College Game

Keith was 17. His high school academic record was mediocre at best; at the time of the interview, he was not certain he had enough credits to be officially called a senior. His principal ambition at the time was to obtain his driver's license, but he lacked the academic skills and ability to pass the "rules of the road" part of the driver's test, which he had failed several times.

During the interview with his counselor, he was asked about his postgraduation plans. The counselor expected a reply about the need to find full-time employment; instead, Keith said, "I haven't decided yet what college to go to. I'll decide next year." The counselor was speechless. Meanwhile, Keith gave the counselor one of those "are they going to buy this or not" looks, a look familiar to those who work in high schools.

The gulf between Keith's abilities and his stated postgraduation plans leads one to conclude that this young man was seriously adrift; fantasy is an inadequate description of his plans. Then again, perhaps he wasn't fantasizing; perhaps he was just playing the one way to win game, saying what he thought the adults, like his peers and possibly his parents, wanted to hear. Perhaps he really knew that college was not a viable option for him.

At any rate, not long thereafter, Keith left school and left home. He may have realized the folly of the idea of going to college and decided to spare himself the embarrassment—a hint of the human cost of providing only one way to win. He and literally millions like him, most of whom are blessed with considerably more academic ability, see only one way to win. These teens call this situation "the college game." "College mania" seems more appropriate. There needs to be more than one game, more than one way to win.

CHAPTER TWO

Recognizing the Forces Behind One Way to Win

> We have made Wal-Mart our model for higher education with 30,000 students swirling about in the education equivalent of a Big Box store . . . Almost any student can get into the big box or at least a wanna-be big box, hunker down and emerge with something called a degree. . . .
>
> —*Alan Contreras*[1]

The vast majority of today's high school students who populate the academic middle are acting out postsecondary plans that are clearly unrealistic and that stem from the one way to win mentality. Having been taught that there is only one road to the American dream, the majority (94.7%) express the intent to continue their education; most (83.9%) want a degree from a 4-year college, and most (57% of men and 74% of women) say they will seek jobs in the professional ranks (National Center for Education Statistics [NCES], 1992).

For many, particularly those in the academic middle, this plan is clearly fantasy. Unless U.S. high schools suddenly become so instructionally effective that 84% graduate with the requisite skills to complete a baccalaureate degree and unless the structure of the future labor market changes dramatically to provide twice as much professional work, they have no realistic reason to expect to achieve these goals. Meanwhile, the costs of this fantasy for the United States, its youth, and their parents are increasing. These costs are high in terms of their negative impact both on the nation's future competitiveness and on personal, federal, and state budgets. They are also high in terms of the human cost of failure, limited opportunities, unmet expectations, and resulting pessimism, cynicism, and low self-esteem for the college bound, not to mention the outright pejorative attitude directed at the 30% who do not go to college but to work. If the damage done by the one way to win mentality is to be undone and if its costs are to be brought under control, the factors that make this ideology so pervasive must be understood. That is the purpose of this chapter.

UNDERSTANDING THE ONE WAY TO WIN MENTALITY

Although the magnitude and effectiveness of the current pressure or "press" to go to college (see Figure 2.1) may be historic, the factors that influence youths' decisions to seek higher education have been of interest to researchers for some time. For example, Hossler and Stage (1992) developed a statistically valid model for the "predisposition" to go to college. This model explains the decision as a reaction to parental or peer pressure coupled with an individual's academic ability or high school record. Pressure from parents and peers, in turn, results from pressures applied by social messages and morals, as well as conventional economic wisdom. Using the Hossler and Stage model as a starting point, we offer an expanded model to explain the factors that make the one way to win philosophy so prevalent in the 1990s.

In our college choice model, the decision stems from ubiquitous pressure to go to college; this pressure comes from parents, relatives, friends, teachers, the media, and even federal No Child Left Behind (NCLB) educational reform policy. The consistent message from all of these groups is that there is only one way to win: go to a 4-year college and pursue a career in the professions.

In the past five years, the message has, if possible, gotten even stronger. The federal NCLB legislation has in effect institutionalized the one way to win philosophy as national policy. If one believes, as we do, that elected officials and everyone else promoting the one way to win mentality are well intentioned and sincerely believe in this advice, then one must assume that their beliefs are based on a rationale that comes from some rather convincing economic arguments,

Figure 2.1   The "Push" to Go to College

Note: Illustration by Denise Dorricott. Reprinted with permission.

from some deep-seated ideologies and values, or from both. In our model, we suggest three such variables: economic uncertainty, social status, and the ideology of equity and the right to fail.

Academic skills are conspicuously missing from the factors that we argue fuel the one way to win mentality. This was not an oversight. In these times of excess capacity in higher education (despite the rhetoric of higher education seeking more public money, there is no shortage of space in U.S. colleges) and resultant open admissions at all but a small fraction of 4-year colleges, academic ability no longer seems to be a consideration in the decision to pursue a 4-year college degree. Although academic ability may well determine which 4-year college a student will attend, lack of academic ability no longer means not going. On many campuses, remedial education has become the dominant aspect of the freshman-year experience.

Thus we view open admissions accompanied by financial aid based on need and not academic skills as the two most important factors that facilitate or enable the one way to win mentality. They do not cause it, but they make it possible.

One reason for the popularity of the one way to win mantra is that there are no obstacles to trying it. Open admissions have given virtually all a seat in higher education, regardless of academic skills. There are undoubtedly teens from rural America and urban centers who are not in college but should be, but with over 70% of all high school graduates matriculating somewhere within two years of graduating from high school, it is hard to believe that access is still an issue in the United States, as higher education would like the taxpaying public to believe. National polls do indicate that the American public believes everyone who is "qualified" should be able to go to college. It is doubtful, however, that the public understands that its tax dollars are being used to ensure that all who are "not qualified" can go as well.

In the rest of this chapter, the causes and enablers of the one way to win mentality are discussed. We begin with a discussion of the pressures applied on teens by parents, educators, peers, and the popular press.

SECTION I

The Pressure to Go to College
From Parents and Others

The go-to-college message in today's society is everywhere. Faith in the axiom that college is good has converted nearly everyone. According to one Gallup Poll (Gray, 1993), 93% of respondents said college was important to individual future success. The reinforcement to the go-to-college message pops up when one least expects it. Even our local automatic teller machine greets patrons with the question, "Need money for college?" It hints of possible profits from college mania.

The pressure on high school seniors to continue their education is intense and relentless. It takes a lot of courage not to go to a 4-year college, especially if one is academically blessed. Perhaps the best evidence lies in the sheer number of students who want to go on to higher education. Anyone who has ever worked with high school students knows that the likelihood of getting 95% to agree on anything, even pizza and rock and roll, is about as likely as successfully herding cats. Thus, when 95% of graduating seniors say they plan to go on to higher education, and nationally, 70% actually do, the intensity and effectiveness of the press to go to college can be appreciated.

This pressure is applied in the form of well-intentioned advice first from parents.

Pressure From Parents

Although most teens who go to college will say they made the decision themselves, their decision was not made in a vacuum. Parents seem to be the important group influencing them. For example, Hossler and Stage (1992) found that parents' expectations were the single best predictor of students' going to college; this was particularly true in low income homes. Although parents may have little influence on fashions, choice of music, or friends, when it comes to the decision about going to college, particularly when they are footing the bill, they call the shots.

If the importance given to parental advice is true, one would expect that, given the dramatic increase in college attendance, more parents are recommending college. NCES data confirm this hypothesis (see Table 2.1). Comparing the 1980s with the 1990s, the go-to-college message from parents increased from 15% in the 1980s to 20% in the 1990s. In the 1990s, 85.2% of young women reported that their mothers had recommended college, as compared with 68.6% in the 1980s. It is also worth noting that, for both genders, mothers are stronger supporters of the go-to-college movement than fathers.

Table 2.1   Percentages Recommending College in Sophomore Years for 1982 and 1992 High School Graduates

	Father		Mother		Counselor		Teachers	
	1980s	1990s	1980s	1990s	1980s	1990s	1980s	1990s
Total	59.1	77.0	64.8	82.9	32.3	65.2	32.3	65.5
Male	55.6	74.0	61.6	80.7	32.2	64.0	32.1	64.2
Female	63.5	80.0	68.6	85.2	32.7	66.3	32.5	66.8
Test quartile								
Lowest	40.4	59.9	47.6	64.7	26.1	56.4	28.2	57.2
Second	49.7	71.7	55.6	79.3	26.1	61.1	26.5	60.7
Third	63.9	83.1	69.2	89.7	31.3	66.4	30.1	65.5
Highest	79.8	90.6	85.1	95.9	43.1	74.3	41.7	75.3

Sources: Compiled from *High School and Base Year Student Survey,* by the National Center for Education Statistics, 1982, Washington, DC: U.S. Department of Education; and *National Educational Longitudinal Study of 1988, 1992 Second Follow-Up,* by the National Center for Education Statistics, 1992, Washington, DC: U.S. Department of Education.

The focus of this book is students from the academic middle. Thus we are interested in the extent and growth of parental pressure on high school graduates from the middle two quartiles. The growth in the percentage of parents recommending college actually increased fastest among students with the least academic ability. Cases in point are students in the second to lowest quartile, the bottom of the academic middle. The percentage of students in this category who reported that their fathers had recommended college increased 22% in 10 years. Even among those in the lowest quartile, 59.9% reported that their fathers had recommended college, whereas 64.7% reported that their mothers had recommended college.

No doubt, parents of high school students from the academic middle have their children's best interests in mind when they recommend college. They believe in the validity of the one way to win paradigm. Our model suggests that this conversion to college mania stems from a number of economic issues and social values. Before turning to these issues, we note other sources that exert the college press on academically average students. One such source is the one major social institution they all attend: their local high school.

Pressure From High Schools

The second most powerful source of pressure to go to college comes from the high schools themselves. Despite rhetoric to the contrary, high school staff have always viewed preparing students for college as their most important mission. Typically, the community agrees. Today, the instructional effectiveness of high school and college attendance rates has become one and the same in the public eye. Although high school educators will point to the community for this "college-or-nothing" criterion for success, it is largely self-imposed and historic in nature. When high schools began to proliferate at the turn of the century, most high school educators saw themselves as saving students from the "dreaded influence of the shop floor." This attitude was so common that industrialists openly accused high school educators of discouraging students from entering the trades (Gray, 1980).

Whereas high school teachers and administrators have set themselves up to be judged by the number of students who go to college, it is not surprising that high school staffs themselves exert significant overt and covert pressure on students to go on to college. Some of this pressure is institutionalized. High schools, for example, sponsor all types of activities aimed at helping students decide to attend college: college fairs, campus visitations, financial aid and college-choice workshops for parents, providing adult mentors for students interested in professional careers, and hosting college recruiters. Similar services and efforts are not made for teens who wish to go directly to work.

In some cases, the institutional pressure exerted by high schools on students to go to college is not particularly subtle. At some high school graduations, for example, the program includes a list of graduates, the colleges they are planning to attend, and scholarships they have been awarded. Now that's pressure. How would you like to be a parent with no college listed after your child's name? How would the child feel?

Perhaps the most repugnant method of institutionalizing the one way to win message by high schools is the weighted grading policies that give extra value to grades earned in special college prep courses typically taken by the academically blessed. Thus an A in accounting, a career-related course, counts less than an A in honors English, a college prep course. The message to the student body could not be more obvious: Value is placed on preparation for college; those who are valued here take these courses.

The go-to-college message that is pervasive in high schools also comes directly from the faculty. Among the "true believers" in one way to win are high school teachers and even some guidance counselors. Both should know better. Even the pecking order among high school faculty reflects the value placed on college. The teachers with the highest status teach only those preparing for college. According to disturbing research by Oakes (1985) and others, teachers in the average high school have a pejorative view of non-college-bound teens. This view is ironic since workers from the academic middle literally construct and maintain our communities. These are the persons who build our homes and roads, maintain our public health infrastructure, provide police and fire protection, and manufacture and distribute the goods we consume. Apparently, Taylorism (Gray, 1993)—the belief that the wealth of the nation depends on the contributions of the academically blessed, whereas those from the middle and lower ends of the academic spectrum are relatively less important—is alive and well. This theme is explored in later chapters.

This bias in favor of the academically blessed—the college bound—elite is not new; thus it contributes little to explanations of the recent and dramatic increase in college attendance among students from the academic middle. What has changed is the extent of teachers' and counselors' enthusiasm for advising students to go to college. Again, of particular interest is the advice given to students in the lowest three quartiles. The same pattern of advice observed among parents is found among teachers and counselors. The percentage of students in the lowest three quartiles who reported that their counselor had recommended college doubled or tripled between the 1980s and 1990s (see Table 2.1).

State-Mandated High Stakes Testing

If the one way to win, go-to-college overt and covert message that is communicated by most high schools were not strong enough already, recent developments at the state level serve to make the message even stronger. Responding to what were perceived to be shortcomings of their public school systems and long before the passage of NCLB, the majority of states instituted testing programs that included at least one test in the 10th or 11th grade. The content of these tests is purely academic subject matter. The rationale, a rationale that would be echoed in the NCLB legislation, was that the advanced academic skills were necessary to succeed in higher education that in turn was necessary for economic success in life.

The point to be made here is that such tests in effect relegated all post–high school alternatives other than college, particularly those that did not require advanced academics, to a second-class status. And most distressing, those students who did not do well on such tests have come to be viewed as school system liabilities. As will be discussed later in this chapter, testing made some alternatives in the high school curriculum, especially those that had anything to do with preparation for work, viewed by test-conscious administrators as, if anything, the cause of poor test scores.

The go-to-college message heard by academically average teens at home is reinforced by the culture at their high schools and most recently by the state-mandated testing that focuses on skills related to college admissions. This point is rather perplexing because, if any group could be expected to realistically assess an individual student's ability to benefit from higher education and to value all teens regardless of their postsecondary intents or academic ability, it would be high school teachers and counselors. These individuals appear to have assessed the politics and decided instead to look the other way. This situation is discussed in Chapter 4. Of course, parents and teachers are not the only important influences on today's youth. Media and friends also deliver the message that "there is only one way to win—you had better go to college."

Pressure From Peers and the Media

The influence of peer pressure on adolescent behavior is legendary. Especially as graduation approaches, all conversation among teens eventually turns to one question: "What are you going to do next year?" It is the rare teenager who is willing to say anything but "I am going to college."

Added to the go-to-college din from parents, teachers, counselors, and friends is a constant barrage of one way to win propaganda in the public media. The press constantly reminds youth that 4-year college grads earn more. Often what is written is misleading. For example, as the economy rebounded in early 2003 and 2004, a headline in the press reported that the job outlook for 4-year college grads was never better and signing bonuses were at an all-time high. A closer reading, however, reveals that the outlook for those with specialized skills related to information technology was never better; the prospect for those with degrees in soft-skill college majors—which was and still is the majority--was terrible. The underemployment rate among arts and science majors, for example, is 68%.

Equally important, the popular press plays an important role in the delivery of the go-to-college message from politicians. Even presidential campaign rhetoric promotes "go to college." When presidential candidates state, "All who want to go to college should be able to," the message is all too often interpreted as meaning that all students are academically prepared to do college academics and that those who do not wish to go to college are therefore deficient in some way.

The go-to-college message from parents, teachers, and friends is nothing new. What is new is its persuasiveness and the fact that it is now delivered to all students regardless of academic ability or achievement. This change in attitude toward the appropriateness of "college for everyone" can be traced first to increased anxiety about the economic future of the nation, globalization and the exporting of jobs, and conventional wisdom that developed about future career opportunities. Second, it can be attributed to several deep-seated cultural values about equal opportunity, the right to fail, and the status of nonprofessional work.

SECTION II

The Economic and Social Forces Behind One Way to Win

The pressure on teens to pursue the one way to win strategy comes from parents, teachers, peers, government, and the media, who in turn preach the philosophy because they believe it. Understanding the biases of this belief is important for those who wish to suggest other ways to win.

Four variables are discussed here: economic uncertainty, globalization, the relationship of education and status, and the ideology of equal opportunity. Each of these variables leads to a predilection to support the one way to win mentality. We begin with an examination of the role of economic uncertainty.

Diminishing Economic Opportunities

The fact that the growth in the percentage of students entering higher education began about the same time as the massive economic restructuring in this country is more than a coincidence. One result of this restructuring was the permanent loss of many high wage/low skill jobs. As a result, the earnings of all except college graduates began to slip. The majority of today's youth and their parents, and perhaps almost everyone else, really are not sure where good work, both rewarding and high paying, will be found in the future. The only thing that now seems certain is the mathematical fact that those with a college degree, on average, earn more than those without one. This well-publicized fact, coupled with murky information about the rise of technical work, has led to several widespread labor market beliefs or assumptions that are mostly myths.

Labor Market Misconceptions

The one way to win or college mania mentality has been fueled by misinformation or myths about the future world of work. Seven such misconceptions seem to underlie much of the rhetoric behind the one way to win mentality.

Labor market myths:

1. In the future, most jobs will require a 4-year degree.

2. In the future, most new additional jobs created will be in technical areas that require a 4-year degree.

3. In the future, all high wage occupations will require a 4-year degree.

4. The total labor force demand for college graduates will be sufficient to ensure commensurate employment for all who receive a 4-year degree.

5. In the future, there will be so many persons who have a 4-year degree that they will take all the good jobs, including those that do not require a baccalaureate degree.

6. Four-year college graduates earn more than high school graduates because they graduated from college.

7. Getting a 4-year degree is worth the cost to get one.

As will be discussed in detail in Chapter 7, all seven of these labor market beliefs are false, particularly for most of the academic middle. It is people in this group who enter 4-year colleges—despite mediocre to poor academic skills—who are the least likely to graduate in the first place. But if they do, they are also the least likely to find commensurate employment. They would be better off considering other ways to win, such as postsecondary pre-baccalaureate technical education, military service schools, and other routes to high skill/high wage employment.

The sobering reality is that only 24% of all work in the future will require any postsecondary education: almost half of all work requires less than 2 weeks' on-the-job training. And although the fastest-growing type of high skill/high wage employment is in technical areas, most employment will be at the technician level; only about 25% of technical jobs will require a 4-year degree or higher.

Globalization

The economic uncertainties of the 1990s that fueled the one way to win philosophy have, in recent years, been compounded by widely reported loss of jobs to other countries. Currently, it is estimated that a million or more jobs have been lost overseas, the greatest job loss since the Depression (Garten, 2002). While this number is a relatively small percentage of the total American work-force of nearly 140 million, it is predicted that another 4 or 5 million jobs will be transferred offshore by 2015. Many of these jobs are, to be sure, low skill occupations that move to countries with the lowest wage rates; many others, however, are high wage professional/technical occupations, suggesting the very real prospect of high skill/low wage jobs in the future. And while some argue that although jobs are going overseas, other countries are exporting jobs to the United States, and although the net gain or loss is admittedly uncertain, it does not matter—the public believes that jobs are being lost to other countries. They rightly sense that for this generation and future generations of young adults, the competition for good jobs will be international in nature. It is especially true for those in the so-called knowledge economy, the very segment of the economy that is projected to create the most "new jobs." Telling was the 2004 testimony of the Head of the Federal Reserve. When a member of Congress asked him what could be done about globalization job flight, his response was that a better-educated workforce should be created. In other words, college.

MISPLACED FAITH IN THE JOB OUTLOOK FOR 4-YEAR COLLEGE GRADUATES

Relatively few teens have taken the time to think about their career plans, even though getting a good job is why they enroll in college. Most have this faith—perhaps hope is a more appropriate term—that there will be ample commensurate employment for 4-year college graduates. Thus all they have to do is get a degree in just about any field, and a high paying professional job is guaranteed.

Unfortunately, their faith or optimism is unfounded. As will be discussed in Chapter 7, statistics from the federal departments of education and labor demonstrate clearly that there will be only about half as many jobs for 4-year college graduates as are needed to accommodate them. The number to remember is 57. That is the predicted number of jobs requiring a 4-year degree for every 100 people who earn one. This means that 43 people will go underemployed, taking jobs that do not require a 4-year degree. Importantly, this is just a year-by-year number and does not take into account that each year, the underemployed from previous years are still looking. Thus the true labor market outlook for 4-year college graduates is actually worse.

THE FUNDAMENTAL FEAR: ALL DECENT JOBS WILL REQUIRE A BA

Some teens and many parents sense this reality that there will not be enough jobs that actually require a 4-year college education to go around. At work, parents have seen college-level jobs vanish due to downsizing of middle management and have seen other jobs go abroad, and many have acquaintances whose children have graduated with a 4-year degree only to move back home unemployed. While they understand this, they also reach the pragmatic conclusion that a college degree today is synonymous with what a high school degree was to previous generations.

The chief concern behind the one way to win mentality is that, as the number of those who hold a 4-year degree grows, a baccalaureate degree will be needed to compete for any type of decent employment. Of course, there is some truth to this belief. Rumors abound that supposed low level jobs now require a 4-year degree. One of the more popular is the one about the want ad for a warehouse job that requires a BA and the ability to lift 30 pounds. Though probably not true, tales such as these are becoming more and more common and do not go unnoticed by teens and parents. To some extent, their fears are justified. Today, most bank clerks and many telemarketers—not to mention truck drivers and waiters—hold university degrees.

There is an important counterpoint to be made, however. Whereas it is certain that 4-year college graduates will be forced to take jobs that do not require the degree, they will be primarily in low skill or soft-skill, low wage occupations. It must be emphasized that university graduates will not take jobs away from those with specific job skills in demand. In particular, those with 4-year degrees will not displace those with occupational skills that are in short supply. Four-year college graduates with degrees in arts and science will not displace technicians educated at the certificate, diploma, or associate degree level.

This latter point is critical for teens, parents, and those who would promote other ways to win to understand. In the future, only academic degrees or credentials that equate to skills in demand will lead to advantage in the workplace. Thus many information technology firms care little about a person's degrees but are very concerned about what technology certificates he or she holds. As will be stressed again and again in this book, the secret to other ways to win is acquiring the job skills necessary to compete for high skill/high wage employment.

The importance of misconceptions and fears regarding economic security as the root cause of the one way to win mentality cannot be overstated. Economic uncertainty about future labor market opportunities alone, however, does not adequately explain the go-to-college press that existed to a lesser extent even during the post–World War II economic golden years and the GI bill that paid for millions of veterans to attend college. Other forces are at work that center on social status and a prejudice against nonprofessional work, as well as on deep-seated cultural values.

EDUCATION, SOCIAL CLASS, AND STATUS

Even before the onset of economic uncertainty, the push to go to college was still very strong. Obviously, something other than economic uncertainty is at work. One such factor in the United States—and around the world as well—is the relationship between social class and prestige (see Table 2.2) and college attendance. Academicians are fond of portraying the benefits of higher education in terms of a more fulfilling and rewarding life. In reality, however, long before college had anything to do with careers other than medicine, law, or the clergy, higher education was popular for an entirely different reason: it was a vestige of education, social class, and status. As the British aristocracy grew, for example, and the number of titles that could be bestowed by the monarch did not, a new vestige was needed—something less vulgar than just money—and college was ideal. Because at first few could afford to attend college, it was the perfect status symbol separating "gentlemen" from the masses. This value was brought to the United States and is still alive and well.

Even though higher education is very accessible now, having a college degree is equated with class structure more than ever. David Brooks (2000) argues that in fact, the increased number of college graduates has promoted the rise of a whole new social structure he

Table 2.2   Occupational Classifications by Prestige

	Number of occupation titles	Average prestige scores
Managerial and professional specialty occupations	132	62.3
Executive, administrative, and managerial occupations	26	53.5
Professional specialty occupations	106	65.4
Technical, sales, and administrative support occupations	102	40.5
Technicians and related support occupations	22	51.2
Sales occupations	23	35.8
Administrative support occupations, including clerical	57	38.2
Service occupations	43	35.0
Private household occupations	5	27.8
Protective service occupations	11	48.4
Service occupations, except protective and household	27	30.8
Precision productions, crafts, and repair	103	38.5
Mechanics and repairers	27	39.3
Construction trades	30	39.2
Extractive occupations	5	37.6
Precision production occupations	41	37.7
Operators, fabricators, and laborers	103	33.4
Machine operators, assemblers, and inspectors	52	33.4
Transportation and material moving occupations	25	35.9
Handlers, equipment cleaners, helpers, and laborers	16	29.4
Farming, forestry, and fishing	19	35.6
Farm operators and managers	4	43.3
Farm occupations, except managerial	4	31.0
Related agricultural occupations	5	33.2
Forestry and lodging occupations	3	38.0
Fishers, hunters, and trappers	3	33.3

Source: "Upgrading Occupational Prestige and Socioeconomic Scores: How the Measures Measure Up," by K. Nakao and J. Treas, 1994, *Sociological Methodology, 24,* pp. 1–72.

calls the educated class. Unlike in the past, when social status was a function of family or money, the new class today is defined by having a college degree and the shared values it implies; thus an Ivy League graduate who is a clerk in a secondhand bookstore is more likely to be accepted among the new educated class than a high school graduate millionaire.

Thus the relationship among social class, status, and college is a strong force behind the one way to win college message. This force is a particularly powerful reason for parental advice to go to college (more about this in Chapter 4). A related aspect of the correlation among social class identity, status, and college is a less overt but no less powerful prejudice against "dirty," blue-collar, non-professional work.

THE PREJUDICE AGAINST NONPROFESSIONAL WORK

Although the public may support the platitude that there is dignity in all work, the only work given much status is professional work. "My daughter, the doctor" or "my son, the lawyer," is still the standard against which all else is compared. Evidence for this point of view could fill several books, but for the sake of brevity, let's examine a standard occupational listing that ranks occupational fields according to the status that American society assigns to each (see Table 2.2).

It is not surprising to find professionals at the top and unskilled labor at the bottom. The middle rankings, however, are the interesting ones. Notice that skilled occupations are listed below semi-professional occupations despite the fact that most skilled occupations pay higher wages than most semiprofessional jobs—higher even than some professional occupations. Skilled precision workers continue to have higher average earnings than schoolteachers, so why are colleges full of students preparing to be teachers when there are jobs for only a fraction of them? Why is hardly anyone preparing for careers in the crafts? The reason is related to status. Teachers may not have the status of a doctor, a lawyer, or even an accountant, but they have more status than a precision metal worker who earns considerably more than they do.

This message is conveyed to youths: White- or striped-collar jobs are valued; all others are not. Furthermore, the belief is that those who do nonprofessional work are not very bright and are ill-mannered and generally unsophisticated. These stereotypes are reinforced in the media by the likes of Al Bundy and Homer Simpson, the so-called Joe Six-Packs. Aside from education, social class, and status, several other deep-seated cultural values create a fertile climate for the one way to win mentality. Chief among them is the importance given in the United States to ensuring "equal opportunity" and the related belief in the "right to fail."

THE IDEOLOGY OF EQUAL OPPORTUNITY

The United States of America is frequently referred to as the land of opportunity. Such platitudes reflect a basic value in U.S. culture that affects the public's thinking about many things, including higher education. This basic value also creates a climate for acceptance of the one way to win mentality. In a nation where, excepting those whose ancestors were brought as slaves, almost everyone's ancestors came from somewhere else voluntarily because of the promise of a better life, keeping open avenues such as college has strong public support. The population in general and educators in particular have traditionally discouraged youths from making career decisions too early, for example, because they think that it could limit future opportunity. This view is one basis of the belief that as many students as possible should be sent to college. In recent times, opportunity and college have come to be viewed as one and the same. College recruiters know this and play on it heavily. Marketing slogans such as "Imagine the impossible, then do it" and "This fall is not too late to turn your life around" (both gleaned from the *New York Times*) are typical plays on the doctrine of equal opportunity. This doctrine not only promotes college mania but also makes the topics of rising costs, lack of ability, inadequate preparation for college, and lack of career direction difficult to deal with, even though it is obvious that encouraging everyone to go to college while ignoring these factors may not be such a good idea. This is especially true since college has come to be viewed as the great provider of equal opportunity.

As suggested more than 40 years ago by the eminent sociologist Burton Clark (1962), a consistent problem in democracies is that although the culture encourages aspirations, it is ineffective in providing equal opportunity to achieve them. This dilemma, argues Clark, is a strong motivator behind the conventional wisdom he calls the "ideology of equal opportunity." It argues that society should provide unlimited access to higher education. As Clark points out, "Strictly interpreted, equality of opportunity means selection [to college] according to ability, without regard to extraneous considerations. Popularly interpreted, however, equal opportunity in obtaining a college education is widely taken to mean 'unlimited access'" (p. 580).

This ideology of equal opportunity is a strong force behind the one way to win mentality. Even suggesting that unlimited access to higher education may not be in the interests of either the nation or its citizens puts one at risk of being politically incorrect. This fear may be one reason that few question college mania. Instead of confronting the problem, society has chosen what Clark refers to as the "soft response": funds are provided to ensure unlimited access and thus allow a sort of higher education Darwinism to take place as half slowly drop out or, as Clark suggests, "cool out." Of course, the irony is that those who cool out are those whom the doctrine of opportunity was supposed to help the most; instead, they are most likely to fail. It is difficult to understand how they are supposed to benefit from the experience (this reality is discussed in Chapter 3). Even raising these questions is problematic because of the second deep-seated belief about youth—that they have the right to try and the right to fail.

In most countries, the idea of supporting the attendance of large numbers of youths in college who do not have the academic ability or preparation to be successful would be unimaginable, and dropout rates of 50% would be intolerable. But this belief is not shared in the United States, at least not yet. Why? First, it is because we are perhaps the only nation that can afford these social inefficiencies. Second, this situation is tolerated because of a basic value that career development specialist Ken Hoyt (1994) calls the "right to try" and the "right to fail." That "1 in 100" individual who "battles the odds" and succeeds despite a poor high school record seems always to be in the back of the minds of Americans. Because of such outside possibilities of success, the nation has been willing to let the Darwinian "cooling-out" process in higher education take its course. Of course, for that to happen, two final enabling ingredients are needed: open college admissions and student financial aid.

SECTION III

The Enablers Behind One Way to Win: Open Admissions and Financial Aid

In this chapter, we have discussed the various groups that deliver the one way to win, go-to-college message and the economic fears, misconceptions, ideologies, and values that lead them to do so. It is interesting to observe that, to varying degrees, these pressure groups, economic uncertainties, and social values exist in all other nations. The United States leads the world in the percentage of youths who go on to a 4-year college, partly because (a) it is the only place that totally disregards academic ability by allowing open admissions, (b) it awards financial aid on the basis of need—not academic ability, and (c) it disregards the fact that only one in four who begin a 4-year degree program graduates or finds commensurate employment. In France, for example, 28% go on to college; in Great Britain, 13%; and in Germany, 20% (Hoyt, 1994). Why? Obviously, factors in the United States that enable graduating high school students to play the one way to win game regardless of academic ability do not exist abroad. Two enablers predominate: empty college seats and government-supported student financial aid.

Open College Admissions

As frequently as college faculties deny it, higher education is a business in which the number of suppliers—colleges—continues to grow out of proportion to the number of traditional customers— graduating high school seniors. By way of illustration, between 1981 and 1991, the number of colleges and universities in the United States actually increased by 328, whereas the number of high school graduates decreased by 250,000 (NCES, 1992). According to Paul Fussell (1983), writer, social commentator, and a leading cynic about college mania, more institutions in the state of Ohio call themselves universities than there are in all of unified Germany.

This excess of college seats supercharges college mania in two ways. First, it removes the obstacle of admission standards: As enrollment declines, colleges take in fewer qualified applicants, and finally, they take virtually all applicants. This situation led Albert Shanker to comment that everyone might as well be given a college degree at birth because academic ability and achievement in high school are no longer needed.

Second, it promotes the one way to win mentality in a subtler way. Declining enrollments have become the principal issue at most colleges. "Enrollment management" is a big issue in higher education. Make no mistake: the goal is to keep the classes and dorm rooms full.

Marketing efforts to fill empty college dorms and classes have become sophisticated and extensive. The most prevalent advertising tactic used in these campaigns is to play on the hopes and fears behind the one way to win mentality. The net result is that, in the effort to fill seats, higher education spends millions of dollars each semester promoting the go-to-college message. By doing so, it reinforces the one way to win mentality. Thus, aside from parents, high school faculty, and friends, colleges themselves are probably the biggest source of go-to-college rhetoric. The product they are promoting is expensive, but this is not a problem because the government is more than willing to pay for much of the cost.

Need-Based Financial Aid

Because the doors to higher education are wide open, the only problem is obtaining the money to pay tuition bills. Even this is not quite the problem it could be, because of the availability of financial aid. As reported earlier, the majority of students in college now receive financial aid. Significantly, this aid is awarded not on merit or on need and merit, but just on need. Thus, although in the distant past excellent academic credentials were needed to get a scholarship or grant, this is no longer true. Right or wrong, this need-based rather than merit-based philosophy of financial aid, coupled with excess higher education capacity, has put college within reach of marginally qualified students from the academic middle. It is not that costs are not a problem (they are an increasingly important issue with parents), but need-based financial aid softens the risks of going to college unprepared and is an important enabler of the one way to win mentality.

Section **IV**

No Child Left Behind

Whereas the No Child Left Behind Act is undoubtedly the most significant piece of federal education policy to be enacted for some time and whereas it is based largely on the one way to win mentality and thus has served to cast the paradigm in cement, it is necessary to discuss its implications on high school kids from the academic middle. For those who may be unfamiliar with the Act, the pertinent point for this discussion is the general philosophy that all children should take academic courses that would prepare them for college. Anything less, it is argued, limits students' options. Thus, as in the late 1800s, when there was only one curriculum in the American high school, namely, the classical curriculum, the intent of the NCLB Act at the high school level is to drive the students higher in the academic program of study, which is considered all-important to their and the nation's future. The other pertinent fact is that the Act requires a number of academic tests that students will take. These tests are used to evaluate individuals but also schools and school systems. The intent here, however, is not to give an exhaustive, detailed description or critique of the Act but to focus on its impact on students in the academic middle.

No Child Left Behind Legislation

No Child Left Behind is a double-edged sword for teens from the academic middle: good for some, bad for others. Clearly, it is in the interest of all students to be as proficient in math, science, and communication as possible. In particular, those who would seek other ways to win in high skill/high wage technical-level fields need to take advanced math courses. Thus it is a positive development that state testing and increased graduation requirements have required many teens in the academic middle to take more math and science courses. For example, while it was feared that such requirements would lead to a decline in high school career and technical education (CTE) course-taking, the result was the opposite. Of the 24% of students who take three or more CTE courses in a single occupational area, 80% also complete the academic program of study. Likewise, programs such as High Schools That Work which emphasize such things as homework for all students, have also led to increased academic rigor and achievement for teens in the academic middle.

Largely, however, whereas increased graduation requirements and state testing programs were in place prior to NCLB, it is difficult not to conclude that the high stakes that NCLB requires states to adopt have had a number of unintended consequences that are harmful to some if not all in the academic middle. In general, the overall impact of NCLB has been to make all but the college-bound student liabilities of the high schools they attended. While the title suggests the focus of the Act is individual children, the goals and methods of assessment are macro in nature. By 2005, a consensus had developed that the best way to comply with the testing requirements and avoid being labeled as a failing high school was to treat every teen as if he or she were going to college. One state actually uses the ACT test, a college admissions test, as its state high school assessment. At the school and district level, passing the state test mandated by NCLB and thus avoiding being labeled as a failing or needs-improvement school or district has become all consuming. Programs of study, such as high school vocational education, now called CTE, too often provided districts not with a valued alternative for some kids but with an excuse for low test scores and a reason to scale back or elim-inate these programs. In some instances, teens who did not do well on the test and thus threatened the school's reputation were with-drawn from the career preparation course so that they could take more academic courses.

The problem, of course, is that not all kids want to go to college, not all kids are good at academics, not all kids like school, and in fact, nine years of nothing but academics is why most who drop out do so, and those who do not leave do outrageous things like not even trying on state-mandated tests. It seems less than a coincidence that the national dropout rate rose from 29% to 33% during the 1990s, when most states instituted increased graduation standards and test-ing. In fact, it is not a great leap to suggest that it was no longer in the interest of high schools to do much to prevent academically defi-cient and otherwise difficult kids from dropping out. Most high school faculties would deny that this is the case, but a comparison of the number of kids entering ninth grade at any high school with the number of kids handed a diploma four years later suggests in most cases that a quarter to a third have disappeared—transferred out, say the schools. But logic would suggest that just as some transfer out, other teens should be transferring in, unless the overall population of the community is declining. The fact is that kids who leave do not take the test and do not drag school scores down. NCLB has created, though unintentionally, an incentive for schools to ignore if not encourage some kids' dropping out of high school.

Then there is the reality that, of those who hang on to graduate, 30% go to work rather than college. While some would argue that these kids also need better academic skills, which is true, they also need—and deserve—assistance from their high school in preparing for work. NCLB seems to ignore that these kids exist at all. Their mere existence is contrary to the logic of the Act. The recommendation of the federal administration that hatched NCLB also proposed eliminating high school CTE. Federal officials are quick to point out that when asked, most teens say they want to go to college, but a better gauge of teens' true intentions is not what they say—they say what adults want to hear—but what they do, namely, go to work in 30% of cases. The fate of work-bound teens is somewhat similar to that of those who drop out. Going to work is not the game plan of NCLB. Work-bound kids in general do not perform as well as the college bound on state-mandated tests. Because they also serve to drag school scores down, they become persona non grata in all too many high schools. NCLB has also, although unintentionally, created an environment in today's schools where work-bound teens are viewed as liabilities, not assets. And the CTE programs they take in high school are often the scapegoat for poor school test scores.

The point to be remembered is that when one adds together those who drop out without graduating and those who go directly to work after graduating, the result is half the kids. In many states, it is more than half the kids. NCLB has not been of much value to these students. They need better academic instruction, but they also need curriculum pathways that open other ways to win that are equally valued by their high school faculty. It is interesting to note, for example, that the largest number of students drop out after the 9th or 10th grades. Most teens, in fact, try the 9th or 10th grade in hopes that something of more relevance will be provided. Many, in fact one-third, find instead only more academics. All too many give up and leave, and all too many educators are relieved.

One final and more general observation needs to be made regarding NCLB. In addition to largely turning kids at risk of dropout and those who are going to work into liabilities for school systems, NCLB, by its single focus on an advanced-academics, single college preparatory curriculum, has legitimized the one way to win mentality. State testing has become the all-important preoccupation of many schools. Critics no longer need to worry about high schools' preoccupation with athletics—testing has taken over. One high school educator reported that because many students cannot concentrate long enough to take the test in a single one- or two-day session, the school must spread the tests over many days; as a result, they lose 20 or more days of instruction a year. Thus, when one seeks to understand the roots of one way to win, NCLB must be considered, if not one of the leading causes, one of the most visible results.

OTHER WAYS TO WIN

In this chapter, we have explored the forces behind the one way to win mentality. National survey research suggests that the most direct reason for increased college attendance among seemingly unqualified students is a change in attitude among parents, teachers, and counselors about the need to go to college regardless of preparation. This change in attitude can be traced most directly to economic uncertainty and related myths about future labor market opportunities and the not unfounded conclusion that a college degree now is equivalent to a high school degree in the past, namely, a needed credential for any decent job. These fears and the one way to win solution are then buttressed by deep-seated cultural values about class identification, the superiority of professional work, the perceived relationship between college and equal opportunity, and the right to choose and the right to fail. Most recently, NCLB legislation has certified the validity of the one way to win message.

The United States has created a form of higher education Darwinism that allows all to try. From admission onward, the emphasis is on survival of the fittest among students. The costs of this cooling-out process were described in Chapter 1. It is particularly costly to those who need help the most, namely, those from the academic middle of the nation's graduating high school senior classes. The irony is that, in this group, youths from disadvantaged homes—and females in general—bear the brunt of the damage done by providing only one way to win. These groups would benefit most from the creation of other ways to win.

NOTE

1. Contreras, A. (2004, November 26). A question of degrees. *The Chronicle of Higher Education*, p. B24.

CHAPTER THREE

Limited Options for Special Populations

Sometimes when people start out to do good, evil follows.

—Daniel Patrick Moynihan[1]

If the percentage of graduating high school seniors enrolling in
4-year colleges immediately after graduation is any indication,
the one way to win paradigm—the conventional wisdom that a
baccalaureate degree and professional work are the only ways to participate in the American dream—has become a pervasive, widely
shared belief. A close look reveals also that the largest group of
recent high school graduates enrolled in 2-year colleges is actually
taking general studies programs designed to prepare them for transfer to 4-year baccalaureate degree programs, rather than technical/
occupational programs.

Although the validity of the paradigm's advice is questionable,
the true cause for concern is the resultant costs. The one way to win
paradigm is not benign to those who would follow this advice, especially those who do so with little regard for their likelihood of success. These costs are measured in terms of decreased international
economic competitiveness, questionable use of public funds, tuition
dollars, student loans, and human failure, alienation, and unmet
expectations and underemployment. Although these frequent

negative consequences of following the one way to win path take their toll on all youth—surprising numbers of the academically blessed drop out during their freshman year, and among those who graduate, almost half fail to find commensurate employment—those students who comprise the academic middle of the nation's high schools are disproportionately harmed. Within this group, three subgroups—those who are "at risk" of dropping out of high school, those from economically disadvantaged households (majority or minority, urban or rural), and young women in general—are particularly vulnerable. These three subgroups are the focus of this chapter.

Our argument is that, although sincere, those promoting the pursuit of a 4-year degree and professional work as the end-all strategy for achieving equal opportunity for disadvantaged youth, lowering dropout rates, and closing the wage gap between men and women are naively optimistic and ultimately harmful. Ironically, by advocating and valuing only one alternative, they may be doing more harm than good to many of those they seek to help the most. The youth in these three subgroups are the most likely to be hurt by indiscriminate advisce to academic middle to go to a 4-year college in the hope of landing a job in the professional ranks.

Section I

Disadvantaged Youth

While at the federal and state level elected officials and those they appoint have been more and more obsessed with academic performance, mandated testing, and enrolling every teenager in college, little public notice has, so far, been given to the rather shocking fact that one-third of all youth in the United States do not graduate from high school. The national high school dropout rate in the year 2000 was 33%: a 4% percentage point increase from 1990 (Haney, Madaus, Wheelock, Miao, & Gruia, 2004), meaning that comparing national ninth grade enrollments in 1996 to national graduate numbers in 2000 reveals that one-third of the kids are gone. Among Latino students, the dropout rate is estimated to be 45%, or almost one out of every two (Greene, 2002).

Figure 3.1   National Dropout Rate in 1980, 1990, and 2001 (%)

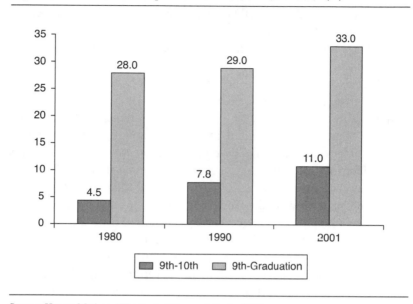

Source: Haney, Madaus, Wheelock, Miao, and Gruia, 2004.

Youth "at Risk" of Dropping Out of High School

Youth "at risk" of dropping out are defined as those whose test scores and grades are one or more standard deviations below the mean. There are many reasons why students fail to graduate, but as suggested in Chapter 1, the one way to win mentality lurks behind many of them. The largest numbers of dropouts leave between the 9th and 10th grade. This fact is important. Almost all teens try high school, meaning they show up for the first year, be it the 9th or 10th grade. Those who find reason to stay do so and graduate; those who do not, mostly leave. Again, the reasons are many and individual, but research regarding what holds at-risk youth in school is telling as to why they leave in the first place.

Multivariate research examining factors associated with at-risk youth beating the odds and graduating suggests that a lot has to do with whether these teens find alternatives—other ways to win—in the high school curriculum, alternatives that are relevant to their goals and that offer an environment that values what they are good at or at least what they are interested in. Plank (2001), using National Center for Education Statistics (NCES) national data sets, found that, in general, at-risk youth who take career and technical education (CTE) are less likely to drop out than their peers who do not. This effect was positive for any ratio of CTE to academic courses but was maximized at a ratio of 3 CTE credits to 4 academic, or a 40% CTE to 60% academic ratio.

The success of CTE in holding at-risk kids in school leads to the conclusion that at-risk students will stay if the school offers and values more than one way to win. If these students find a program of study that welcomes them and is relevant to them, they will stay. Of importance are that these programs are valued, that students are welcomed, and that their teachers understand them. CTE is one example of a program that meets such criteria. Many kids take CTE, not necessarily because they have a well-thought-out career interest, but because it is the only place in the high school program where the teachers remember their names and they feel welcomed.

The idea that the one way to win, No Child Left Behind (NCLB) ethos of increased academic rigor, improved academic instruction, testing, and putting well-qualified teachers in every classroom is going to reduce dropout rates is clearly naive in most cases. While there may be exceptions in some dysfunctional school systems around the country, in general, most dropouts go to the very same high schools as do the other students who go to college. But unlike most of the their college-bound classmates, these teens find, when they get to high school, just more of the kind of academic courses they have never been good at. Sensing correctly that high school is just more of the same, they leave school. If the national dropout rate is to be reversed, high schools need to provide other ways to win in the high school program of study.

Special Needs Students

In today's high schools, typically 11% or more of those enrolled have been identified as special needs students and have an individual education plan that guides their high school program of study. Some are severely mentally or emotionally challenged, but most are not. Some have limitations that have nothing to do with academic ability and are otherwise academically gifted, but most do not. Some are learning disabled and part of the academic middle, and some are not. Some are potentially at risk of dropping out of high school, and others are not. Almost all, however, have one thing in common: they become victims of the one way to win mentality.

Logic alone suggests that when, after significant evaluation, professionals and a child's parents agree that the child has special limiting educational needs, the one way to win message is clearly inappropriate in most cases. But talk to any high school special education teacher and you find that the one way to win message is as much believed by these kids and especially their parents as it is by the school population in general. It is not at all uncommon, in fact it is common, that special needs kids and their parents, especially if they are enrolled in an ultimate one way to win high school in the suburbs, are planning to go to college. Seeing a market and another way to fill empty seats, many colleges, and not just 2-year colleges, are more than happy to take their money and enroll them. And of course, what you might expect happens: most fail—no, not all, but most.

That large numbers of special needs students also go off to college is just plain nonsense. When even special education students, kids who by definition have limited academic abilities, also pursue the one way to win plan, then the real power of the paradigm is apparent. Special needs kids want to do what all the other kids are doing, and their parents hope, against all odds, that college will be the answer for economic security. Meanwhile, a lot of these kids, especially those without strong parental support, are among the one-third who drop out of high school.

Research suggests that many of these special needs teens would benefit from pursuing other ways to win, and many would do so if their high schools provided and valued alternatives. Again, CTE is one example of another way to win and the need for viable alternatives in the high school curriculum. Harvey's (2002) research finds, for example, that special needs kids who complete a CTE program of study are more likely to graduate, more likely to become employed, more likely to be employed in higher paying craft occupations, and more likely to be enrolled in 1- and 2-year college occupational programs than special needs students who do not take CTE.

SECTION II

Economically Disadvantaged Youth

Although statistics regarding poverty among the nation's youth vary due to debates regarding definition and so forth, it is clear that many youths live in impoverished households and that family wealth is a strong predictor of success in school and later life. While children make up 26% of the population, they account for 39% of the poor. In any randomly assigned classroom in the country, one would expect to find at least 20% of the students living in households that are below the poverty level. In classrooms in counties in some states, it could be more than half, and in some rural and urban school district classrooms, it could be virtually all.

Though progress was made in lowering the poverty rate in the late 1990s, the decrease was measured only in tenths of a percent and began to climb again with the economic turndown in 2001. And, although the poverty rate for African Americans (26.5%) and Hispanics (27.1%) exceeds that of whites, the experience of all economically disadvantaged children is pretty much the same regardless of race. They enter elementary school at a disadvantage and face the same future. For example, black and white students who must repeat the first grade are just as likely to drop out of school later.

Breaking the poverty cycle for disadvantaged youth, be they majority or minority teens, has proven to be a perplexing problem. In decades past, the great hope was increasing high school graduation rates. Today, it is the one way to win paradigm. One national study found, for example, that among high school sophomores, a higher percentage of African Americans than white students aspired to college (NCES, 1988). And, of course, the one way to win message means the same for disadvantaged youth as it does for those from higher income families: to get a better, high-paying job in the professions, get a 4-year degree.

Is the indiscriminate urging of all disadvantaged youth to pursue the one way to win strategy a good idea? Just as with more advantaged teens, the answer lies in the results. Again, whereas the one way to win philosophy is certainly appropriate for some disadvantaged youth, and it is certainly a matter of national pride and social justice that these youth are able to purse this path, the question remains: is it good advice for all? Logic alone suggests otherwise. But there are more specific concerns.

In his book *Street Wise*, Elijah Anderson (1990) argues that among urban youth, the best predictor of persistence and success in school is hope for a better future. At the same time, according to other researchers, although low-income youth may have the same ambitions as their more blessed peers, their expectations for achieving these goals are significantly less. Thus, although hope is critical to breaking the poverty cycle, telling economically disadvantaged youth that their only hope is a bachelor's degree is counterproductive. For many, a 4-year college degree is beyond their perception of the possible. As a result, they end up with no hope. Some drop out for a life on the streets or dead-end jobs; others find it safer and socially acceptable to stay in school with their friends. The latter group comes to school each day but tunes out when in class. These youth deserve better. Holding out only one valued alternative—a 4-year college degree—is cruel and unethical and does them more harm than good. For one thing, they are the least likely to be academically ready for such a challenge.

While hard to accept, the reality is that the likelihood of being prepared to do 4-year college academic work is directly correlated with family household income. For example, 53% of 1992 low-income (less than $25,000) high school graduates have sufficient academic qualifications for admission to a 4-year college, compared with 68% of middle-income ($25,000–$74,999) graduates and 86% of graduates from high-income families (NCES, 1998, Indicator 8).

The unavoidable fact is that low-income students are the least prepared for a university education. As a result, high percentages of those students who try the one way to win strategy end up taking remedial courses in college. These courses cost the same as standard curriculum courses but do not count toward a degree. Although justified on the grounds of providing opportunity or a second chance for these students, the problem is that they are largely ineffective at doing so: most who take these courses never graduate.

The plight of economically disadvantaged youth from the academic middle who pursue the one way to win paradigm is about the same as that of more advantaged teens from the middle—the majority of both groups fail to graduate—but there is one important difference that seems to be totally disregarded. For teens from low-income families, the consequences of trying the one way to win path and then failing are a lot worse. Why? Because those from middle- and upper-income families are (a) much less likely to have student loan debt, and (b) if they do, they are more likely to have financial help from their families. Thus while the one way to win mantra is not benign for all youth, it can be particularly devastating for those from low-income families who fail and have accumulated significant student loan debt.

Does this grim picture mean that low-income youth should be discouraged from 4-year higher education? Of course not! Although some argue that everyone should have an equal right to fail, we argue that until society can ensure equal probabilities of success and equal costs of failure for all youth, indiscriminately promoting a 4-year college education to low-income youth from the academic middle of the nation's high schools sets up too many for failure. Such a situation could, in fact, be construed as a conspiracy to ensure their failure. Youth from economically disadvantaged homes desperately need hope, alternatives, and other ways to win.

The good news is that, arguably, economically disadvantaged youth have the most to gain from considering other ways to win. Why? Because they are generally dramatically underrepresented in the second and third highest-paying occupational group, namely, crafts, precision manufacturing, specialized repair, and technical support (see Table 3.1). This is particularly true for women, but it is also the case for African Americans and Hispanics. Their share of jobs in these occupational groups should be similar to their percentage of the total labor force, specifically women (46.2%), African Americans (10.8%), and Hispanics (9.8%). Obviously, this is not the case; all three groups are underrepresented. As a result, many employers are actively seeking women and people of color. Most occupations in these two groups do not require a 4-year degree; in some cases, no degree is required at all. They all require formal training, as verified by completing a high school CTE program, which is linked to a 1- or 2-year postsecondary pre-baccalaureate technical education, a formal apprenticeship program, or relevant military training while in the service.

Section III

Women and the Gender Wage Gap

Among the true believers in the one way to win philosophy, young women appear to be the most zealous. In 2004, there were 2 million more women in higher education than men. They earned 57% of all bachelor's degrees. The female/male higher education enrollment ratio has become so lopsided that some 4-year colleges are now actively recruiting males. Like their male counterparts, women are in college primarily to "get a better job" (see Table 1.1). In some studies, young women are actually more apt than young men to say that "being successful in work" and "being able to find steady work" are "very important" to them.

Again, we ask, is this development good or bad? Again, the results suggest that celebrations may be premature. For example, census bureau data indicate that while women outnumber men in college, their overall graduation rate from 4-year colleges (26%) is lower than that of males (29%). Overall, the prognosis for young women from the academic middle who pursue the one way to win strategy is about the same as for young men; they enroll in third-or fourth-tier institutions, they take remedial courses, only slightly higher percentages graduate, and their prospects are few when they do graduate. As an indication, despite rising educational levels, women are twice as likely as men to be at high risk of underemployment and eight times as likely to be at medium risk of underemployment as men (Mohammed, 1998). One reason for high underemployment is the choices women make in college. According to the American Council on Education, women are five to eight times more likely to choose majors related to the helping professions than those in engineering, management, computer science, or nonprofessional technical areas such as drafting, construction, or manufacturing.

Women still cluster in low-paying professional occupations. A population survey conducted by the federal government found that only 28% of computer systems analysts and 31% of computer programmers were women, even though 70% or more of these workers were younger than 44. Young women are three to four times less likely than men to major in electrical engineering or computer science and six times less likely to major in 2-year associate-degree technical programs.

One of the reasons so many young women try the one way to win game is that they seem not to know of other ways to win. It is worth noting, for example, that among entering college freshmen, women are 25% more likely than men to be undecided about careers. When pressed to make a choice, they all make the same choice: 68% hope to land a job in the helping professions.

Meanwhile, some researchers who seek to narrow the gender wage gap have concluded that the problem is no longer too few

Table 3.1   Percentage of Labor Force and Occupational Groups Comprising
Women, African Americans, and Hispanics, 2004

	Women	*African Americans*	*Hispanics*
Total labor force	46	11	13
Managerial	50	8	6
Professional	56	9	6
Service occupations	56	16	19
Sales and office	64	11	10
Construction/repair	5	7	22
Production and transportation	23	14	19
Farming, fishing, and forestry	21	5	39

Source: Labor Force Participation, by the U.S. Department of Labor, Bureau of Labor Statistics, 2004. Retrieved August 22, 2005, from ftp://ftp.bls.gov/pub/special.requests/lf/aat11.txt

women executives but too few women in other high skill/high wage occupations. Thus Terrell (1992) argues that narrowing the wage gap in the future will depend on breaking up sex segregation among occupations. Although some of the unequal representation of women in high-paying professional occupations may still have to do with gender barriers, or "glass ceilings," in the case of many other high-paying occupations, one major reason is that few women aspire to, and thus do not prepare for, these careers.

The problem is that, although women are gaining parity in the professions, they are seriously underrepresented in high-paying nonprofessional careers. Table 3.1 lists the six occupational groups (used often in this book) identified by the Department of Labor. In the table, the occupational groups are not listed alphabetically, but rather from highest to lowest according to the average yearly income of those who work in each group. The table reports the percentage of women employed in each occupational group. The message is clear: although women have gained parity in the highest paid managerial and professional group, they represent only 5% of the labor force in the third highest-paid group—crafts, precision metal, and specialized repair.

Breaking down the barriers to occupations that do not traditionally include women will be the real feminist challenge in the future.

Telling all women that they should go to college in the hope of entering the professional ranks—the one way to win message—is counterproductive. History has already proven that too many women take this advice, only to end up employed in clerical positions because they could not obtain a teaching job or get into law school. Meanwhile, the demand for women in high skill/high wage occupations that require only a pre-baccalaureate postsecondary education is staggering. But the typical profile of a woman who begins a career in a nontraditional occupational area for women is that she is 32 years old, is divorced, and has children (Sternberg & Tuchscherer, 1992). Young women are six times less likely than men to major in 2-year associate-degree technical programs (American Council on Education, 2004). Obviously, young women currently are seeing only one way to win. Those who seek to improve young women's plight in the labor market would do well to help them consider other ways to win.

OTHER WAYS TO WIN

One major way the one way to win mentality is promoted is from the well-intended efforts of government, advocacy groups, and individuals who hope that a single focus on academics in high school—such as dictated by NCLB—that prepares all for college is in the best interest of all students. They think such a focus will break the poverty cycle and improve the earnings of females relative to males. In such a scenario, teens at risk of dropping out, special needs students, and those who want to go to work after graduating from high school are largely forgotten. Unfortunately, the pursuit of a 4-year college degree in preparation for a professional career is an appropriate strategy for only some low-income youth, some special needs kids, and some young women; it is not realistic for all, particularly for those from the academic middle. And, unfortunately, the one way to win plan increases high school dropout rates and leads many parents of special needs students to make plans that are both expensive and doomed.

Importantly, many other impoverished and special needs youth view college as an impossible "wannabe" dream and, without alternatives, they lose hope. Meanwhile, the teens whose parents push them to follow the one way to win path and enter college are, on average, the least prepared to be successful, the most likely to have to take remedial course work, the most likely to drop out of college, the most likely to end up underemployed if they do earn a degree, and the least able to cope with the financial consequences.

Likewise, some argue that the one way to win mentality is leading a majority of young females from the academic middle of high school seniors down a labor market path to professions that are too narrow to accommodate them. Meanwhile, other more promising career paths for women, especially in technician-level employment, go untraveled. The real gender gap issue is not the glass ceiling but too few women in high-paying nonprofessional occupations outside of the helping professions. The one way to win mantra makes even the consideration of such alternatives very difficult for young women.

Of course, these arguments demand proof that (a) those in the academic middle are unprepared to do college-level work, (b) when they go to college they do not do well, and (c) those who do graduate will face a very overcrowded labor market for 4-year college graduates. We provide this evidence and discuss the reasons for the public's blind eye toward this travesty in Part II of this book. Our discussion begins in Chapter 4 with an honest look at the academic preparation of high school students who make up the academic middle.

NOTE

1. Purdum, T. (1994, August 7). Moynihan's mouth and muscle. *New York Times*, p. 26. Copyright © 1994 The New York Times Company. Reprinted by permission.

PART II

Counting the Losers in the One Way to Win Game

CHAPTER FOUR

Questionable Academic Preparation

> Long-term trends show that as the "A" average becomes the norm, the "C" grade is becoming a thing of the past.
>
> —*Higher Education Research Institute*[1]

A t one time, going to college was unusual; today, the high school graduate who goes directly to work is the oddity. Throughout the period from 2000 to 2005, on average, around 1.8 million or 65% of all high school graduates enrolled immediately in higher education, whereas 30% of all graduates went to work or entered the military. Of those in higher education, two-thirds enrolled in 4-year colleges, and at least one-third of those who enrolled in 2-year institutions were not taking occupational programs but general studies courses. Thus of all high school graduates, the vast majority go to college, and the largest group enrolls in 4-year colleges or 2-year programs in preparation for transfer to a baccalaureate degree program. Is this a positive development? Perhaps not, if many are academically unprepared to benefit from the experience. Thus it seems prudent to ask this question: how many of these 1.8 million new college freshmen are prepared to do college work? Our focus of analysis is the effectiveness of the revered and respected high school college prep curriculum.

Section I

How Effective Is the College
Prep Program of Study?

Today, most youth aspire to baccalaureate education. Not surprisingly, the majority, including those in the academic middle, also say they took the college prep program in high school in order to prepare for college. Using National Center for Education Statistics (NCES) national high school transcript data, Table 4.1 summarizes high school course-taking patterns. More than two-thirds of students take the academic program of study. Twenty percent take both (combined) academic and career and technical education program of study.

If grades in high school are any indication, the college prep program is very effective. Among college freshmen involved in the annual UCLA college freshman survey in 2004, a record high 47% indicated they graduated from high school with an A average. But

Table 4.1   Demographic Distribution (%) of High School Graduates by Program of Study: 1998 High School Graduates

	Entire sample	Academic	Combined academic and CTE	Traditional CTE	General
1998		70	20	4	6
Female	53	56	43	32	55
Male	47	44	57	68	45
White	75	76	72	81	61
Black	14	13	17	9	15
Hispanic	11	11	11	10	24
4 E, 3 SS, 3 M, 3 S, 2 F	44	54	34	0	0
4 E, 3 SS, 3 M, 3 S	55	64	53	0	0
4 E, 3 SS, 2 M, 2 S	75	83	80	15	15

Source: 1998 Transcript Study Tabulations, NCES 2001-498, by the National Center for Educational Statistics, 2001.

Note: By definition, it is not possible for a vocational or general student to take course combinations in rows 6 and 7.
CTE = career and technical education; E = English; F = foreign language; M = mathematics; S = science; SS = social studies.

there is room for skepticism: these students also indicated that the amount of time they spent studying remained low. Only 34% indicated they spent six or more hours per week studying in their senior year.

The question is, how many high school students actually graduate prepared to do college-level academic work? Everyone? Some? A few? If not everyone, then maybe the one way to win strategy, at least, as pursued directly after high school, is, for some, ill-advised. Table 4.1 provides a beginning clue. Of the 70% who are in the supposed academic or college prep program, only a little over half (54%) take what would be called a minimal college prep set of courses that includes three years of math and science and two years of a foreign language. These students, and especially their parents, may think they are in the college prep program, but few grasp that in most high schools, there are actually two.

Part of the subterfuge caused by the growth of the one way to win mentality and the corresponding growth in the number of students wishing to take college prep courses has been the bifurcation of the college prep curriculum to distinguish between the academically blessed and those from the academic middle. Today, in virtually all U.S. high schools, at least two college prep programs are going on simultaneously: One consists of the regular college prep courses; the other is the college "honors" or "advanced placement" (AP) courses. Most would consider the latter to be the college prep program of old.

The mere existence of these two levels of college prep programs hints that one group of students may not be getting quite the same preparation as the other. Many teens and their parents may be deluding themselves. Just because teens are enrolled in college prep programs does not necessarily mean they graduate prepared to do college-level work, even when they got good grades in high school, which is a reality that often becomes brutally apparent only when disappointing college board entrance test results arrive in the mail. Surprisingly, no one seems concerned about, or at least has questioned, the effectiveness of the college prep curriculum. In fact, No Child Left Behind (NCLB) seems to promote its expansion to all teens based on the assumption that it is effective. It seems appropriate, then, to take a closer look at the effectiveness of a college prep program of study in the light of the large number of academically average students enrolling in it.

THE COLLEGE PREP PROGRAM
AND THE ACADEMIC MIDDLE

Increases in enrollment in college prep programs and NCLB-led proposals that all teens should take this program of study have only recently resulted in investigations about its effectiveness for the academically diverse cohort participating in it. Specifically, if the objective of the college prep program is to prepare students for college admission and success in college-level academic work, how many of those who enroll actually achieve these outcomes? No doubt some do, particularly if the academically blessed are separated into honors classes with the best teachers. But what about the rest?

This question is important for those who suspect that the one way to win paradigm may, in fact, encourage many academically average teens to pursue postsecondary plans that are unrealistic and doomed to fail.

Several national studies suggest that if 72% of recent high school graduates are in college within two years of graduating, two-thirds of whom are supposedly working toward a university degree, many are academically ill prepared. One indicator is the National Assessment of Education Progress. Table 4.2 indicates the percentages who scored at proficient and advanced levels in reading, mathematics, and science. Level 300 in reading is defined as being able to understand complicated written information; Level 350 is the ability to learn from specialized reading materials (such as college reading lists). Most would agree that wannabe college freshmen should be able to read at these levels, but in 2002, only 31% could read at this level—down 8% from 1998. Proficiency in mathematics is the ability to solve mathematics problems using algebra; 60% had mathematics skill at this level. Not all that impressive, considering that around 65% of this group will enter college when they are 18 years old.

Equally interesting is a study done by the NCES (1998, Indicator 8) that sought to determine the percentage of youth who graduated from high school qualified to do college-level academics. Importantly, this study included only students who were already enrolled in 4-year colleges. The criteria included high school class rank, courses taken, and standardized test scores. For example, minimally qualified students need only have graduated in the top 50% of their high school class, have a C average, and have a combined SAT

Table 4.2   National Assessment of Educational Progress: Percentage of
1998 and 2002 17-Year-Old High School Seniors Scoring at
College Levels of Proficiency

Subject	1998	2002
Reading		
Level 300: Proficient	39%	31%
Level 350: Advanced	6%	5%
Math		
Level 300: Proficient	60%	61%
Level 350: Advanced	7%	8%
Science		
Level 300: Proficient	21%	18%
Level 350: Advanced	3%	2%

Source: National Assessment of Educational Progress, 2004 Long-Term Trend Assessment
Results, by the National Center for Educational Statistics, 2005. Retrieved August 22, 2005,
from http://nces.ed.gov/nationsreportcard/ltt/results2004/

Note: *Proficient* represents solid academic performance for each grade assessed.
Students reaching this level have demonstrated competency over challenging subject
matter, including subject matter knowledge, application of such knowledge to real-world
situations, and analytical skills appropriate to the subject matter.

score of 820 or a composite ACT of 19. Table 4.3 shows the
results.

Table 4.3 suggests that, of all those students in 4-year colleges,
only two-thirds are even minimally qualified. If one argues, as we
do, that the minimally qualified are really not academically qualified
to succeed in college, the result is rather sobering. More than half
(52%) of students pursuing the one way to win dream at 4-year
colleges are not academically prepared. If we were to take the
old-fashioned view that only highly qualified students should be
pursuing a 4-year degree, then the unavoidable conclusion is that
only 32% are qualified to do so. It is little wonder that in some institutions, two-thirds of entering freshmen are in remedial education,
and six years later, only about half have graduated.

Additional insight into just how many so-called college prep
students graduate from high school prepared to do college-level
academics is supplied by a high school follow-up study done for this
book. This study examined in detail the experiences of 1998 high
school graduates.

Table 4.3   Academic Readiness of Enrolled College Students

Race/ethnicity and family income	Marginally qualified or unqualified	College qualified				
		Total	Minimally	Moderately	Highly	Very highly
Total	35.5	64.5	16.6	15.9	18.2	13.8
Race/ethnicity						
White	53.1	68.2	16.1	16.6	20.3	15.2
Black	53.1	46.9	16.7	14.0	9.9	6.3
Hispanic	47.0	53.0	20.7	13.6	10.8	7.9
Asian/Pacific islander	27.3	72.7	14.6	15.0	20.2	23.0
American Indian/ Alaskan native	55.2	44.8	22.2	15.8	5.9	1.0
Family income						
Low (less than $25,000)	47.5	52.5	18.7	12.8	13.6	7.3
Middle ($25,000-$74,999)	32.4	67.6	16.1	17.0	19.9	14.6
High ($75,000 or more)	14.1	5.9	11.5	18.4	27.0	29.0

Source: National Center for Education Statistics, 1998.

FOLLOW-UP STUDY OF RECENT HIGH SCHOOL GRADUATES

The best indicator of the need for promoting other ways to win at any particular high school is to look at what happens to its students the first year after graduation. However, unless it is based on what courses they took in high school, such evaluation is meaningless. For example, the implication of large numbers of students taking remedial courses in college depends clearly on what they did or did not take in high school. If most were quasi-general/academic students, then it is understandable. If, on the other hand, many were in honors courses, the implications are quite different. Thus rather than just sending graduates a questionnaire regarding their first-year experiences, a better approach is to also collect information regarding courses taken, grade point averages (GPAs), absences, test scores, and so forth, for each graduate. This information is then used to develop a longitudinal data set that links students' high school records with their post–high school experiences. This was the approach taken in the follow-up study discussed below.

Seven high schools that included inner-city urban, rural, and suburban locals participated in the study. Regardless of the demographics, sending as many teens on to college as possible was the criterion of success. None of these high schools had an official general track program, and typically less than 15% of the students completed a concentration in vocational education. Thus, by default, most students must be considered to have been in the academic/ college prep program of study.

The question we are asking is, how many were actually prepared? Unlike the NCES study that evaluated just those enrolled in 4-year colleges, this study looked at all high school graduates in the participating high schools.

Table 4.4 indicates the range of students at various high schools assigned to three levels of preparedness to do college-level academics: namely, prepared, marginally prepared, and unprepared. The criteria used were three years of college math and two lab sciences,

Table 4.4   Percentage of High School Graduates Prepared to Do College-Level Academics

Range of Preparation for College

	A: prepared	B: marginally prepared	A + B	Unprepared
	10–27%	8–28%	28–55%	72–45%

Criterion

	3 years college prep math	2 years college lab science	2 years same foreign language	Combined SAT scores	High school GPA
Prepared	Yes	Yes	Yes	1100	B
Marginal	Yes	Yes	Yes	800	C
Unprepared			Default		

Source: Gray and Xiaoli, 1999.

GPA = grade point average.

two years of the same foreign language, cumulative GPAs, and combined SAT scores. Because of wide differences in demographic/ socioeconomic settings of the participating high schools, ranges are provided instead of averages.

To be assigned to the academically prepared group, a student must have taken the required courses, earned a GPA of B or better, and had a combined (verbal + math) score of 1100. At the best-performing high schools, 27% of graduates had these credentials; at the other end, only 10% did. Of course, it can be argued that these criteria are too difficult. And it could also be argued that they are too lax; clearly, they would not be sufficient to gain admission to colleges that still have competitive versus open admissions.

Nonetheless, a second count was conducted to identify students who were marginally prepared academically for college, meaning that they probably could survive in college, though some remediation might be necessary. To be included in this category, students needed to take the courses but needed only a C average and a minimum combined test score of 800. Again, at the best-performing high school, these more lax standards added 28% versus 18% at the poorest-performing site. Perhaps most important is the column (A + B) which combines these two levels: prepared and marginally prepared. In the "best case," only 55% of the graduates were either prepared or marginally prepared to succeed in college (see Table 4.4). It is to be remembered that these data are for teens from a state that has had increased graduation requirements and state testing long before NCLB, yet there is little evidence to suggest that the result has been anything other than perhaps grade inflation.

GOING TO COLLEGE: DO ACADEMIC CREDENTIALS MATTER?

From the information provided in Table 4.4, it is clear that, at best, about half of high school students graduate even semi-prepared to do college-level academics. But most, two-thirds, were in college anyway. Not surprisingly, virtually all of the prepared and semi-prepared graduates were in college (see Table 4.5).

But what about the group that interests us the most, those who graduate with credentials suggesting that they are not prepared to pursue the one way to win strategy? Amazingly, more than half were also

Table 4.5   Post-High School Pursuits of Respondents (%)

	Full-time student	Full-time student working part time	Full-time employment	Part-time employment	Others
Total	46	32	14	6	2
Prepared (academically competitive)	71	27	1	1	0
Marginally prepared (semicompetitive)	55	36	4	5	0
Unprepared (noncompetitive)	23	33	29	10	5

Source: Gray and Xiaoli, 1999.

in college. This finding is startling for three reasons: None of these graduates (1) had a combined SAT score of over 800, (2) had taken a complete sequence of college prep courses, and (3) had maintained a C average. The expectation at this point may be that these students enroll mostly in 2-year institutions such as community colleges or technical schools. This is not the case; many of these students are in 4-year colleges. Apparently, the idea that it takes good academic credentials to get into a 4-year college is old-fashioned.

In general, the data confirm the wide acceptance of the one way to win paradigm: The only way to win is to have a 4-year college degree; 78% of all graduates were in 4-year colleges. What is astounding, however, is that almost half (47%) of the students who graduated with academically noncompetitive credentials were also in 4-year colleges. Of those in 2-year institutions, we can be only somewhat certain that the 15% in business and technical schools were not taking general studies courses in the hope of transferring to 4-year degree programs.

Looking at the analysis of high school transcripts discussed previously illustrates the persuasiveness and results of the one way to win paradigm. Consistent with national data, most students in this study were in the academic/college prep program of study. But, at best, only half graduated from high school even marginally prepared to do college-level work, and of this group, about half had credentials that suggest college was going to be an academic stretch. Even though the other half (and in some high schools it is two-thirds) are not prepared, at least half of this group are in college, and half are in 4-year colleges. How do they do in college?

In addition, we should not forget the students who went to work without having taken vocational education in high school. How do they make out in the world of work? We examine these questions in Chapter 5. But before turning to the postsecondary experiences of those in the academic middle, a closer look at the high school experiences of those who graduated with academically noncompetitive credentials is worthwhile. After all, these are the students most likely to be hurt by the presence of only one way to win.

SECTION II

The High School Experience of
Those in the Academic Middle

How many math and science courses did the academically average students in this study take? As part of the Class of 1998 Follow-Up Study, data regarding levels of mathematics, science, and foreign language courses taken were collected from each student's transcript. After these patterns were summarized for just those who failed to earn either "marginally" prepared or "semi-competitively" prepared credentials, we found that the overall levels of math, science, and foreign languages taken by the remaining unprepared students were often quite high.

College Prep Course–Taking Patterns

But something seems odd, doesn't it? If these students had this much math and science, why did they do so poorly on the SAT? The data suggest that although these students were often enrolled in higher levels of math and science courses, they were somewhat untouched by the experience. Stated in another way, traditional college prep courses seem to be less effective for those in the academic middle. Unlike their more academically blessed peers, those in the academic middle may take a course but not master the content. This conclusion is substantiated by the low grades obtained by this group in these courses and by the fact that (as is reported in Chapter 5) half of those who graduated unprepared but went on to college had to take one or more remedial courses in higher education.

The point is that simply driving these students higher in the traditional curriculum—an oft-expressed goal among educational reformers—may not do much to improve their skills. Those who take solace in the fact that more academically average students are now in college prep courses are perhaps celebrating prematurely; students may be in the courses, but they may not be learning much. National grade inflation data discussed earlier suggest that in some high schools, this may be the case even when their grades indicate the opposite. In fact, they often seem to be almost unaffected by the experience. This statement brings us to another important variable: the general degree of involvement of these students in the high school curriculum.

Involvement in the Curriculum

As researchers probe the results of the steady increase in the number of students who succeed in graduating from high school, it becomes increasingly apparent that completing high school and actually learning something are two entirely different things. This reality suggests that the goal is not only to keep young people in school—or even in class—but also to engage them in the academic content as a prerequisite to learning (Anderson, 1983). Thus those seeking to improve the instructional effectiveness of schools are increasingly focusing on students' degree of involvement in, or attachment to, the curriculum.

In the light of the growing body of literature suggesting the relationship between educational achievement and involvement—and common sense tells us that it is tough to learn by not paying attention—the researchers involved in the Class of 1998 Follow-Up Study employed statistical techniques to test the degree to which students were involved in the curriculum. They did this by testing the degree to which traditional variables, such as attendance, satisfaction with high school, and working part time, affected students' grades. The rationale was that if the students were not very involved with learning in school, it would make little difference whether they were absent, liked school, or worked part time. In fact, when compared with their more academically successful peers, those who graduated with academically noncompetitive credentials had grades relatively unaffected by the variables tested. Although absences, dislike of school, and working part time all negatively affected the grades of those graduating with competitive or semi-competitive credentials, only absences affected the grades of noncompetitive students. Even then, the magnitude of the effect on grades of not coming to school was considerably less for these students than for the rest.

A pattern thus emerges. A large number of high school students take rather high levels of college prep courses, but their participation is passive, at best. They might as well take high school correspondence courses. These students are playing the one way to win game without much enthusiasm. In fact, when asked, they agreed: 75% of those in the Class of 1998 Follow-Up Study who graduated unprepared for college said they wished they "had worked harder while in high school."

Career Uncertainty

Passivity and lack of engagement by academically average students may be partially explained by the fact that, compared with their more academically successful peers, they are less certain about why they took college prep courses in the first place. Indicative of this situation is the degree to which the academically unprepared were significantly more likely to express feelings of career uncertainty. For example, these students were twice as likely to volunteer on the follow-up survey that they wished they had "thought more about their future" while in high school. Likewise, a majority (60%) of all respondents wished that the high school had provided opportunities to explore careers. In fact, a much higher percentage (80%) of those graduating with academically noncompetitive credentials thought this way; this finding suggests a higher level of both career uncertainty and anxiety.

Thus, although we cannot say with certainty that career immaturity or uncertainty was a factor in their lack of academic success, it may be something more than a coincidence that the more successful the students were in the college prep program, the less likely they were to express a need for opportunities to explore careers. Studies of community college undergraduate and graduate students, for example, indicate that at least half of America's postsecondary population indicates a need for assistance with career planning, career choice, or both (Herr, Cramer, & Niles, 2004). One wonders, then, about these students' level of commitment to preparing for college, in the light of their relative uncertainty about their future. This speculation adds weight to the argument that many pursue college prep because they have been provided with only one way to win. It would seem that if they needed guidance, they did not get it in high school. In fact, in high school, they were largely asked to take a back seat.

Second-Class Status

If the academically average seem largely uninvolved, it is because they are treated this way within the social framework of the U.S. high school. Basically, they are largely ignored and treated as second-class citizens.

In the true Taylorist tradition, high school educators appear to be preparing the academically less blessed for future roles as quiescent, anonymous subordinates. As is pointed out in the still classic work, *The Shopping Mall High School* (Powell, Farrar, & Cohen, 1985), these students are relegated to the role of "spectator." While these authors' study was conducted 20 years ago, not much has changed. If a high school has an awards assembly, and they all do, one does not have to attend to know what happens. Ninety percent of the individual awards go to five percent of the kids. The role of the rest, those average kids in the academic middle, is to sit passively during awards assemblies while their more blessed peers receive all the awards. They are expected to show "school spirit" by filling the stands at pep rallies for more honored student athletes. Even the uniqueness that should fall on those in the academic middle because of enrollment in revered college prep courses does not occur: today, virtually everyone is enrolled in this curriculum. The awards are reserved now only for those enrolled in honors or AP college prep courses. This Taylorist modus operandi is not lost on students, particularly those relegated to second-class status. As part of the Class of 1998 Follow-Up Study, graduates were asked whether they thought "some students were treated better than others"; 78% of all graduates and 84% of those graduating with noncompetitive credentials responded affirmatively.

How is it possible for nearly half of the teens in any high school to be lost, even when they are in a college prep program of study?

Some researchers suggest a masked bias by teachers in favor of the more academically talented. Evidence suggests that teachers do describe and treat the blessed in significantly more positive terms than the less blessed (Oakes, 1985). But, in most cases, the situation is probably due more to benign neglect than to covert plots or sinister prejudices. Perhaps there are simply too many teens and too few teachers. Regardless, few would debate that when it comes to academic performance, the standards for those in the academic middle are lower, there is little demand for excellence, and the teens know it. And while NCLB penalties are designed to correct this situation, it is just as likely that when a large number of kids fail prescribed tests, the test and the penalties will be changed. In fact, by the spring of 2005, several states were threatening to sue the federal government over NCLB, and the U.S. Office of Education was signaling greater flexibility. The reality is that as long as open admission is the rule, not the exception, in higher education, and teens know that they will get in somewhere, there is little incentive for high school students in the academic middle to worry about the tests.

Low Academic Expectations

As part of the Class of 1998 Follow-Up Study, graduates were asked whether they wished they "had worked harder in high school." Seventy-five percent of academically unprepared students said they wished they had. Equally important, they apparently were not asked to. When asked whether they felt "pressure to get good grades," fewer than half of this group said yes. Even in college prep courses, these students are not held to the same standards as the academically gifted cohort sequestered in honors and AP courses. Homework is a good example.

Although the academically less blessed may not be able to achieve at the same level as the blessed, they should be expected to invest equal amounts of time in trying. One indicator of institutional expectation of effort is whether or not homework is regularly required. Any number of studies have documented the lower amount of homework, if any, expected of less academically blessed students (Bottoms, Pressons, & Johnson, 1992). Some researchers have gone so far as to suggest that an unwritten deal has been struck between those who make up the academic middle and their teachers. The authors of *The Shopping Mall High School* (Powell et al., 1985) call these agreements "classroom treaties," whereby unmotivated students agree not to hassle the teachers and, in turn, the teachers agree not to hassle them. Thus much less is required of these students than would be required of more academically able students.

Sedlak (1986) argues that the lack of rigorous academic standards for those in the academic middle, together with the classroom standoff between teachers and those from the academic middle who now enroll in college prep courses, represents a logical adjustment to contradictory social expectations. Specifically, in the face of unrealistic expectations of universal attendance and now universal success in preparing all students for college, high schools simply have adjusted. The academically gifted, those who are blessed with the cognitive skills to succeed in the one way to win game, are placed in honors courses and provided with a demanding and rigorous program. The rest, if they choose, are allowed to enroll in college prep courses, but the daily routine and standards within these courses are quite different from those populated by the academically blessed. Honors courses are challenging and competitive, whereas courses for the less blessed are passive, generally unchallenging, and noncompetitive. Debate and cooperative or group learning are common in advanced college prep classes, whereas lectures and predictable routine dominate classes for the average student in the college prep program. When discussion does occur in the regular college prep classes, it is often at the concrete recitation level, whereas in advanced courses, students are challenged to interpret and extrapolate. At both levels, some homework is required, but the complexity and level of thinking required in honors courses are more advanced (Powell et al., 1985). In advanced college prep classes, both the academic content and teacher expectations are what would be expected of those preparing for serious college work. The same cannot be said of regular courses populated by academically average students. This finding explains why many of those who graduate having taken college prep courses are still not prepared to do college work.

OTHER WAYS TO WIN

In this chapter, the academic credentials of high school graduates have been examined to determine the degree of readiness to pursue the most popular goal after graduation, namely, a 4-year college degree. Of particular interest was whether high school students were graduating with the advanced academic credentials needed to predict academic success in college. A study of 1998 high school graduates from seven public high schools where virtually all were supposedly preparing for college revealed that, at most, only 27% earned the academically advanced credentials normally associated with admissions and success at Level 1 colleges (those that are still selective and rigorous). At best, another 24% graduated with credentials that might predict readiness to do higher-education academic work at Level 2 institutions, those that accept virtually everyone. The remaining students graduated with credentials that suggested inadequate preparation for higher education.

Of particular importance to those seeking to create other ways to win is evidence that simply enrolling these students in traditional college prep high school courses is not instructionally effective. Although students may take the courses, they do not necessarily master the content. Furthermore, this group is largely unengaged in the high school curriculum in general, perhaps because they are largely ignored or unchallenged by high school teachers. These students report not being pressed to do well in high school and wishing they had worked harder. They also wished they had thought more about their future and had been given more opportunities to explore careers while in high school. This information suggests that, compared with their more academically successful peers, they lack career maturity. The point is that if educators are to create legitimate other ways to win, it will be necessary to devise not just postsecondary alternatives but also focused, rigorous academics that prepare students to succeed by providing well-planned and focused career exploration. Evidence suggests that this creation calls for higher expectations and new instructional approaches, all of which are explored in detail in Part III.

Data reviewed in this chapter demonstrate the unavoidable conclusion that, even in elite public high schools, only about half of graduating students are even minimally prepared to do college-level work. One can assume that, in lesser high schools, the percentage is lower. But, like their counterparts across the United States, faced with only one way to win, most students go on to higher education anyway, mostly to 4-year colleges or to 2-year general studies transfer programs. Clearly, this decision by those with noncompetitive academic credentials seems unrealistic and thus very risky. These students seem to require better alternatives or other ways to win. Of course, the validity of this argument necessitates evidence, such as data about the level of success experienced by academically average students in higher education. This topic is the focus of Chapter 5.

NOTE

1. Higher Education Research Institute. (2004, January 26). Political interest on the rebound among the nation's freshmen, UCLA survey reveals, p. 2-2-2. Retrieved August 16, 2005, from http://www.gseis.ucla .edu/hcri/03_press_release.pdf

CHAPTER FIVE

Winners and Losers in the One Way to Win Game

Diplomas from most American universities are a devalued
currency in the marketplace. It no longer means what it
used to.

—Hudson Institute[1]

I f enrollment projections are any indication, 4-year college enrollments will continue to climb through 2012. This may well be one
of those rare cases, however, where more may not be better. By the
late 1990s, some writers were suggesting that so many were pursuing
a 4-year college degree that its value, particularly in the social
sciences and liberal arts, was about equal to a high school diploma.

Indeed, by the end of the 20th century, as many persons, including politicians of all stripes, had come to associate college graduation as essential to success in the labor market, there were, on the
other hand, a growing number of criticisms of this one way to win
focus on a 4-year college education. These critics (see Boesel &
Fredland, 1999) contended that the public had come to believe that
almost all high school graduates should go to college; this go-to-college
movement was sweeping many marginally qualified or unqualified
students into college, and hence the overall academic ability of college
graduates was declining; as a result of these declines, both college
remedial academic courses and college dropouts were increasing;

many of these dropouts did poorly in the labor market and would have been better advised to pursue other types of education and training; they were often burdened with debt from college loans; and finally, even among those who did graduate, many failed to find a job that required a 4-year degree or paid a wage that made the expense of going to college worthwhile.

In general, this inventory of criticisms about the one way to win mentality provides an outline of this chapter. Among those who try the one way to win path, which is the majority of those who go to college, who then are the winners and losers?

It is argued in this book that the one way to win advice passed along to all teens and the continued growth of baccalaureate education that has resulted requires public scrutiny. If increased enrollments are resulting in more students' entering 4-year colleges unprepared, ending up in remedial courses, and flunking out after accumulating significant student loan debt, or if greater percentages of those who do graduate end up underemployed, then this growth is, in fact, both wasteful and harmful. The purpose of this chapter is to provide evidence to objectively answer the question, among those who pursue the one way to win paradigm, how many win and how many lose. If the justification is to provide opportunity, just how much opportunity is being provided?

Section I

Remedial Education and College
Dropouts: The First Losers

The conventional wisdom of one way to win is the belief that the only route—at least the only socially acceptable route—to the American dream involves getting at least a baccalaureate degree in the hope that it will lead to a job in the professional ranks. Thanks partly to the one way to win focus of No Child Left Behind, a large majority of today's high school students are taking one form or another of the academic/college prep program. Aided by open admissions at most institutions of higher education, most enroll in 4-year colleges or 2-year programs that hold a promise of leading to a 4-year degree. This is true despite the fact that many young people graduate from high school with academic credentials demonstrating a lack of preparation for college-level work.

Is the unprecedented growth in higher education enrollments, particularly in programs leading to a 4-year degree, a positive development? And is this a wise investment of both individual and public funds? The answers seem to depend first on the degree to which a reasonable number of those who enroll are academically prepared and how many graduate, and then on how many actually find a job that pays a wage that is commensurate with completing a 4-year college degree.

ACADEMIC ABILITY TO BENEFIT

One test of the wisdom of one way to win for all and, conversely, of the need to create other economically legitimate and socially acceptable alternatives to pursuing a 4-year degree, is how well freshmen, particularly those from the academic middle, perform in college. Our review of the effectiveness of college prep programs in Chapter 4 gives us reason to suspect that many who head off to college are not ready to do college-level work. College faculty, when polled, agree: only 20% of faculty at baccalaureate institutions agreed that incoming freshmen were adequately prepared in "written and oral communication skills." Only 15% felt the same way about undergraduate preparation in mathematics (Boyer, Altbach, & Whitelaw, 1994). Perhaps the best evidence of the academic deficiency of many entering freshmen at all types of higher education institutions is the number who must take remedial courses during their freshman year.

Remedial Education in Higher Education

One of the best kept secrets in higher education is the large amount of course work taken by entering freshmen that does not count toward a degree. Of the 2.4 million college freshmen in 2000, 671,000 took one or more remedial courses. Parents in particular are often shocked when they find out that their teenager, who got mostly B or even A grades in high school, is required to take remedial courses in college. According to the National Center for Education Statistics (NCES, 2000b), 80% of public and 59% of private 4-year colleges now offer remedial courses. At public 2-year colleges, where many teens from the academic middle start in hopes of transferring to a 4-year college, the rates are even higher: 98% of these institutions offer remedial courses. Forty-two percent of students at public

Figure 5.1   Remedial Education in Higher Education, Fall 1995

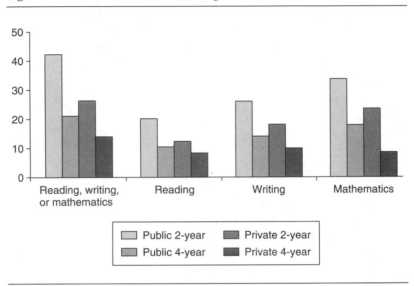

Source: National Center for Education Statistics, 2000.

2-year institutions and 20% at public 4-year institutions were taking one or more remedial courses in 2000 (see Figure 5.1). Importantly, these figures are based on data provided by the colleges, and thus there is the possibility of undercounting; other sources have reported even higher figures. Also of note, the rate of remedial course–taking in college did not change much at all between 1995 and 2000.

Our purpose is not, however, to question the merits of offering remedial education at the collegiate level or to add fuel to the debate about whether remedial education at the taxpayers' expense makes any sense at 4-year colleges. But we do ask, just how effective is this remediation? Although colleges report that three-fourths of participating students pass these courses, it does not seem to matter. Having to take remedial education courses is a strong predictor of one thing: dropping out. An Ohio study found that only about a third of students who were required to take remedial courses ever graduated.

Of particular interest to this discussion is what happens to those from the academic middle. How many must take remedial courses? One answer is provided by the high school Follow-Up Study discussed in Chapter 4 (see Table 5.1).

Table 5.1   Higher Education Freshmen: Remedial Courses and Sophomore
Status, Class of 1998 Follow-Up Study

	Remedial English	Remedial math	Any remedial	Achieved sophomore status
Unprepared	26%	31%	46%	52%
Marginally prepared	22%	5%	27%	66%

Source: Gray and Xiaoli, 1999.

Respondents in the study were asked several questions to determine their academic success in the freshman year. As a group, the participation rate in remedial education was a little less than the NCES-reported average of 28%. Few students from the prepared and about a fifth of those from the marginally prepared took remedial education. However, when one looks at the students we are interested in—those from the academic middle—the numbers are much higher. About half of the unprepared group was taking remedial courses. Similar to other national data, this study's data showed mathematics was the most common area of weakness.

So, what is the point? Our intent is not to point the finger at high schools for poor preparation. In all fairness, it must be said that high schools prepare well those blessed with the academic ability to do legitimate college-level work. Although we could fault the colleges for admitting ill-prepared students, college administrators would argue that they are providing equal opportunity through open admissions, though others argue that the true motive behind remedial education is not altruistic but tuition dollars (Roueche & Roueche, 1999).

Instead, then, our intention is to suggest that if these large numbers of students are not prepared to do baccalaureate degree academic work, then maybe—just maybe—they should be doing something else. And if, given some legitimate, socially valued alternatives that make economic sense, perhaps many of these students *would* do something else. Without other choices, what happens to those who start college having to take remedial courses? Many fail. As Burton Clark (1962) argued, "The initial move in a cooling out process is pre-entrance testing: low scores lead poorly qualified students into remedial classes . . . which slows the students moving into bona fide courses . . . and cast doubt regarding ever graduating" (pp. 569–577).

Although in Clark's time remedial courses were confined to 2-year junior colleges, today they exist virtually everywhere in higher education except truly selective 4-year colleges. Their effect, however, has not changed over time. Enrollment in remedial courses is the first sign of trouble in the one way to win game. The second sign is the number returning home after completion of the freshman year who have not earned a sufficient number of credits to be classified as sophomores.

College Dropouts

Of high school graduates who go directly on to higher education, the first losers are those who must take remedial education courses. The second group of losers is those who fail to persist to graduate. These include many who take remedial education and also many who do not. How many actually graduate?

Table 5.2 shows the percentage of students who actually graduate with some type of a degree five years after they start, based on the degree they were pursuing; of those who pursue a 4-year college degree, 54% graduated in five years. A newer NCES study that tracked whether those who transfer to other colleges graduated increased the five-year graduation rate to 67% (Adelman, 1999).

Table 5.2   Highest Degree Obtained Within Five Years

By Students Seeking a Bachelor's Degree

	Highest degree completed in five years (%)			
Level of first institution	Bachelor's	Associate	Certificate	Any
Total all institutions	45.8	5.1	3.3	54.3
4-year colleges	57.1	2.5	2.1	61.7
2-year colleges	7.9	13.9	7.2	29.0

By Students Seeking a 2-Year Degree or Certificate

	Highest degree completed in five years (%)			
Degree	Bachelor's	Associate	Certificate	Any
Associate degree	7.5	23.7	11.4	42.6
Certificate	0.5	4.3	49.7	54.5

Sources: National Center for Education Statistics, 2000a and 2005.

A higher percentage of those who start at 4-year institutions earn a degree than those who start in transfer programs at 2-year institutions (7.9%). In fact, of those who start a transfer program at a 2-year college, only 29% earn any type of degree five years later. This latter point is important to dwell on. Teens from the academic middle, especially those with academic credentials that predict failure in college, those from low-income families, and those who have no well-thought-out reasons to go to college in the first place are more often than not counseled by well-meaning adults to start at a community college transfer program. The problem is that most of these students fail.

At the same time, Table 5.2 provides insight into other ways to win. Of those who pursue an associate degree or certificate at a 2-year institution, the success rate is about the same as that for the more academically blessed who enroll in 4-year colleges. This suggests that the persistence rate is dramatically better for those from the academic middle if they pursue a certificate or associate degree program, most of which are typically career related, rather than prepare to transfer to a 4-year college. To quote Boesel and Fredland (1999),

High school graduates of modest ability or uncertain motivation who are thinking of enrolling in four-year colleges would be well advised to consider attending two-year colleges instead. If they did so, they would probably realize the same earning and cognitive skills at lower costs with less debt. (p. ix)

Of course, students drop out of college for a variety of reasons. Some of these would exist even if there were other ways to win. Of interest here are the variables that cause students to drop out and that can be influenced in high school. One way to focus on these variables is to examine students who drop out during their freshman year because, arguably, these are the ones whose failure is most related to their high school preparation.

Many parents of college freshmen spend their child's first year in college in various stages of apprehension, waiting for the dreaded "I am coming home" call. They sense, without being told, another one of higher education's well-guarded secrets: basically, combining both 2- and 4-year colleges, one-third of all college freshmen drop out during their freshman year (Noel & Levitz, 1985). Many drop out before they even really begin. If the number of all freshman dropouts is subtracted from the number of those who leave between semesters, half of the rest drop out during the first 6 weeks. It is a mistake to think that these students simply flunk out. In fact, some data suggest that the first-year dropout rates for college freshmen are just as high for academically able students as for marginal students.

The huge number of entering freshmen who fail to return the following year suggests that many youth are making what they later decide was a bad decision. They do not necessarily fail; that can take a couple of years. Instead, they drift away. They have played the college game and made everyone happy, but high school graduation is over and the pressures are not as intense; they throw in the towel and leave school, but not without costs. According to the General Accounting Office (GAO) (1991), an important predictor of those who will default on student loan debts is whether they failed to complete their first year. Thus, for at least one-third of all college freshmen, going to college proves, in the first year, to be a very expensive mistake. One wonders how many of these, even among those who are academically gifted, did not really want to go in the first place and would have made other choices if they had had other ways to win that adults were willing to value their pursuing.

The good news is that 4-year college graduation rates may not be a bleak as was previously thought. When those who transfer to other 4-year colleges are not counted as dropouts, the six-year graduation rate is reported in one study to be 68%. While the survey of households by the U.S. Census Bureau suggests this number is high, nevertheless, at least two-thirds of those who start a 4-year degree may well finish. So these are the winners in the one way to win game. Well, yes, some are, but unfortunately for some, the real bad news comes after graduation. The bad news is that almost half of those who do graduate from college will end up underemployed.

SECTION II

Underemployed College Graduates: The Second Losers

National survey data (see Table 1.1) of both high school graduates and entering college freshmen show that the principal reasons for going to college is to get a high-paying job. In fact, economic uncertainty regarding future employment opportunities and the conclusion that only a 4-year college degree offers any opportunities have been largely responsible for the growth in college enrollments since the early 1980s. Overwhelmingly, high school graduates place their hopes for a secure economic future in one set of occupations: the professions.

In a study of graduating seniors, 49.3% of males and 68.8% of females expected to be employed in the professions (see Table 1.2). No other occupational choice was even close. Only 6.7% were inspired either to own their own businesses or to be managers or technicians (6.0%). Only 2.8% expected to enter the well-paying skilled trades. For all practical purposes, everyone has the same career plan, and its folly is obvious. Major league baseball players make lots of money, but (a) not everyone has the talent to be one, and (b) even if everyone did, there are only so many jobs in the big leagues to go around. The same is true of professional work.

The public in general and students and parents in particular seem to have faith that if one earns a 4-year degree that includes a professional credential, such as a teaching certificate or a law degree, a job will be waiting. The assumption is that the demand for professionals will increase to accommodate the rising percentage of the population who hold these credentials. By the turn of the new century, signs indicated that this faith was not well placed. At the 2004 meeting of the American Economic Association, much time was spent by presenters discussing the leveling-off of returns to a college education, and while college graduates do earn more than high school graduates, the gain is mostly due to a decrease in wages of high school graduates, not a dramatic increase in wages of university graduates (Uchitelle, 2005).

The Labor Market Outlook for College Graduates

Students, parents, and all those promoting the one way to win strategy take note. Evidence suggests that, even among those who persist to graduate, many will end up losers. The reality is that there are not enough jobs that require a 4-year degree to go around. Projections by the U.S. Department of Education regarding degrees awarded annually, with projections by the U.S. Department of Labor regarding the demand for jobs at various levels of education (see Table 5.3),

Table 5.3   Comparison of Occupation Supply and Demand by Higher
Education Credentials to the Year 2010

	Supply	Demand	% Underemployed
First professional	81,600	69,100	15
Doctoral	47,100	76,000	0
Master's	439,000	63,400	86
Bachelor's	1,324,000	730,400	45

Sources: Supply data are from *Projections of Education Statistics to 2010,* by the National
Center for Education Statistics, 2000. Retrieved August 21, 2005, from http://nces.ed.gov/
pubs2001/2001048.pdf. Demand data are from "Occupational Employment Projections to
2010," by the U.S. Department of Labor, Bureau of Labor Statistics, 2004, *Monthly Labor
Review, 127,* 80–105.

Note: Demand data reflect projected average annual job openings due to growth and net
replacements; total job openings due to growth and net replacements during 2000–2010
was divided by 10.

predict a dramatic oversupply of those with advanced degrees in
general and those with a 4-year college degree in particular.

Table 5.3 provides a comparison of the projected supply of
degrees awarded at the bachelor's level or above and the labor market
demand for individuals educated at these levels. Our main interest is
the 4-year degree level. The annual demand for 4-year college graduates is substantial: 730,000 jobs annually. That number sounds like
a lot until one takes note of the supply numbers. Annually, the nation's
colleges are projected to graduate 1.324 million individuals. The
implication is clear. On average, 45 of every 100 who persist to get
a degree will not find commensurate employment. This amounts to
over half a million persons annually and, of course, this number
compounds each year. Thus, between 1998 and 2006, there are
projected to be well over 4 million underemployed 4-year college
graduates.

The stark reality is that, while the percentage of teens trying the
one way to win paradigm increases each year and the percentage of
young adults who have a 4-year degree grows each year, the percentage of all work that requires education at this level does not; the
total number of jobs grows, of course, but not enough to provide jobs
for all who graduate. Despite all the rhetoric about the need for further education, labor studies suggest that the percentage of all work
that requires a 4-year degree is only 12%, which is only 1% higher
than it was 15 years ago (Silvestri, 1997). In fact, only 24% of all

jobs in the United States require education beyond a 2-year degree; 40% of all work can be learned in only two weeks on the job.

Thus not surprisingly, an ongoing NCES study of recent 4-year college graduates, Baccalaureate and Beyond (McCormick & Knepper, 1996), found that almost half (43%) said that they held jobs that did not require a 4-year degree one year after they graduated. In the second follow-up of the same cohort, now four years after they graduated, almost half were still saying they were in jobs that did not require a 4-year degree and had no career potential.

The mismatch between projected demand and supply of credentialed college graduates becomes even more dramatic when one looks at data for selected occupations. Table 5.4 also provides the projected average annual job openings for specific occupational groups, the number of education and training credentials awarded annually, and the resultant net demand or surplus of candidates. Notice immediately the projected net demand in professional occupations. Most high school graduates who go to college say they expect to work in the professional ranks, but there clearly are not enough jobs to go around. For example, the economy is expected to generate 623,000 jobs in the professional specialty category, but it is also projected that the higher education system will award more than 1.1 million professional undergraduate and graduate degrees. Considering that these supply figures do not include other sources of employees for these professional jobs, such as professionals trained abroad, or project the number of these jobs that may well go overseas as globalization and free trade play themselves out, it is clear that, at best, only one of two who prepare for the specialized professional ranks will find commensurate employment.

The sobering bottom line for 49.3% of male and 68.8% of female high school graduates with ambitions to enter the professions (Table 1.2) is that, at best, even among those who actually graduate from college, there will be twice as many individuals graduating with professional credentials as there will be jobs available. In fact, the data reveal many widespread misconceptions about the need for certain types of professionals. Although the oversupply of lawyers is widely known, the popular belief is that there is a national shortage of scientists, engineers, and related workers. This is a misconception (see Table 5.4). Even in the hard sciences, the supply of graduates greatly exceeds the demand, a fact that leads some, such as Rustum Roy (1992), world-renowned solid state scientist, to argue that the shortage of people in the sciences is just a myth created by the National Science

Table 5.4   Projected Average Annual Job Openings, 1990–2005

	Openings	Number of credentials awarded	Net openings
Professional managerial			
Executive, administration	436,000	506,830	−70,830
Construction managers	7,000	825	+6,175
Marketing, advertising, and public relations managers	23,000	66,416	−43,416
Professional specialty	623,000	1,120,063	−497,063
Physical scientists	8,000	35,163	−27,163
Lawyers	28,006	44,314	−16,308
Blue-collar technical			
Craft, precision metal, and specialized repair	455,000	133,057	+321,943
Mechanics, installers, repairers	160,000	91,758	+68,242
Service occupations	882,000	237,062	+644,938
Operators, laborers	477,000	41,504	+435,496
Farming, forestry, fishing	90,000	14,547	+75,453

Source: Data compiled from Eck, 1993.

Foundation to obtain greater funding from Congress. Similarly, when Congress asked the GAO to investigate claims of a dramatic shortage of college-trained information technology workers in the late 1990s, the GAO reported that the demand had been grossly exaggerated. Most recently, the *Chronicle of Higher Education* (Monastersky, 2004) carried an article questioning the supposed shortage of scientists and mathematicians in general. Of note, 67% of the arts and science majors in the Baccalaureate and Beyond study, for example, said they were underemployed.

As will be discussed in Chapter 7, although serious shortages do exist, they are primarily for technicians trained at the pre-baccalaureate level. In fact, the only major professional occupations in which demand for college graduates was strong in 2005 were in the health fields, computer science, information technology, and accounting.

The bad news is not confined to the professions. When looking at other occupational groups normally associated with 4-year college-level preparation, one finds similar oversupplies. An example is professional managerial occupations. In this category, demand will exceed supply (see Table 5.4). A close look at the managerial occupational group, however, reveals some interesting exceptions that hint at other ways to win. For example, there is an oversupply of people preparing to be marketing, advertising, and public relations managers— popular majors at 4-year colleges. Conversely, the demand for individuals with the skills necessary to manage construction projects, which are well-paid positions, greatly exceeds the supply. These positions do not require a 4-year college degree. They may not be as glamorous, but they are high-paying and offer good opportunities for advancement, a fact discussed in Chapter 7.

Certainly, some who earn a 4-year degree will find commensurate employment in the future. And who are the lucky ones? More than likely *not* those from the academic middle but those who attend the better colleges (see NCES, 2000a) and those who are focused enough to select and then get admitted to the specialized majors that are in demand in the labor market. David Autor, economist at the Massachusetts Institute of Technology, suggests that the demand for these academically blessed teens will always be high and they will therefore always have high earnings because there will always be a shortage of these elite teens. But while the elite are mostly all college graduates, not all college graduates are among the cognitive elite (Uchitelle, 2005).

In most cases, those populating the ranks of the losers will be from the high school academic middle who go on to try the one way to win path at institutions sometimes described as the "colleges of the forgotten Americans" (Lovett, 2005). If labor market projections are at all accurate, more and more from the academic middle will graduate from college but never find work commensurate with their 4-year degree. They will not go unemployed; many will take the better jobs that high school graduates used to hold, but these jobs will not pay wages that begin to justify the costs in terms of the time and money it took to earn a 4-year college degree. Meanwhile, as will be pointed out in Part III of this book, there are tremendous career opportunities that many of these teens would be both capable of and happy doing that pay very well and require less than a university education. There are other ways for these young people to win.

Section III

More Losers: Those Who Prepare for College but Go to Work Instead

The percentage of high school graduates who pursue full-time employment directly after high school has hovered around 30% nationally for 15 years, and in some locales and in some states, it is much higher. Significantly, more than half of those who pursue full-time employment do not take career and technical education (CTE) in high school, but in fact are quasi–college prep students. How do these students who take just academic courses in high school fare in the labor market? The question becomes important in determining the need for other ways to win. Research on this point is clear that the significant economic rewards of attending college, be it diploma, certificate, associate degree, or above, accrue only to those who graduate. The only economic certainty for those who go to college and drop out is that many will end up with student loan debt that must be repaid. To probe this issue further, we return to the High School Follow-Up Studies.

Dead-End Jobs for Those Without Career and Technical Education

In our follow-up studies of high school graduates, we have been particularly interested in the postsecondary experiences of graduates who did not take CTE but went to work full time. Indicative of the persuasiveness of the one way to win press, 60% of this group had taken the SAT. This group contained a small percentage of very academically able students. The majority (82%), however, graduated unqualified for college. Those who went to work but had not been enrolled in CTE course work were the most marginal of college prep students. How did they do? Not well. Their average yearly income was $16,303, which would be poverty level for a family of four. Of course, many were earning even less: one-third were making between $8,000 and $15,000. The majority were working in services and transportation industries, followed by food service or retailing and manufacturing.

Importantly, the experiences of this group, particularly those who graduated with academically noncompetitive credentials, were significantly poorer than the experiences of those who took CTE. Those completing CTE programs of study were less apt to be unemployed and earned higher salaries. No doubt, the latter resulted from the fact that CTE graduates were more likely to be employed in work that required some prior skills. CTE graduates, for example, were more likely to have found employment in the skilled trades, health occupations, and food industries (not to be confused with fast-food service jobs).

Almost all of the high school graduates in these studies who were in the labor force worked in small firms: 39% in firms with fewer than 19 employees and 79% in firms with fewer than 500 employees. This finding is important because of the often-heard argument that high school students do not need courses that teach job skills because employers will provide on-the-job training. Small firms cannot afford to provide on-the-job training and are the least likely to do so (Carnevale, Gainer, & Villet, 1990). Indeed, studies indicate that American employers, compared with their foreign counterparts, invest less in new entrants to the workforce and in only limited cases provide extensive on-the-job training (Hilton, 1991). Many employers, particularly but not exclusively small firms, tend to expect young workers to come prepared with the necessary employment skills (Herr, 1995). Thus it was not surprising to find that only 22% of those in the labor force reported receiving formal training. The importance of training and its relationship to work that pays a living wage were illustrated by the data: those who reported having been trained by their employer were earning on average $19,982 a year, versus $10,000 for those who had not. Confirming other studies (Gray & Wang, 1989), the data suggest that those who think employers will train high school graduates are largely mistaken and that those who need training the most are least likely to get it unless it is in high school.

In summary, what can be said about those who take the traditional college prep program of study but go to work? Do they win or lose as a result of preparing for the one way to win game instead of for full-time employment? Compared with those who take CTE, they mostly lose. In general, they end up in unskilled jobs in small firms, mostly in the service industries. They receive no formal training and earn only minimum wage. As a group, they are more likely to be unemployed, and, if they are employed, they are more likely to earn less than students who took a comprehensive CTE program. For those seeking to create other ways to win, it is important, therefore, to note that the most at risk among those who went to work are those from the academic middle who graduated without any work training experiences. Such findings suggest that the expectation that all high school students should or will go to college and pursue a baccalaureate degree has blurred the reality that there are many students, potentially a great many, who are employment bound immediately following high school graduation. Ironically and importantly, treating all students as college bound increases the probability that high schools will *not* serve all students and will leave a lot of teens behind.

OTHER WAYS TO WIN

In this chapter, data from the postsecondary experiences of recent high school graduates have been studied to evaluate the merits of the one way to win philosophy. The data suggest the wisdom of questioning the one way to win paradigm among both those who head off to 4-year colleges and those who, without adequate preparation, go to work. The losers outnumber the winners.

For example, the data reveal that, of those who begin a BA program, only slightly more than half of whites and Asians and fewer than half of other people of color graduate. Furthermore, of the group that does graduate, 43% will still lose because the economy will provide too little college-level work. When one looks just at those who aspire to the professions, the majority of whom are women, the odds of winning are even worse. Of those preparing for the professions—accountants, chemists, elementary school teachers, engineers, and so forth—only one of two will find work.

Who will be the winners? Common sense and good research suggest the winners can be identified in high school. The winners will be those who graduate with academically competitive credentials that enable them to go to better colleges; these credentials will, in turn, give them advantages in the labor market when competing for a limited number of professional and other 4-year college-level jobs.

Who will be the losers? The losers likely will be among those who graduated from the academic middle—those who were pressed into attending 4-year colleges even though they lacked adequate academic preparation or the ability to succeed. The losers will also include those who, for whatever reason, prepared in high school to go to college but went to work instead. Thus it is difficult not to conclude that losers outnumber winners in the one way to win game.

We make one final point. If so many young people in the academic middle are being hurt at great cost to themselves, to their parents, and even to the United States as a whole by the one way to win paradigm, and if those who need help the most are hurt the most, why isn't corrective action being taken? The answer lies in the politics of the academically average in U.S. high schools, which is the topic of Chapter 6.

NOTE

1. Hudson Institute. (1997). *Workforce 2020*. Washington, DC: Author.

CHAPTER SIX

Who Cares? The Politics of Average Students

> A great many people think they are thinking when they are merely rearranging their prejudices.
>
> —*William James (1842–1910)*

In terms of achieving their expressed postsecondary education and career goals, more than 50% of all high school graduates fail. Nationwide, 85% of high school graduates want to obtain a 4-year college degree, but only 40% graduate from high school with the academically advanced credentials to indicate adequate preparation for college-level academic work. While 30% of teens never graduate from high school and 30% of those who do graduate go to work, all the rest go on to college, mostly to 4-year colleges, despite inadequate academic preparation. Thus it is not surprising to find that among those who go to a 4-year college, one-fifth have to take remedial courses sometime during their freshman year in college; among those who start at 2-year colleges with the intent to transfer to a 4-year college, it is almost one in two. Five years later, of those who started at 4-year colleges, about 65% actually graduate. Of those who start at public 2-year colleges with the intent of transferring to a university, only 7% have earned a baccalaureate degree five years later (National Center for Education Statistics, 2005). The rest of the students "cool out" of the higher education system, but not before most have accumulated significant debt.

Meanwhile, the employment prospects for those who do persist and obtain a 4-year degree worsen. Whereas in the past one in every five persons with a college degree failed to find commensurate employment, today it is almost one in two. Department of Labor data indicate that in fact, only about a fifth of all occupations require a baccalaureate or graduate degree. Although 4-year college graduates do not go unemployed, more and more end up in jobs that require only a high school diploma or less and that do not pay wages college graduates were led to believe would be there for them.

Meanwhile, the nation faces an unprecedented shortage of technicians trained at the pre-baccalaureate level. Non-native-born workers in the 1990s filled almost half of all openings in these areas. And, while the nation's firms search the world to fill high skill/high wage technical occupations, growing numbers of American college graduates end up in low-paying occupations struggling to pay off student loan debts.

Not a very pretty picture, is it? Yet few want to talk about it. It is the "quiet dilemma." Quiet because students, parents, the education community, and, of course, elected officials running on education reform platforms are largely silent about the consequences of providing high school students with only one way to win. Meanwhile, politicians continue to speak and act as though it were the 1980s; they sense little advantage in taking on a problem no one wants to acknowledge even exists. Others take financial advantage of the situation. These are the strange politics of one way to win, or the "must go to college" mentality. While the nation's elected officials talk about opportunity, the facts seem to suggest instead that there is a conspiracy going on. More specifically, it is the strange politics of "average students," the most common victims of providing only one way to win.

SECTION I

High School Politics and the Academic Middle

To understand the politics of the one way to win conventional wisdom, it is first of all important to understand that the kids whom it hurts the most, namely, those who make up the academic middle, have no advocates either locally or nationally. At the federal level, the Washington, DC, advocacy (a fancy name for lobbying) scene is a good illustration. At least 30 groups promote themselves as advocates for children with special needs. There are lobbyists for college students, for Ivy League colleges, for land-grant universities, and for unemployed engineers, to name a few. But as far as we know, there is no advocacy group for academically average students in general and in particular kids who go to work directly upon graduating from high school. In fact, the No Child Left Behind (NCLB) legislation seems to view the latter as school system failures that confound the view "that everyone should prepare to go to college."

At the local level, the academically blessed have many advocates— for example, their parents who serve on public school boards, high school teachers who love to teach advanced placement (AP) and honors courses, and school administrators who see admissions at prestigious colleges as the zenith of educational effectiveness—but average teens have no one. For example, at high school graduations, it is rare that a listing is provided of students who have obtained full-time jobs. Meanwhile, it is very likely that a detailed account will be provided about each student who has been admitted to college and even more accolades given to those who have gotten scholarships to do so.

Whereas special needs students have an army of advocates— laws and lawyers seeing dollar signs—to safeguard their rights, average students have neither, a situation that led the authors of *The Shopping Mall High School* (Powell, Farrar, & Cohen, 1985) to label them the "unspecial." In reporting the results of an ethnographic case study of several high schools, Powell et al. (1985) were struck by the invisibility of average students; in fact, they were so invisible that high school educators had difficulty describing them:

> Indeed, one important characteristic is the very absence of precision [in high school teachers' minds] about exactly who they [the unspecial] are. They were variously the "invisible people," "the middle of the class," and "that great gray-mass area," those who don't belong anywhere, the people who don't fit into any . . . categories. (p. 174)

Powell et al. (1985) go on to confirm the argument made here, that the unspecial are the majority:

Words like average, middle, normal, and regular were often used to describe quite different kinds of adolescents. Some enrolled in college-preparatory programs but were not in advanced or honors courses and therefore were no longer special because post-secondary education was a mass expectation. Others saw the unspecial as a contemporary version of traditional "general" students—shaped neither by clear college expectations nor a focused vocational education program. To others the unspecial were those on the top end of the bottom spectrum. (p. 175)

And they have no advocates:

Another fundamental characteristic of the unspecial is that they have no important allies or advocates. Top track students are blessed with a strong constituency of parents. The handicapped and those with a highly focused vocational interest, even the unruly, had their spokespeople, usually organized lobbies or political groups that generated money or mandates from legislatures and courts. (p. 176)

While we would hope that the findings of this study of the American high school, probably the best ever done, have been corrected in the intervening 20 years, data suggest that if anything, conditions for students in the academic middle have gotten worse. Data from the Economic Policy Institute (Rothstein, 1997) confirm this observation. Between 1967 and 1996, the percentage of school budgets spent on regular education (that part of the budget that supports education for the academic middle) dropped from 80% to 57%. Meanwhile, the percentage of the budget spent on special education, bilingual education, and other programs for special students increased from 4% to 22%. In other words, while education budgets have grown over the years, the percentage of dollars spent on those in the academic middle has actually decreased.

The parents of these youth are largely silent, either because of the feeling that no news from school is good news or because they lack the savvy or the combativeness to effect change. For example, whereas parents' organizations are the norm at all elementary schools and are typical at middle or junior highs, they seldom exist at the high school level. Why? One reason is that high school educators do not encourage them. Another reason is that the parents of the silent majority are, by now, almost completely silent. It's not that they don't care; they just seem to give up. As one counselor said, "Most parents are too busy trying to survive [raising a teenager] to try to tell the schools what to do" (Powell et al., 1985, p. 177). This is too bad because high school educators also have largely given up trying to advise students, particularly those from the academic middle, on what to do. In the worse case, NCLB has made many of these students liabilities to schools desperate to avoid the dreaded "needs improvement" label.

WHY HIGH SCHOOL EDUCATORS LOOK THE OTHER WAY

Conversations with high school principals, counselors, and teachers (the authors of this book have, at various times, served in all of these positions) leave little doubt that these professionals are aware of the growing number of academically average youth in the college prep programs who do not do very well but still go on to 4-year colleges. In fact, school guidance counselors are increasingly amazed at the ease with which students with mediocre academic credentials gain admittance into what used to be fairly selective colleges and universities. They also are well aware that few high school students know why they are going to college except that their parents want it, everyone else expects it, and there appear to be no alternatives. Here we get to the heart of the matter.

High schools are public institutions and, as such, are quite responsive—better yet, vulnerable—to community desires. The old saw among superintendents of schools was and still is that as long as the band plays on tune, the football team has a winning season, and the students get into college, the public is happy. It's true. National data indicate that most parents want their children to go to college, and in this day and age there is little stopping them. In the light of the politics that exist today in most high schools, few principals are willing to deliver this message: many students enrolled in the college prep program are not prepared to do baccalaureate-level work. In a society in which "kill the messenger" is the rule, the lack of willingness to deliver this message is understandable. In fact, parents often do not wake up until the dreaded SAT or ACT college admissions test scores arrive. Meanwhile, school personnel are thankful that this insight is coming from someone else.

If the high school culture was not already highly unfavorable to those in the academic middle, along comes NCLB. Now high schools have something new to worry about, and it is definitely a good news/bad news situation for kids in the academic middle. The Act requires that not just students but schools be assessed and that schools where the kids do not meet standards are judged as needing improvement. Of course, all this is grist for the press, hungry for any negative local news.

The implication of the Act is that students in the academic middle are academically average because they do not have good schools and qualified teachers, that they are not held to high expectations in school (meaning they are lazy), and that they will improve if held accountable (tested). Now, in at least one respect, the assumptions of this Act are correct: for those in the academic middle, there is little incentive to apply themselves in high school. By the eighth grade or earlier, they know that they are not going to ever be the kind of student who gets into the better colleges or even graduates in the top 20% of their high school class, thus enabling them to negotiate a lower tuition at colleges with empty seats (which is most of them). They also know, however, that getting into college somewhere is a certainty, and it does not matter much what course they take or what scores they get on state-mandated or college entrance tests. School systems and schools may be concerned about NCLB, but most of the kids in the academic middle aren't. In fact, among those less blessed with academic ability, the tests are a joke, they know their results before they even take the tests, and many just blow them off. So much for the NCLB's master plan!

Now for high school teachers and administrators, these students, particularly those who are not the most motivated to take these tests, become a real problem. They become the enemy from within who drags down the school's test scores. Unless they happen to be an important member of some athletic team—and thus of some specific value—the reality is that their high school would be better off without them. So, when they stop coming to school, there is little incentive for the school staff to make much of an effort to find them. While this sounds like a harsh indictment of the American high school staff and hopefully completely unfair to most of them, the data are clear. In virtually every state, the four-year ninth grade to senior dropout rate went up in the 1990s era of state and federal testing programs.

ARE SCHOOL GUIDANCE COUNSELORS THE VILLAINS?

Over the years, in talking about the one way to win problem with employers, employee groups, educators, and even some parents, the natural question is, "Whom can we blame?" The number one suspects are almost always high school guidance counselors, who are viewed as the professionals responsible for providing teens with reality therapy. Realistically, parents have only themselves to blame. A typical explanation given by counselors goes this way,

> For years, all we counselors hear are digs about the supposed case of successful college graduates who report that their guidance counselor told them not to go to college. After 20 years of this abuse and criticism, most counselors are a bit gun-shy about presenting any information, let alone advising that anyone should not go on to college.

Then there is the "kill-the-messenger" attitude of all too many parents that leads school counselors to look the other way when kids make plans that are clearly quixotic. It is easy to understand such attitudes. An increasingly frequent story told by counselors is about the calls they get from irate parents because the counselor even suggested to their child that they consider anything other than the one way to win strategy. Neither school officials nor school board members see any reasons to push the issue. What they observe is that colleges are admitting kids no matter what their credentials are, and as long as that is the case, who wants to fight the battle to change the one way to win mind-set of students and parents?

One other issue is more difficult for high school educators to duck: how can students be in a college prep program of study and get good grades, yet end up in remedial courses in college?

THE POLITICS OF GRADE INFLATION

Perhaps the best example of schools caving in to the one way to win mind-set that everyone should go to college is the grades kids get. Periodically, the media write about something called grade inflation. The term means that grades go up without requisite evidence that learning is increasing too; in fact, data often suggest just the opposite. For example, although SAT entrance test scores have stagnated over the years, the grade point averages (GPAs) reported by entering college freshmen keep going up. In a survey conducted by the Higher Education Research Institute (Engle, 2004), 47% of entering 2003 college freshman reported that they graduated from high school with an A average; in 1968, only 18% so indicated. Again, one wonders what an A average really means because as grades go up, the amount of time students say they spend studying continues to go down. Only 34% of entering 2003 college freshmen indicated they studied at least six hours or more per week. What is going on? Some authors (Sedlak, 1986) suggest that a stalemate exists between teachers and the academically average youth in their classes. Teachers ask little of academically average students; in return, these students ask little of their teachers.

THE STALEMATE IN HIGH SCHOOL CLASSROOMS

Understanding the stalemate that exists between high school teachers and average students in college prep classes requires an appreciation of the impossible catch-22 situation that high school faculty find themselves in because of public demands. High schools are asked to do the impossible: be rigorous but ensure that everyone gets grades that will enable him or her to get into college. The situation has gotten even worse. Now, some states have scholarship programs that guarantee significant financial grants to all those who earn a certain GPA. Guess what happens? The percentage of kids who get this average miraculously goes up every year, but their college entrance exam scores do not. Meanwhile, colleges do whatever it takes to fill seats, including discounting tuition cost to students who have a certain high school GPA, which adds even more pressure for high school teachers to give out inflated grades.

Maybe it is possible for high schools to be rigorous yet ensure all students will earn good grades, and at the same time prevent one-third from dropping out (high school bashers have made careers of suggesting that such action is possible), but under the circumstances, it is not. As the experience at colleges (where most high school bashers work) has shown, grade inflation is difficult to control. This point was aptly illustrated by cartoonist Garry Trudeau in his panel about a fraternity member who sued the university because he got a B+ instead of the expected A. Obviously, problems with grade inflation are not confined to high schools.

The public simply will not accept one basic reality: if a normal population of high school students is put into college prep courses that carry high academic performance standards (not to be confused with high expectations, which should be the norm for all students), not everyone is going to do well. Thus if everyone is to do well as indicated by the grade received, the only solution, at least given the current student-to-teacher ratio in U.S. high schools, is to lower standards. This is exactly what is occurring in the college prep classes taken by those in the academic middle of U.S. high schools. Academically average students and their parents ask no questions as long as everyone gets above-average grades and gets into college; today, that is virtually ensured. If no one looks too closely at the learning that may or may not be taking place in classes populated by the academic middle, then everyone is content.

One reason for this complacency is that parents of the academically blessed know that their kids receive a different college prep curriculum from those in the academic middle—one with real standards and failing grades—offered under code names such as AP or honors courses. These are the courses and grades the few really selective colleges look at.

The politics of the situation allows no other solution. The public wants all students in high schools to graduate with high academic credentials so that they can go to college, but for a variety of reasons, this task cannot be done. All but a few of these reasons are outside the schools' control, so high school faculty compromise: they offer a real AP or honors college prep program for those who have the ability to do it and a less rigorous college prep curriculum for those who cannot or will not do as well. In the latter classes, teachers ask less of the students; in return, students and parents do not hassle the teachers. This standoff will not be easy to change as long as one way to win goes unchallenged and most colleges practice overt or covert open admissions.

Section II

Taking the High Ground:
The Role of Elected Officials

Whereas the one way to win paradigm is costing the government billions, hindering economic growth, and resulting in more youth failing than succeeding, one might expect elected officials to speak out about the need to consider alternatives to a 4-year college education. As columnist Robert Samuelson (1991) suggested—no doubt with tongue in cheek—all government officials have to do to solve the problem is to announce that they will no longer support higher education budgets without performance standards and that they will no longer fool our students or waste taxpayers' money by sending people to college who are not ready. Not surprisingly, none have taken his advice.

Some states are now looking at higher education expenditures in relation to strategic economic development plans. And in such states, more taxpayer money for colleges is not as automatic as it was in the 1990s. Even Congress is coming to view higher education as a sector similar to health care in that costs are out of control and increases in federal financial aid lead to higher tuition costs, not more affordability for students. But then there is NCLB, which suggests that while elected officials are increasingly skeptical of ever-increasing tuition costs, they still believe—at least for the record—in the one way to win philosophy.

When it comes to one way to win, the rhetoric is classic political smoke and mirrors, at least at the federal level. Congress passes legislation that increases the dollar amounts for student aid, and then its members hit the campaign trail to bring the good news to their constituents. They fail to tell the whole story, however, that although Congress has passed a bill to increase student aid benefits, there is no money to fund it. Thus, in late 2004, the U.S. Office of Education added more restrictive regulations regarding student financial aid eligibility, disqualifying tens of thousands of student who would have gotten aid in the past.

In the light of the political hay to be made from supporting the one way to win mentality, it is clearly unrealistic to think the federal government will urge the public to consider alternatives to a 4-year degree leading to a career in the professional ranks. In fact, often the political returns from promoting college attendance are so high that they actually lead to proposals that make no sense. For example, in the mid-1990s, one proposal called for a payback schedule for direct student loans that did not cover loan interest; over time, then, student loans would actually increase in size!

One final and important point should be made regarding politicians' use of the one way to win mentality to increase public approval of their performance. By doing so, they in effect lend considerable credence to the validity of the one way to win paradigm. When the president of the United States asserts that anyone who wants to go to college should be able to, the message is interpreted in a far larger context than may have been intended. In the country's classrooms and households, the message means that everyone should go to college. Some believe it even insinuates that something is wrong with anyone who does not aspire to college. If there is a positive sign in all this, in the 2005 budget proposal, the federal administration proposed legislation designed to increase attendance in high skill community college programs that were to be coordinated closer with industry; a very encouraging sign.

Section III

One Way to Win: Opportunity or Opiate

Ultimately, the bottom-line origin of the one way to win mentality is fear. Public opinion polls of teens and their parents regarding the economic outlook for this generation are consistently pessimistic. Neither teens nor their parents expect that they will be able to maintain the same level of lifestyle that their parents enjoy. The majority think programs such as Social Security will be long gone before today's teens reach retirement.

Fueling the pessimism is economic globalization. For example, many parents of kids in the academic middle worked and earned a respectable living in the textile industry. In 2005, the last tariff regulations that protected what remained of these industries were forced to expire due to mandates by the World Trade Organization. These jobs have gone overseas and will not return. Predictably, exporting of jobs was a major issue in the 2004 presidential elections. In fact, the position of both candidates is telling. While bemoaning the loss of jobs overseas as the other candidate's fault, they both were on record as supporting free trade. Neither candidate had an idea of what to do to stop job loss, nor does anyone else, it seems.

While there is much debate regarding the pluses and minuses of globalization, one thing seems clear: wage rates for similar work and thus standards of living worldwide will regress to a mean. For highly developed countries such as the United States, this is not very good news. Yes, some countries and some firms will benefit handsomely from globalization, but, despite much free-trade rhetoric to the contrary, it is hard to understand how it cannot hurt just as many. The reality is that jobs will go to localities where, for a given skill level, wages are the lowest. The implications are dramatic. Were it not for federal farm aid, there would already be much less produced in the United States; almost any agriculture product can be produced cheaper somewhere else in the world and shipped to the United States overnight.

Politicians know this, of course; they are clever people. The problem is that they do not know what to do about it. There is definitely an attitude that nothing can be done about it: the typical response is the old saw, "The horse is already out of the barn." Even the revered Alan Greenspan, head of the Federal Reserve Board, was at first stumped when asked at a congressional hearing if he knew what could be done about job flight. Guess what he finally advised? Send more teens to college. Lester Thurow, the renowned economist, says much the same thing in his book *Fortune Favors the Bold* (2003).

To modern day geniuses such as Greenspan and Thurow, and seemingly to everyone else, college has become the last great hope. Unfortunately, it is a false hope. More and more college graduates will not lead to more and more jobs that pay a college-level wage, only more and more college graduates with more and more debt taking jobs that pay a high school wage. This generation is in the competition of its lifetime, namely, the competition for high wage employment. There is not enough of this kind of work to go around. And with globalization, virtually any qualified person from any country can compete for the limited amount there is.

This is rather dismal news. It is not the kind of uplifting message politicians like to deliver; it does not tend to get votes. To them, the solution by which to appease the voters is to make it possible for everyone to go to college, even though those who try and fail will greatly outnumber the winners. Faced with the fearsome reality of a not-too-bright economic future and the political necessity of keeping it to themselves, elected officials, with few exceptions (Congressman John Peterson of Pennsylvania being one such exception), endorse the one way to win solution. And it works.

Given these political realities, it seems justified to conclude that in the United States today, the primary function of the "one way to win/everyone needs to get a university degree" message is *not* that of providing sound advice regarding career opportunity, for clearly this advice leads the jajority of today's youth to make bad career decisions, but instead to make them and the populace in general complacent to the fact that there is not enough opportunity in the new global economy to go around. Its major role is that of a social opiate.

Baccalaureate education in general and open admissions in particular serve to deaden the common sense of the populace. It deadens their justified fears of hard times ahead. And unfortunately, like most opiates, it works. Public opinion polls find, for example, that when students fail in high school, they blame the schools, and when they fail in college, they blame themselves—not the system, not the government, not economic policy. They conclude that they were given a chance, but they screwed up. The fact that they had little real chance in the first place is a reality they are never told; what they are told is that there is only one way to win and, for whatever reason, they blew it.

Of course, there are other ways to win, ways that have greater odds of winning. But most teens and parents have been so convinced by the one way to win message that they are afraid to take a different path. It is a difficult situation.

SECTION IV

Behind the Scenes: Those With Vested Interests

Each year, higher education in the United States is a multibillion-dollar business. Revenues for higher education institutions alone are now over $120 billion. This amount may be just the tip of the iceberg because untold billions are generated by products and services related to higher education. College sports on national television, college and financial planners, moneylenders, T-shirt manufacturers, textbook publishers, beer distributors, and providers of cram courses for entrance tests, to cite a few, all add up to staggering amounts of money. The one way to win mantra is essential to keeping this market booming, and promoting the one way to win philosophy is a marketing essential not just for colleges but also for firms of all kinds that feed off college students.

Thus colleges and universities have become big business, and, as with all businesses, a steady supply of customers is essential. In turn, a steady flow of customers requires a product in demand. The one way to win paradigm provides the rationale for the demand for a baccalaureate education. The point is that, although most endorse one way to win because they believe it is sound advice for today's youth, others promote the value of college because their jobs depend on it. It is in their interest to promote the myth.

No doubt, the largest vested interest in one way to win is the higher education community itself. Higher education is a huge service industry. It sells a service (education)—or more accurately, products (degrees)—employs people, and portrays itself as meeting a need and creating opportunity. If someone dropped in from another world and observed this activity, however, these efforts would more resemble marketers' efforts to create a need for a product in a saturated market.

Obviously, all is not well in this multibillion-dollar enterprise. The industry has overexpanded; classes are underenrolled in small but expensive liberal arts colleges; in big university branch campuses and other such higher education backwaters, classroom seats and dorm rooms are empty, and revenue is down. Thus recruitment and retention, not excellence, are the priorities at all but relatively few colleges. Although administrators at most colleges act as if admissions were selective, admissions are truly selective at only about 250 of the more than 3,000 institutions of higher education. In fact, most higher education institutions practice open admissions. Most take the best that apply even if the best of these are not well qualified to do college work; as the adage goes, "Poor students are better than no students." What other explanation is there for the fact that 80% of all public 4-year colleges "offer" (a code word for require) remedial courses for entering students?

One major tactic used by higher education in its increasingly sophisticated marketing efforts to keep colleges and universities full is to reinforce and play off the one way to win mentality. These efforts have been very successful. Opportunity and college have become synonymous, thanks in part to these efforts. Suffice it to say that higher education is a strong political force working overtly and covertly to sell and perpetuate one way to win.

Questions about the sincerity of these efforts are left to the reader to decide. The point is that those who seek to promote other ways to win should understand that the United States has an over-supply of baccalaureate degree–granting colleges; between 1980 and 1990, the number of public and private baccalaureate-level colleges actually increased despite a decreasing number of high school grad-uates. You can expect these institutions to push hard the one way to win concept.

One final group deserves mention among those with a vested interest in one way to win: the moneylenders and financial planners for whom college mania has become a source of growth and profit. In December 2004, Sallie Mae, the largest, now private, student financial aid lender, alone held 110.5 billion dollars in student loans, most all of which were guaranteed by state or federal gov-ernment. Need money for college? Plan now for college, and ask about student loans. Are tuition bills due? Consider a home equity loan. These messages are heard day after day. A house used to be the largest purchase made by a family; now, for many, it is their children's education. By promoting their services, these financial institutions are reinforcing the message and keeping public faith in higher education alive and well; after all, doing so is a dollars and cents issue. Were the one way to win myth exposed, it would result in declining profits.

OTHER WAYS TO WIN

In this chapter, we have explored the political realities behind the apparent lack of public concern for the plight of those from the academic middle of high school graduating classes and the almost universal faith in the one way to win message. Aware of no other socially acceptable and economically promising alternatives, many in the academic middle are heading off to college despite being unprepared for it. Even among the academically blessed, many also head off to college by default and would make other choices if given a chance. Most in the academic middle never graduate and are only successful in accumulating significant student loan debt.

But no one seems to voice much concern. There are few, if any, advocates for these students; teachers largely ignore them, and their parents are by and large powerless. Meanwhile, elected officials, even when faced with the economic realities of too many 4-year college students and too few jobs, take the high ground and sidestep the problem. Also, for many individuals employed in primary, secondary, or higher education, ensuring a steady stream of students is essential for job security. Political realities of locally controlled public schools and conflicting community expectations prevent high school educators from actively raising concerns about the appropriateness of student high school course-taking decisions, let alone postsecondary plans; it is just easier to look the other way. Most recently, NCLB has not only institutionalized the one way to win mentality, but it has also made teens who do not share this vision or do not do well on standardized tests liabilities of the school system.

These political realities make the creation of "other" ways to win more of a challenge but in no way diminish the need. In the one way to win game, most lose. The first losers are those who, early in their high school years, see college as an impossible reach. Unaware of alternatives that may be equally valued by teachers or the community, they give up, drop out, or stay in school but tune out. The second losers are those who go to college unprepared, end up in remedial courses, and slowly cool out of the system and never graduate. The final losers are those who actually persist, only to discover that few jobs are available in their major; these people typically end up underemployed, forced to take jobs that do not pay the kind of high wages they were told that 4-year college grads would get and would make student loans worth the cost. Most of the losers are from the academic middle. Although assuredly some from the academic middle do graduate and do find commensurate college-level work, they are the minority; the majority would have benefited from alternatives, from other ways to win.

In Part III of this book, we discuss ways to restructure the high school curriculum and high school guidance and placement services to provide these alternatives. We begin in Chapter 7 by outlining an economic rationale for alternatives that can be used to persuade the public—particularly students and parents—that there are other ways to win.

PART III

Creating Other Ways to Win

CHAPTER SEVEN

The High Skill/High Wage Rationale

[It is] just possible we have a surplus of graduates and a
scarcity of [youth] with real skills.

—*R. Samuelson*[1]

One of the best clues to other ways to win is to observe what
many 4-year college graduates do when they cannot find commensurate employment. Many for the first time take a hard look at
the job market for occupations that pay high wages and then go back
to school, but not graduate school. Instead, they enroll in what is a
far better bet for most: 1- or 2-year technical programs. These young
adults are termed reverse transfers, and they are one of the fastest
growing groups of students in higher education. A reverse transfer
is a student who is working on or already holds a 4-year or graduate
degree but still decides to matriculate in a 2-year associate degree
program—even a 1-year diploma/certificate program—at a community/
technical, public, or private college. National data are not available
in this area, but some 2-year postsecondary institutions report that,
in certain programs, reverse transfers represent the majority of their
students. On speaking tours the authors have made around the
nation, some community college administrators have told us that
up to 34% of their students have at least a college degree before
enrolling in 2-year associate degree technical programs.

Why would anyone with a bachelor's or advanced degree invest additional time and money in a lesser degree when doing so seems illogical? One clue can be gained by noting the specific technical programs that reverse transfers enroll in, namely, occupation-specific technical programs in fields such as medical technologies, information technology, and automated manufacturing. These students have discovered, albeit a bit late, that there are other ways to win. They have learned from experience that four or more years of college do not necessarily lead to a high-paying career but that an associate degree or even a 1-year certificate program can if it is in a technical field.

These college graduates have learned an all-important labor market fact the hard way: Earning high wages is a result of having occupational skills that are in demand, not of education per se. This relationship between skills and wages is the concept implied by the term high skill/high wage work. The skills required in many high skill/high wage occupations can be learned in associate degree programs in the technologies. They can also be gained in workplace employer and employee training programs such as apprenticeship programs in the skilled crafts or in the military. Each of the military services is now a learning organization pervaded by the use of advanced technology to perform its mission. Therefore each branch of the military offers many different career fields. Importantly, military service schools provide excellent instruction, and more often than not, these skills are in high demand in the civilian labor market. This high skill/high wage rationale forms the economic basis for the creation of alternatives or other ways to win for high school graduates.

The purpose of this chapter is to explain the high skill/high wage rationale for creating alternatives for high school graduates who make up the academic middle. Our intention is to provide a rationale that can, in turn, be effectively communicated to students and parents. This chapter begins with an examination of five economic myths held by students, parents, and educators that have led them to conclude there is only one way to win. Those who seek to promote alternatives must understand these myths if they hope to argue for reasonable consideration of other ways to win.

SECTION I

Five Myths About the Future Labor Market

Myth 1: In the future, most jobs will require a 4-year degree.

Fact: Of the 57 million job openings projected between 2000 and 2010, only 21% will require a 4-year degree or higher (see Figure 7.1).

There is a widespread myth that in the future, most jobs will require a 4-year degree. The dismal truth is that according to Department of Labor figures, through 2010, most jobs (70%) will in fact require no formal higher education at all. Important for those who preach the one way to win mantra, only 12% of all job openings will be in fields that require only a university degree without experience.

Figure 7.1   Percentages of Work Requiring Various Levels of Education and Training

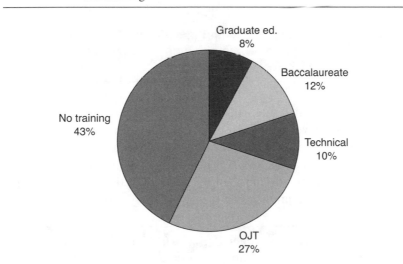

Source: Hecker, 2001, p. 83.
OJT = on-the-job training.

In other words, the vast majority of all youth plan to go to a 4-year college that, when and if they graduate, will qualify them to compete for only 12% of all job openings.

> *Myth 2:* In the future, most new additional jobs created will be in technical areas that require a 4-year degree.
>
> Fact: Jobs that require any higher education will account for a little less than half of all job growth through 2010.

While it is true that the growth rate for jobs requiring some higher education will grow at a faster percentage rate than those that do not require higher education, the total number of jobs created will still be less than those created by slower growing occupations that do not require a degree. Importantly, among the fastest growing jobs that require some training beyond high school, just as many, paying just as much, will require not a 4-year or graduate degree but an associate degree, diploma, industry certification, or the like.

> *Myth 3:* In the future, all high wage occupations will require a 4-year degree.
>
> Fact: Many occupations requiring less than a baccalaureate degree pay as much as or more than the average of all jobs that require a university degree.

The reality is that many occupations that do not require a 4-year degree pay very well. As one general example, 83% of workers holding associate degrees have the same or higher annual earnings as those with a 4-year degree (Carnevale & Desrochers, 2001). For example, a professional chef earns more than the average college graduate, as does a journeyman in the building trades.

> *Myth 4:* The total labor force demand for college graduates will be sufficient to ensure commensurate employment for all who receive a 4-year degree.
>
> Fact: Between 2000 and 2010, the labor market is projected to provide only about half as many jobs that require a 4-year degree as are needed to employ the numbers who will graduate (see Table 5.3).

It is widely and dangerously assumed by students that the economy will generate enough jobs to accommodate them when they graduate with a university degree. The reality is quite the opposite. Labor Department projections indicate that there will be 730,400 jobs annually through 2010 that will require a 4-year degree, but the nation's colleges and universities will award 1.3 million bachelor's degrees annually. For every 100 university grads, there will be just 55 jobs that require this level of education, and this assumes a perfect match between job openings and college majors, which does not seem to be the case considering the nation's growing reliance on highly educated foreign-born workers. Job openings are a function of the demand for goods and services, not the supply of workers. More college graduates than jobs will mean more underemployed and overeducated young adults.

Myth 5: In the future, there will be so many persons who have a 4-year degree they will take all the good jobs, including those that do not require a baccalaureate degree.

Fact: University graduates will not displace workers with specialized skills that are in demand.

This final myth is the pivotal fear that fuels the mania for a 4-year college degree. It must be vigorously corrected if the "one way to win" mantra is to be exposed as a myth. Parents and students worry that an increase in the number of 4-year degree holders will result in a situation where those with less or no higher education will not be able to compete for any decent job. At first glance, there is good reason for them to reach this conclusion. For one thing, the largest segment of the labor force is those with some college. But data indicate that almost half of those with a 4-year degree are underemployed or overeducated for the job they hold, which suggests that they must be taking jobs that employers would have filled in the past with high school graduates.

But there is evidence that there may be another explanation. For example, about 15% of high school graduates earn more than college graduates, and as mentioned above, over 83% of those with an associate degree have the same or higher earnings than those with a university degree. Why do some persons earn more than others despite the fact that they have less formal education? The explanation is that they have skills in demand that university graduates do not. University graduates are and will continue to displace those with lesser education for low- or middle-level skill employment but not for high skill/high wage employment. A person with a 4-year degree in psychology, for example, is not going to displace an individual with an information technology industry certificate or an associate degree in a technical area. As noted in a national survey of employers in the 13 largest industrial sectors, "10 of 13 industry groups ranked the need for vocational training higher than the need for a college degree" (Stern, 1992, p. 25), confirming the importance of skill, not degrees, in the hiring decisions made by firms.

TWO MORE MISUNDERSTANDINGS

While the five myths outlined above are the backbone of the one way to win myth and thus the most important to refute, there are two others that need mentioning. They relate to the constant and seductive message that college graduates earn a lot more than those who graduate only from high school.

> True or false: Four-year college graduates earn more than high school graduates because they graduated from college.
>
> Mostly false: A college degree actually has a very low correlation with earnings.

The latest numbers in the press indicate that college graduates now earn, on average, $17,000 more a year or nearly 45% more than high school graduates. Most assume this is because they have a college degree. But a simple observation should cast some doubt on this assumption. If high earning is the result of a college education, then those who do the best in college, those who get the best grades, and so forth, should be earning the most money. But the opposite is more often the case. It has been reported, for example, that the grade point average of Fortune 500 company CEOs was an unimpressive C−.

Such things as socioeconomic level of parents, marital status, and economic sector of employment are much stronger predictors of earnings than degrees. It could well be that a college degree gets you a place in the line, but other things, like college major/skills in demand, ambition, sheer brainpower, or family wealth, are the real factors involved in higher earnings. One observes, for example, that virtually all children of the rich and connected go to college. Thus it would be wise for many teens and their parent to look beyond baccalaureate education and consider all the available alternatives.

A 4-year college degree does not guarantee economic success, nor is it the only route to economic success. Students and parents would be wise to heed the caution given by Massachusetts Institute of Technology economist Lester Thurow (2003), who points out that while college graduates as a whole may seem to earn more, many earn less, and while the national go-to-college message poses few if any risks to the nation as a whole (and elected officials in particular), the risks of losing for individuals are in fact quite high, and the results of losing, in terms of financial aid debt, not to mention self-esteem, are also quite high.

> True or false: Getting a 4-year degree is worth the cost to get one.
>
> Maybe true, maybe not.

Colleges and universities are fond of publishing job placement data; in fact, they are required to do so. The numbers are always pretty good. But they do not tell us much. Why? Because the issue is not whether a university graduate is employed but whether he or she is employed in an occupation that either pays enough now or at least has prospects for paying enough in the future to make the investment of time and money it takes to get a university degree worth it.

While some types of higher education institutions are required to provide data on how many find jobs in the area they studied, 4-year degree–granting institutions are not. We must therefore rely on national data suggesting that perhaps as many as half are in jobs that they are overeducated for and that have no career potential.

Furthermore, the logic of pursuing a 4-year college degree because it may lead to a labor market advantage in competing for low skill/low wage work makes little sense, dollarwise. A 4-year college degree can cost from $50,000 to $120,000 and take five or even six years of full-time study, thus preventing any work experience or earnings in the labor force. Add to this scenario the interest costs from student loans and forgone earnings while in college, and it makes even less sense. Thurow (1996) points out that, in general, the return on investment for a 4-year college degree is so low that no corporation would invest money in such a venture.

This last point is not a small concern. An acquaintance of one of the authors is a single mother working two jobs, trying to help her son complete a degree in engineering. While he receives financial aid and student loans, the mother herself has had to take out a second mortgage on the home. She would have preferred that her son went to technical college, which was much more affordable. She is worried. She wonders whether all the sacrifice will be worth it. She hopes he actually graduates, and she worries that even if he does, he may not find work that will make it possible to pay off the resultant debt. She is right to worry. Despite the rhetoric, there is a worldwide surplus of engineers. But for most occupations for which training is offered at technical/community colleges and proprietary schools, the opposite is true.

Section II

The Labor Market Rationale for Other Ways to Win

If the goal of students is future economic security, the focus of their postsecondary planning should be on obtaining job skills that prepare them to compete for a limited supply of high skill/high wage work. This focus differs significantly from that of getting a 4-year college degree on the basis of the naive faith that it will lead to a good job. This advice is particularly suited for high school graduates from the academic middle of their graduating class because odds are that they will not be among those who ultimately will find a college-level job even if they do actually graduate with a university degree. Many of those in the academic middle would have been better off if they had considered other alternatives. And they, their parents, and the population in general would be better off to heed this message from the U.S. Department of Labor:

> Workers with less education, but who are employed in jobs that require special skills or training, earn as much as [4-year] college graduates who do not require [skills] training to get their jobs. (Eck, 1993, p. 37)

This single sentence sums up the pivotal rationale for other ways to win. All high schools ought to be required to put it on the wall in every classroom. No, on second thought, it should be on the wall of every elementary school classroom as well. The key to high wage occupations is having a skill set that is in demand in the labor market. College degrees that do not equate to skills in demand may help individuals to compete successfully with high school graduates for low skill/low wage jobs, but it will not allow them to qualify and thus compete for high skill/high wage employment, nor will it allow them to displace those with lesser education but who have skills that are in demand by employers.

But what skill sets for what occupations? Knowing the basic rationale, outlined above, is not very helpful without knowing the answers to these questions. We suggest a two-step process to provide the answers to where in the labor market there are other ways to win—ways that may require some postsecondary education but at the certificate, diploma, or associate degree level.

Two Steps for Finding Other Ways to Win

Step 1: Understand Three Labor Market Basics

The first step in the quest for other ways to win is to understand and keep reminding oneself of three labor market basics.

The Composition of Employment in High Skill/High Wage Firms

The workforce in virtually all segments of the economy is composed of three levels of workers: professionals/managers, technicians, and operatives (see Figure 7.2). Professional/managerial jobs are those that require a 4-year college degree, MBA degree, etc.; they are typically upper management, professional engineers, CPAs, etc. Operatives are those involved in low skill or semiskilled work; these individuals hold the jobs that make up 70% of all work, more than half of which can be learned in two weeks or less on the job.

The best source for other ways to win occupations for those from the academic middle is the third group of workers, the technicians. Here, the title "technician" refers to those who hold specialized skills and typically supervise workers who are operatives. This

Figure 7.2   High Skills/High Wage Workforce

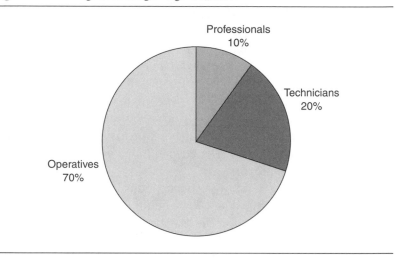

class of worker is found in virtually all industries. In the most recent classification of occupations by the U.S. Department of Labor, occupations with the title "technician" are now found in the classification of professional and related jobs, suggesting their important role in today's economy. Others with similar levels of skills and supervisory responsibility are found in virtually every occupational group and industry. They are found in proportionally large numbers in, for example, the health, crafts, precision manufacturing, and repair classifications and industries (Hecker, 2001).

The Best Measure of Opportunity Is Total Job Openings

The way most occupational outlook information is presented to the public by the press misrepresents the realities of labor market supply and demand and leads to erroneous conclusions regarding where there will be good job opportunities in the future. More often than not, articles stress the "fastest growing" occupations. Because many of the fastest growing occupations require a professional degree, on them data are favored by promoters of the one way to win message. The assumption made is that fastest growing equates to greatest opportunity. But, of course, this is not true. Occupations with very small numbers of jobs can have large percentage gains but in truth add few new jobs and thus have very limited opportunity for employment. The case is made best by a quote from the U.S. Department of Labor's *Monthly Labor Review* publication.

> Employment of environmental engineers is projected to grow twice as fast as employment of accountants and auditors over the 2002–12 period, 38.2 percent, compared with 19.5 percent. However, the accountants and auditors occupation is projected to add more than 11 times the number of new jobs (205,000 compared with 18,000), because employment was so much larger than for environmental engineers in 2002 (1,055,000 compared with 47,000). (Hecker, 2004, p. 80)

The best source of information, therefore, is not the fastest growing data but numbers showing total job openings, which can be found in the job projections of the Department of Labor that include both new jobs created and openings that are due to retirements and so forth. It is important to remember that the largest source of job openings is not from job growth but from the need to replace individuals who retire, etc. For example, the construction trades, which generally pay high wages, are projected to grow at a modest 13% from 2000 to 2010, but due to retirements in particular, this group will generate over 2 million job openings during this period of time. Meanwhile, computer scientist and analyst positions are predicted to grow a staggering 59% during this period but add only around 300,000 jobs.

Also, it should be remembered that all this information reveals only one side, the demand side, of the labor market. Real opportunities exist when demand exceeds the supply of those who are qualified and are in the labor market looking for work. In most cases, there is an oversupply of those credentialed in high skill/high wage occupations that require a 4-year degree, while the opposite is true for technician-level employment that requires an industry certification, associate degree, diploma, or significant work experience such as one might gain in the military. It is worth remembering that because of the lack of native-born and trained individuals with technician-level skills, almost half of high skill/high wage technician-level jobs in the United States had to be filled with non-native-born workers in the 1990s.

Specific Occupational Skills Are
More Important Than Degrees in
Competing for Many High Wage Occupations

Another misunderstanding that fuels the one way to win message is confusion about what it takes to compete for high wage employment. The key word here is "compete." The competition of a lifetime for today's youth has nothing to do with sports or the lead in the senior class play; it is competing for high wage employment. Why? Because there is not enough high skill/high wage employment to go around. And in today's global economy, the competition is not just youth within a country's border but job seekers in all countries. As discussed previously, there is, in general, a worldwide labor surplus that includes many well-educated and technically skilled workers eager to compete for jobs in America. The question then is how individuals can prepare themselves for this competition—to use the economists' term, how they can gain "labor market advantage" over the competition.

There are three typical opinions regarding what employers are looking for in employee and thus what factors give an individual an advantage in the hiring process. One school of thought is that a good work ethic is all that really counts. Proponents of this view point out that when asked, employers frequently state all they need is someone who has good work habits. A second school of thought is that employers prefer to do their own training; thus the best way to prepare to compete is to get a good sound academic education so as to be able to benefit from this training quickly. The final point of view is best understood by perusing the help wanted section of a major newspaper or trade journal. What one sees are job titles many of us have never encountered before and then a listing of very specific job skills required to be qualified. So what is the answer: work habit and ethics, academics, or occupational skills?

As illustrated in Figure 7.3, there are three sources of labor market advantage in competing for employment. For some work, namely, low skill/low wage work, the kind of work that can be learned in two weeks or less on the job, the only prerequisite is good work ethics, such as reliability and cooperativeness.

As work becomes more involved and thus pays higher wages, academic skills do become more important, but mostly because they are needed to succeed in training for high skill/high wage employment. Academics alone are not a major source of competitive

Figure 7.3   Sources of Individual Labor Market Advantage

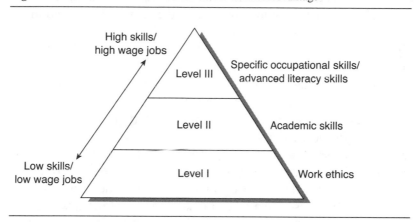

advantage because (a) there are fewer high wage jobs where the only requirement is academic skills, and (b) with the steady increase in university graduates, the supply of those who would seem to have these skills far exceeds the demand.

The primary source of individual labor market advantage, therefore, comes from possessing more relevant and increasingly very specific job skills or relevant work experiences than the competition. It is instructive to note, for example, the increased numbers and, therefore, importance of industry-based skills certifications and licenses. Employers, especially those in fast growing technical fields such as information technology or health, make employment offer decisions based first on whether applicants have the necessary certifications, not what degrees they hold or what impression a candidate makes at a college job fair. The point is that those with all three levels of skill (good work ethics, academic skills, and specific occupational skills) will have advantages in competing for high skill/high wage employment over those who do not have all three. A college degree alone equates only to Level 2 sources of labor market advantage—unless an individual's college major results in learning marketable job skills that employers can document. And finally, those with skills that are in demand in the labor market will have labor market advantage over those who do not; this is the case even if the latter have more formal education.

In general, the goal of all youth and their parents is high wage employment. Unfortunately, as pointed out many times in this book, there is far too little of this type of work to go around. So what decides who gets it and who does not? Putting oneself in the place of an employer makes it quite easy to grasp the answer. If you had more than one applicant for a position, you would hire the one with the highest skill level that is relevant to your firm's business because he or she could be productive immediately. In today's economy, there seem to be two situations: Either there are more applicants than jobs, or there are too few applicants but the job requires a very specific skill set; college graduates with degrees in art history, for example, need not apply. In the first case, firms pick the applicant with the most relevant skill set and/or prior experience; in the second case, more and more, they hire someone from abroad or move the work overseas.

Summarizing, the first step in seeking out other ways to win is to remember these three labor market realities. First, distribution of work is typically one professional, two technicians, and seven operatives. While there are ample numbers of professionals, there are too few technicians, making this level of employment the best source of opportunity for teens from the academic middle. Second, opportunity is determined by the relationship of labor market demand to the number of qualified job seekers. Fastest growing may or may not mean opportunity. Opportunity exists when demand exceeds supply, which is not the case, unfortunately, for most jobs requiring a university degree. Third, labor market advantage over other applicants for high wage employment comes from having the best skill set; some degrees equate to skill sets, but most do not. Those with the necessary skill set will have a competitive advantage over those who do not, even when the latter has more formal education.

Step 2: Investigate Technician Level Occupations Within Key Sectors of Economic Growth

The second step to finding other ways to win, meaning high skill/high wage occupations that do not require a university degree, is to focus on the basic occupational groups in the economy and those occupations within these groups that require formal training but not a baccalaureate degree. The U.S. Department of Labor organizes all occupations, for example, into six groups and provides detailed employment projections for these groups and for hundreds of specific occupations within each group. This classification is, however, a bit technical and difficult to use. A less formal classification system is presented in Table 7.1 and provides some examples of occupations that are high paying but do not require a 4-year degree.

Regardless of the classification scheme, within each group, the 1:2:7 (professional to technician to operatives) relationship will be true. The other way to win and the best way to win for those in the academic middle is preparing for those occupations in the technician and precision/craft classification. More detailed strategies for helping today's youth explore these occupations is provided in Chapter 8.

EXAMPLES OF PRE-BACCALAUREATE HIGH SKILL/HIGH WAGE OCCUPATIONS

The best way for academically average students to win in the fierce competition for above-average-paying jobs in the future is to focus on

Table 7.1   Worker Elite High Skill/High Wage Occupations Not Requiring a Baccalaureate Degree

Craft and Construction
    Construction drafting
    Construction project manager
    Heating/air-conditioning technician
    Plumbing/pipe-fitting technician
    Precision welding
    Specialized carpentry and installation
    Specialized interior finishing and installation

Health Occupations
    Dental assistant
    Dental hygienist
    Emergency medical technician
    Home health aide
    Licensed practical nurse
    Medical laboratory technician
    Medical record technician
    Optometric technician
    Radiology technician
    Surgical technologist

Manufacturing
    Computer-controlled equipment operator
    Drafting technician
    Electronics engineering technician
    Electronics lab technician

(Continued)

Table 7.1 (Continued)

Engineering technician
Manufacturing systems operator
Manufacturing technician

Service Occupations
Accountant
Agribusiness sales
Automated office manager
Commercial design
Computer graphics corrections
Data processing manager
Firefighter
Law enforcement/protection occupations
Library technician
Paralegal
Professionally trained chef
Specialty auto mechanic

Technical Service, Repair, and Installation
Airframe mechanic
Avionics repair technician
Biomedical equipment technician
Computer systems installation and repair
Electromechanical repair technician

Information Technology
Telecommunications installation and repair
Computer systems specialist
Software support specialist
Computer systems installation and repair

---

getting the skills needed to compete for high skill/high wage occupations that require something less than a 4-year college degree. Table 7.1 lists some examples of these occupations by broad industry category.

This list is by no means complete; even within these limited occupation titles, there are thousands of individual job titles for each occupation. All of these occupations pay yearly earnings above the national average. The key to obtaining these jobs and earnings is occupational skills. For example, whereas an untrained short-order cook earns minimum wage, a professionally trained chef from one of the recognized culinary institutes earns a higher starting wage than a schoolteacher. If the chef is even moderately successful, he or she will always outearn public school teachers—and the majority of college professors as well.

Of course, money and the status of going on to postsecondary education are not everything. Aside from monetary rewards from jobs, most individuals also seek and are the most successful in careers that are consistent with their interests, talents, and perceptions of themselves. As indicated by this list, pre-baccalaureate high skill/high wage work can appeal to all types of individual interests and preferences. There are occupational choices for those who want to help people, who like to work outdoors, who like to take things apart, who are artistically creative, who want to work on the East Coast or the West Coast, and who want to dress professionally each day (or not). The choices are endless.

How does one learn the prerequisite skills required in the high skill/high wage occupations? They are learned in a variety of settings. Table 7.2, for example, portrays the occupational structure in the construction and manufacturing fields. Some occupations, particularly in construction crafts, can actually be learned in high school vocational education programs. Still others can be learned in formal work-based training programs, such as apprenticeships organized by employer and employee groups. Most, however, require either 1- or 2-year postsecondary educational training; if they do not require it, having postsecondary training results in a labor market advantage in competing for jobs.

This latter point is important: a majority of today's high school students and their parents have decided that their only option is to attend a higher education institution after graduation, and currently, their preference is a 4-year college education. Although they may be open to alternatives to a 4-year college degree, it is unlikely they will be receptive to plans that do not include some type of postsecondary education. Because many high skill/high wage occupations require postsecondary education—but at the pre-baccalaureate level—those in the academic middle can both go on to higher education and prepare for occupations in which their chance for success is good. Furthermore, many such 2-year postsecondary technical programs articulate with 4-year baccalaureate programs and thus provide an opportunity for those who do well at the 2-year postsecondary level to proceed with further academic study, if they choose.

What about future employment prospects? Compared with the outlook for 4-year college degree graduates, the employment outlook for those preparing for high skill/high wage work requiring less than a 4-year degree is great!

Table 7.2   High Skill/High Wage Occupations in Construction/Manufacturing

Occupational Group	Craftsperson, Blue-Collar, Technical		Technician	Professional Technical	
Preparation Required	High school vocational education Apprenticeships 1-year technical certificate		2-year associate degree	4-year degree	Graduate School
Typical Job Function	Testing Service Maintenance Routine analysis		Manufacturing Production Operations	Complex design Product development Testing and evaluation	
	Repair Assemble Operate Construct	Quality assurance Technical sales Maintenance	Routine design	Basic research Research development Theoretical analysis	
Representative Job Titles	Electrician Factory assembler Tester Machinist Operator Computer operator Mechanic	Engineer's aide Service technician Drafter Foreman Programmer Inspector	System analyst Technical sales/services Project manager Technical operations manager Customer service representative Field operations supervisor Data communications manager Surveyor	Design engineer Systems engineer Product development supervisor Plant manager Engineer	Research scientist Engineer Mathematician Physicist Professor

OCCUPATIONAL OUTLOOK FOR HIGH SKILL/HIGH WAGE OCCUPATIONS NOT REQUIRING A BACCALAUREATE DEGREE

The occupational and earnings outlook for most high skill/high wage occupations that require less than a baccalaureate degree is generally good. To begin with, technical or information workers are projected to comprise one-fifth of all workers by 2005. Most of these occupations do not require a 4-year college degree but do require prerequisite skills; thus those not having a 4-year college degree but who do have relevant skills will not be in danger of being displaced by unskilled baccalaureate degree holders. Meanwhile, the earnings of those holding technician-level high skill/high wage jobs will compare favorably with most college graduates and will exceed those of many 4-year college graduates. These statements are supported by the labor market data summarized in Table 7.3.

Table 7.3 contains important information for those who seek to alert students from the academic middle, their parents, and faculty that there are other ways to win besides a 4-year college degree. In the first column of the table are listed six broad occupational clusters now used by the U.S. Department of Labor.

The second column of 7.3 ranks the occupational groups from highest to lowest according to the average annual salary of individuals who work in occupations contained in each cluster. The highest-earning group is managerial/professional, which includes such occupations as executives, lawyers, doctors, accountants, and schoolteachers. This ranking is probably not a surprise and actually lies behind the one way to win paradigm.

But wait! What is the second highest-paying group? It is technical, sales, and administrative support; this category includes the majority of new economy technician-level occupations, a classification that includes medical lab techs, electronics lab techs, computer support and repair techs, and so forth, most of which require formal education but not at the baccalaureate level. And notice the third highest-paying occupational group—precision production, craft, and repair—a category that includes automated manufacturing, the well-paying building trades, and repair technicians in fields such as refrigeration, auto repair, etc.

It is important to point out that many high skill/high wage occupations that do not require a BA degree can be found in all six clusters—agribusiness, for example, employs thousands of technical workers—but the largest percentages of these occupations are found in the technical support and craft/precision metal/repair clusters. This concentration of high skill/high wage occupations that do not require a BA degree in the second- and third highest-paying occupational clusters provides the fundamental rationale for creating other ways to win. Specifically, it explains the following reality stated by the U.S. Department of Labor:

On average, the yearly income of individuals employed in the craft/precision metal/repair areas and as technicians will be higher than that for all college graduates except those who find work in the managerial/professional ranks. (Eck, 1993, p. 37)

Table 7.3 Occupational Groups Ranked by Earnings, Net Openings, Required Training, Percent Female, and Prestige Scores

Classification	Earnings	Net openings	Required training	% Female	Prestige scores	Occupations
Managerial and professional	1	2	1	50%	62.3	Chief executives, physicians, lawyers, computer systems analysts, science teachers
Technical, sales, and administrative support	2	1	2	65%	40.5	Medical technicians, computer programmers, radiologic licensed practical nurses.
Precision production, crafts, and repair	3	5	3	16%	38.5	Medical appliance technicians, computer repairers, carpenters, electricians, and sheet metal workers
Operators, fabricators, and laborers	4	4	4	13%	33.4	Welders and cutters, printing occupations, rail vehicle operators, ship captains, material moving equipment operators
Service occupations	5	3	4	43%	35.0	Police and detectives, firemen, health aides, welfare service aides, dental assistants, and nurses aides
Farming, forestry, and fishing	6	6	5	19%	35.6	Farm foremen, agricultural products inspectors forestry and logging workers, farm workers

Source: "Occupational Employment Projections to 2010," by the U.S. Department of Labor, Bureau of Labor Statistics, November 2001, *Monthly Labor Review,* 124, 57–84.

The importance of this labor market reality is magnified when one takes into account the occupational opportunity outlook in these clusters (see the third column of Table 7.3). In this column, the six occupational groups are rank-ordered according to net (demand minus supply) job opportunities. Now a more complex and revealing picture unfolds.

Although managerial/professional is the highest-paying cluster, it ranks second in terms of opportunity; in fact, in many occupations, the demand for workers is half that of the yearly supply of new job seekers. For example, each year, colleges graduate 58,000 students with degrees in accounting for only 38,000 projected jobs. Although the public thinks there is a shortage of engineers, there is actually a worldwide glut; in the United States alone, colleges graduate 85,000 engineers yearly for 52,000 jobs. In fact, if college and public school teachers are taken out, the managerial/professional cluster ranks last in terms of net opportunities.

Meanwhile, notice that the second highest-paying occupational group—technical—ranks first in projected net job opportunities. In many occupations within this occupational cluster, wages are high, and the number of job openings greatly exceeds the number of individuals training for these jobs. In fact, in the 1990s, non-native-born workers who came to the United States to take jobs that native-born youth were not trained to do filled almost half of these jobs.

Also note the precision manufacturing, craft, and repair cluster, which ranks third in both pay and net job openings. These numbers take into account that many of the present workers in these areas are baby boomers who are quickly approaching retirement and that few of today's youth are training to take their places. Thus the opportunity is tremendous. It is not uncommon for a cross-skilled electrician in technical manufacturing to earn $80,000 a year with 4 weeks of vacation and job offers that would make many professionals envious.

IMPORTANCE OF OCCUPATIONAL SKILL AND POSTSECONDARY TECHNICAL EDUCATION

Table 7.3 also confirms the high skill/high wage rationale for the creation of other ways to win, specifically the argument that the objective of postsecondary education is to acquire the skills required to obtain high skill/high wage work, not just a degree per se, and that high wages are a return for these skills. In the fourth column of this table, the occupational clusters are ranked from highest to lowest by percentage of workers who reported to the U.S. Bureau of the Census that their job required some degree of formal training. If skills, not education, were the key to high wages, one would expect the rank-ordering of the six occupational groups according to earnings and the percentage of workers reporting that their job required prerequisite skills to be the same. This is exactly what was found for the three highest-paying occupational groups. Importantly, only in the managerial/professional group are these skills learned primarily at the 4-year college degree level; in the other two categories, the majority of occupations are best prepared for at the 1- and 2-year postsecondary level or in formal on-the-job training programs such as apprenticeships.

The high skill/high wage rationale mentioned above provides a strong argument that other ways to win do not require a 4-year college degree. This is the rationale behind creating alternatives for those in the academic middle. Understanding this rationale is critical for those who seek to create alternatives. It is even more critical that the rationale be effectively communicated to parents and students. Thus we conclude this chapter by suggesting five points to present to parents.

OPPORTUNITIES FOR SPECIAL POPULATIONS

In Chapter 3, it was argued that, although it is a matter of national pride that those who can benefit from a 4-year college program be able to do so regardless of socioeconomic background or gender, special populations may well be the most hurt by the existence of a single alternative—a 4-year college degree—and therefore would benefit the most from socially acceptable and economically viable alternatives. The fifth column of Table 7.3 illustrates this point in more concrete terms. It shows the percentage of women in the workforce in each occupational cluster. Women have just about gained parity in the highest-paying occupational group, namely managerial/ professional. As a result, the competition among college graduates of both genders for the few jobs in the professional ranks should get even fiercer.

But notice the percentage of women in the third highest-paying group, craft/precision metal/specialized repair. Only 16% of the workforce are women. The numbers for minorities are similar. Although the growth in the ranks of women and minorities who are chief executives receives most of the press, the real problem is that, aside from health occupations, too few of either are among the ranks of technical or craft workers.

FIVE POINTS TO MAKE WITH PARENTS

Those who seek to create alternatives for students in the academic middle need to know why pursuing a 4-year college degree is not a sound plan for many students and what alternative labor market opportunities exist. Ultimately, however, high school students, their parents, and even many educators must be convinced. To assist in this mission to dispel the one way to win myth, the following five points should be considered before deciding on a 4-year degree program.

Five Things to Consider Before Finalizing Post–High School Plans

Point 1. Because of open admissions, getting into college is relatively easy, whereas graduating is not. Of all those who start a 4-year degree, either at 2-year transfer institutions or at the university level, only about half who matriculate ever graduate in six years.

Point 2. In the decade ahead, the number of 4-year college graduates will far exceed commensurate job opportunities.

Point 3. Technical workers are the fastest growing and economically most promising segment of the labor force. Generally, in high wage/high skill industries, there will be two technical-level jobs for every university graduate–level job.

Point 4. The largest number and fastest growing group of jobs among technician-level workers can be trained for at 1- and

---

2-year community and technical colleges, and some can be prepared for in high school career and technical education.

Point 5. On average, technical-level workers without a 4-year college degree will earn higher salaries than all 4-year college graduates except those who find work in the professional/ managerial ranks.

The point to be made in offering these arguments to students and parents is that, although the decision to attend a 4-year college is theirs, they should understand that (a) they face high odds, particularly when one graduates from high school with poor academic credentials, and (b) there are alternatives. The issue of higher education costs was not included in this argument, but some of you may wish to add it. Data regarding the magnitude of the average student loan debt typically acquired by those pursuing a baccalaureate degree can be a real wake-up call. Thus some people may wish to add this dimension to the argument; others may think that discussion of money is a private matter. Ultimately, each person must tailor this argument and the data to meet his or her circumstances.

OTHER WAYS TO WIN

The dramatic increase in 4-year college attendance by graduating high school seniors can be traced to genuine economic uncertainty about the future employment outlook. This uncertainty has led to the "anxious class"; this anxiety has led to the conclusion that the best bet is a 4-year degree. In previous chapters, we explored the harm done by this one-sided advice. In this chapter, economic labor market data have been presented that demonstrate the presence of a good alternative, namely, 2-year technical education that will lead to high skill/high wage careers in the ranks of the new technocrat/knowledge worker/gold-collar occupations.

The message to students, parents, and teachers is that, on the basis of the five points outlined here, there are other ways to win. Although going to a 4-year college in preparation for the professions is a very good postsecondary plan for some students, is it a realistic plan for all? A good alternative for those who want to go on to higher education, particularly for those from the academic middle as indicated by their high school academic performance, is 2-year technical education in preparation for competing for high skill/high wage work.

Persuading students and parents that something less than a 4-year degree is worth considering will not be an easy sell. It will require significant counseling and career planning involving both parents and students. This guidance is the topic of Chapter 8.

NOTE

1. Samuelson, R. (1992, August 31). The value of college. *Newsweek*, p. 75. Copyright © 1992, Newsweek, Inc. All rights reserved. Reprinted by permission.

CHAPTER EIGHT

Step 1: Providing Systematic Career Guidance for Students and Structured Feedback for Parents

A parent's understanding is an incredible gift.

—*D. Muse*

The fundamental challenge for those who would promote other ways to win is to help students and their parents make more informed secondary and postsecondary academic decisions. As discussed earlier, despite higher education's rhetoric to the contrary, there are few barriers to pursuing the one way to win path. The majority of colleges and universities practice what is de facto open admission: everyone who wants to can get into a 4-year college somewhere. In such an environment, the easiest thing for teens to do is to follow the one way to win advice. Thus changing the one way to win mentality begins with helping parents and students to at least realize there are other ways to win in hopes that this will lead them to make decisions that have a much higher probability of success.

Many teens, if not most, who pursue the one way to win strategy make no conscious decision to do so; for them, pursuing a 4-year degree is a default action. Rather than facing reality—which for many is not as pleasant as ignoring it—and making appropriate secondary and postsecondary choices, they take the easy way out. They do what everyone else does.

Much the same thing can be said for the course they select in high school. Most drift around in the so-called college prep program of study. A widely held misconception in U.S. high schools is that students are tracked into a regimented set of courses that limit their options. In fact, the opposite is more often the problem. Whereas in the 1950s and 1960s students had to complete a structured program of study to graduate from high school, today they need only accumulate a specified number of credits in broad content areas in order to meet graduation requirements established by the states and, in some states, to achieve proficiency on state-mandated tests. The bottom line is that students can take nearly any course they or their parents want. It is, therefore, not surprising that in a 2005 survey of recent high school graduates, the majority indicated that if they had it to do over again, they would have taken different/more demanding courses. One can speculate that if many of these teens had developed at least a tentative career focus, it would have guided them to choose courses more purposefully.

The implication of this trend is that the success of creating other ways to win depends primarily on parents' and students' decisions that these alternatives are worth enrolling in. The most sophisticated and well-intended efforts to provide students from the academic middle with more realistic postsecondary alternatives will fail if students and their parents do not buy the concept and elect the appropriate programs of study.

Nor should one underestimate the difficulty of convincing these clients of the public school system that there is value in anything less than the traditional college prep program of study and pursuit of a 4-year degree. Aside from the genuine parental concern for the economic future of children and coping with the social pressure to go to college, a well-financed higher education primary and secondary industry has a vested interest in maintaining the conventional wisdom of one way to win in order to maintain the enrollments at baccalaureate colleges.

For these reasons, the first step in creating other ways to win is to foster more informed decision making by teens and their parents by providing (a) a systematic career development/guidance program and (b) a means of getting feedback to parents regarding their teens' readiness to pursue postsecondary education. These two activities are discussed in this chapter.

SECTION I

Systematic Career Guidance for All Students

The need for better career guidance for youth is highlighted in many data sources that are easily found. Although 68.8% of all graduating female high school students expect to be working in the professions by age 30, most probably have not thought seriously about career plans. In the original follow-up study of recent high school graduates conducted for this book, most students indicated that they wished they had more opportunities to explore careers. Important for this discussion of the three academic groupings identified in the study, those who graduated with the poorest academic credentials were the most likely to wish they had received more career guidance.

Also supporting the argument for the need for more career development/guidance is a 1999 national survey of high school students. To begin with, the finding indicated that the one way to win conventional wisdom was well entrenched; 81% indicated they planned to continue their education, and 79% expected to go to a 4-year college. Only 50%, however, indicated they felt confident about their choices, even though 84% said they had given some serious thought to the topic. Meanwhile, 40% said they had not received adequate career guidance, and 30% indicated they had not had much help selecting courses in high school. These findings suggest an inconsistency. Whereas most plan to pursue the one way to win strategy—and other studies indicated most are doing so to "get a better job"—only about half are at all sure about their career goals and wish they had had an opportunity to explore careers while in high school. The problem is that the latter, a lack of career focus, predicts success in the former—going to college and getting a college-level job.

CAREER CHOICES AND POSTSECONDARY SUCCESS

There are good reasons for all students and parents to support better career development/guidance programs independent of academic talent. Of the four most important indicators of postsecondary persistence (academic skills, money, involvement, and commitment), it is the last, commitment, that is now the most important. As argued in *Getting Real: Helping Teens Find Their Future* (Gray, 2000), if we are to move beyond just counting how many go to college and begin to take responsibility for how they do once they get there, then career development/guidance becomes as important as college prep academics. And make no mistake about it, graduating from high school and going to college at any level without at least a tentative career plan predicts trouble. Here are some examples from national research.

CONSEQUENCES OF CAREER INDECISION

The vast majority of students who drop out of college do not do so for academic reasons. Typically, students do not flunk out of college anymore. It is almost impossible to flunk out. Keeping students in college (they call it enrollment management), not flunking them out, is the priority at most colleges. Rather than flunking out, students first stop going to class and then stop going to school altogether. The first group leaves during the first six weeks of the freshman year, which accounts for 30% of the 30% who fail to complete their freshman year. Others wait until they must declare a major at the end of the sophomore year. Because upwards of 70% of incoming freshmen indicate that they are not sure what they will major in, it is not surprising that having done little to clarify their goals in two years, many leave at the end of the sophomore year. Still others practice "academic major of the month," changing majors frequently. Although changing an academic major once may be healthy, multiple changes are not. Many who do so make the final choice—not because after four or five years of college they have finally found their vocation but because it is a major that allows them to at least graduate. As they run out of time, they make the choice impulsively, selecting a major even though they have little passion for it. Not surprisingly, when they do graduate, most end up underemployed.

Thus perhaps the number one argument for career development/ systematic guidance programs is that they are important for all students: both the academically blessed and the less blessed. Most students are in higher education for labor market advantage in competing for well-paying and satisfying jobs. Those who go to college, be it for one, two, or four years, with some clarity as to which career they want to pursue, are most likely to succeed.

SYSTEMATIC CAREER GUIDANCE DEFINED

Contemporary views of career guidance suggest that it is more than a set of activities and services; it is a systematic, sequential, purposeful, and developmental program aimed at helping students achieve specific outcomes. The outcome at the junior and senior high school levels is the development of a level of individual career maturity that will lead to realistic high school academic course selection; such selection, in turn, will increase the probability that all students, especially those in the academic middle, will make a successful transition from high school to postsecondary education or a career. Career guidance should be coordinated and coherent in its responsibilities to students and parents. In light of the realities that this generation of youth will face in competing for family-sustaining careers, career guidance should be seen as central to the mission of the schools if they are in fact committed to leaving no child behind.

While there are many approaches to planning the content of comprehensive career guidance programs, both the American School Counselor Association and the National Career Development Guidance Revision Project have provided school counseling models designed to provide content and activities that can facilitate the career development of all students, not just the few students fortunate enough to receive individual career counseling from a school counselor. In these models, the expectation is that career guidance may be reflected in many school activities, with the teaching of academic subject matter that includes examples of how that subject matter is used in the working world as workers solve problems and produce goods and services. In such models, it is also expected that career guidance begins in elementary school, so students are helped to become aware of the characteristics of the occupational structure, how jobs are classified, and the decisions they will need to consider in the future as they create individual career plans and choose courses and curricula to prepare themselves for such choices at each educational level. In broad terms, such development can be thought of as emphasizing in elementary school awareness of opportunities, educational and occupational, that will be available in the future; in middle school, exploration and trying one's interests and aptitudes and their relationship to the requirements of different clusters of occupations; and in senior high school, the importance of specific planning related to the next steps after high school graduation, such as going directly to employment, attending a 2- or 4-year college, or entering the military.

THE AMERICAN SCHOOL COUNSELOR ASSOCIATION MODEL

In 1997, the American School Counselor Association created national standards and, indeed, a national model intended to guide the development and the focus of school counseling programs, including the provision of career guidance. In essence, this national model indicates that the goal of a counseling program in a school is to enable all students to achieve success in school and to develop into contributing members of our society. Further, the model suggests that school success requires that students make successful transitions and that this outcome, in turn, involve the acquisition by students of the attitudes, skills, and knowledge essential to the competitive workplace of the 21st century (Campbell & Dahir, 1997).

According to the model, the areas of student development that underlie such student access are also the areas that school counseling programs must facilitate: academic development, career development, and personal-social development. These three broad areas of student development encompass nine standards, each of which includes a list of student competencies or desired learning outcomes that define the specific types of knowledge, attitudes, and skills students are expected to obtain as a result of an effective school counseling program. The three standards for career development (without the specific student competencies for each standard listed here) include the following: (a) students will acquire the skills to investigate the world of work in relation to knowledge of the self and to make career decisions; (b) students will employ strategies to achieve future career success and satisfaction; and (c) students will understand the relationship between personal qualities, education, training, and the world of work.

These standards and the associated student competencies, implementation materials, and evaluation instruments available from the

American School Counselor Association suggest that regardless of the particular emphasis of counseling in any specific school, there is a core of student knowledge, attitudes, and skills that should be systematically facilitated across grade levels, should be basic outcomes of any school counseling program, should be measured, and are central to the mission of the school. Certainly, a large part of that effort should be devoted to career guidance of all students.

THE NATIONAL CAREER DEVELOPMENT GUIDELINES REVISION PROJECT

Another national approach to systematically connecting schooling to the facilitation of student career development, career planning, and employment was that of the National Occupational Information Coordinating Committee (NOICC), which first released the National Career Counseling and Development Guidelines in 1988 and continued for the ensuing 12 years to provide an array of resources for elementary, junior high, and senior high schools to facilitate the career development of all students. Again, as the foundation for a systematic approach to career guidance, the National Career Counseling and Development Guidelines proposed three program goals that were important to the strengthening of individual career development: self-knowledge, educational and occupational information, and career planning and exploration. These program goals, in turn, were defined in terms of 12 competencies and a series of indicators for these recommended competencies.

The competencies represent general goals, and the indicators represent specific knowledge, skills, and attitudes that individuals should master to deal effectively with lifelong career development tasks. Unfortunately, NOICC was disbanded in 2000.

In 2003, however, the U.S. Department of Education's Office of Vocational and Adult Education instituted the National Career Development Guidelines Revision Project. The goal was to expand and update the original NOICC guidelines. In essence, the development of materials for the components of the revised National Career Development Guidelines was intended to help youth and adults better manage their own careers and to help professionals design and deliver career development programs and services for youth and adults in a variety of settings. In line with the information expressed elsewhere in this book that discusses globalization, changes in the way work is organized, and the expectations that workers increasingly will be expected to manage their own careers, be flexible, and be committed to lifelong learning, the new National Career Development Guidelines emphasize three domains: personal-social development, educational achievement and lifelong learning, and career management. Eleven goals underpin the three domains, and 200 indicators emphasize the knowledge and skills needed to achieve them. Each of these indicators is presented in a developmental sequence of learning stages: knowledge acquisition, application, and reflection. The elements of these guidelines are then used as the framework for materials developed for various audiences: students, teachers, parents, counselors, and others.

The resources just identified give systematic career guidance substantial content, a developmental or systematic framework for presenting career development content and activities, and a rationale for the importance of the career guidance process.

The principal emphasis in career guidance at the high school level should be on secondary and postsecondary academic and career planning. Such planning should begin by elevating the readiness of adolescents to participate in life as independent, goal-directed persons and then move on to help them define tentative career choices. These choices are to be confirmed or modified by academic performance, exploratory experiences, and changing preferences as a student progresses through high school. The point is that career guidance program activities in the senior high school must take each student from where he or she is in coping with developmental tasks integral to career development and lead that person to create a specific set of preferences and plans for achieving those goals (which is the substance of the individual career plan discussed in the following section).

Within a systematic career guidance program are myriad activities that can facilitate career maturity that, in turn, will lead to realistic high school course selection and postsecondary plans. One listing of such career guidance activities of particular relevance to the focus of this book has been advanced by Chew (1993). It includes, in abridged form, the following:

1. Counselors and school districts should implement a comprehensive developmental guidance model for K–12 students, emphasizing technical careers within the career component.

2. Counselors should provide all students with interest and aptitude assessments (beginning not later than the eighth grade) to help them plan postsecondary education goals.

3. Counselors should provide schoolwide activities that promote the awareness of technical career opportunities.

4. Counselors should provide students with information about community or technical colleges.

5. Counselors should give attention to women and minorities by providing them with information regarding unique opportunities for them in technical careers.

6. Counselors should assist special needs students (e.g., learning disabled, physically disabled, teen parents, and economically disadvantaged) in making transitions from secondary to postsecondary education.

7. Counselors must have access to appropriate materials and resources that explain the options of tech prep and technical careers.

8. Counselors should help students develop a portfolio that summarizes their credentials, both educational and experiential. (pp. 32–35)

The career guidance activities identified by Chew can be implemented by using many different types of interventions. For example, Dykeman et al. (2003) developed a taxonomy of 44 commonly used school career development interventions, which could be clustered into four taxonomy groupings: work-based, advising, introductory, and curriculum-based interventions. Each of these clusters adds a somewhat different emphasis to the provision of systematic career guidance in a school. For example, work-based interventions occur in community settings and include such interventions as youth apprenticeships, mentoring programs, service learning, and job shadowing. Advising interventions are typically delivered on an individual basis to facilitate student plan fullness and resolve career conflicts; this cluster of interventions includes career counseling, portfolio/individual career planning, and career-focused parent and student conferences. Introductory interventions are designed to initiate, prompt, or awaken students' interest in their own personal and professional growth and include career field trips, career days or career fairs, and community members talking about careers in classrooms. Curriculum-based interventions are school-based, group efforts to promote and teach career and academic knowledge and skills relevant to the world of work.

For a complete discussion of other alternatives, consult *Career Guidance and Counseling Through the Life Span: Systematic Approaches*, by Herr, Cramer, and Niles (2004). We chose here to emphasize what should be the heart of a systematic career guidance program for all students: the individual career plan (ICP). Before we discuss the ICP, it is important that the reader understand the concept of career maturity, the development of which is the goal of an ICP.

THE PROBLEM OF ADOLESCENT CAREER IMMATURITY

One very important aspect of individual development is career development, the lifelong process of decisions and actions taken to decide on, prepare for, enter into, and be successful in an occupation or occupations. Psychologists and vocational guidance specialists have studied career development and have constructed a model of the typical career development phases of youth (Herr et al., 2004). This model is presented in Table 8.1.

Notice that each phase is associated with a typical chronological age. An individual exhibiting signs of "mature" career development will be learning about and acquiring the self-assessment and career-planning skills relevant to the phase of career development appropriate for his or her age.

According to the model, a mature individual should have moved from fantasy in the elementary grades to realism at the time of

Table 8.1   Career Maturity Through Young Adulthood

	Approximate ages			
Preschool	5–9	10–14	15–18	19+
Formulation of self-concept ⟶	Translation into postsecondary plan			
Developing preferences ⟶	Choice	⟶		Transition
Fantasy ⟶	Tentative	⟶		Realistic

Source: *The Psychology of Occupations,* by A. Roe, 1956, New York: Wiley.

graduation from high school—realism in terms of having made a tentative decision to prepare to enter a particular field of work. Importantly, this decision, though tentative, is mature to the degree that it is based on a realistic assessment of skills and/or preparation at the time of high school graduation, as well as on projected labor force opportunities.

When roughly 70% of all female high school graduates and 50% of all male graduates indicate they expect to work in the professions, one can make a strong argument that massive career immaturity (see Hoyt, 1994) is afoot in U.S. high schools. Understanding the thought process that leads to this massive fantasy is critical to planning efforts to improve the career maturity of those in the academic middle. In this case, psychological decision-making theories are useful.

Career development theories are best thought of as theories about how individuals make decisions—in this case, decisions about what type of work they will prepare for and engage in. Several of the major theories are predicated of the assumption that persons can make logical decisions based on the availability of information and help from counselors or other professionals to assist them in weighing and evaluating their alternatives. Decision theories are also based on economics; they hold that any choice will maximize gain and minimize loss in aspects that are the most important to the particular individual (e.g., income, prestige, security) (Herr et al., 2004).

Some theories, such as Holland's (1985), are optimistic, democratic, and therefore intuitively pleasing. Such characteristics suggest that career decisions are "an expression of personality and not a random event. Individuals choose an occupation that is consistent with an individual's personality or self-concept" (p. 219). But this construct seems inadequate for explaining the current situation; almost two-thirds of high school students are making the same postsecondary choice—namely, attending a 4-year college to gain entry into the professional occupations—but certainly they cannot all have the same abilities or personalities. Nor can they all be receiving the types of systematic career guidance that allow them to clarify their interests, abilities, personality predispositions, or goals.

A theory is needed that explains a seeming suppression of individual differences, one that explains irrational acts and bad decisions or indecision. Cognitive dissonance theory seems to best explain the present state of affairs. Individuals faced with too much, too little, or conflicting information make decisions intended to reduce the personal anxiety created by this overload; in this case, they decide to go to college. As suggested by Herr et al. (2004),

> The magnitude of information and the number of factors to be considered in decision making are so great that the individual chooses prematurely, without fully considering the implications of the choice, in order to reduce the besieging pressures as the torrents of information relevant to the choice are sorted out. The person then reinforces the choice by rationalization: selective attention to those data making the choice appear satisfying to self and to external observers. Although the chooser "knows" there are other options and better ones, particularly over the longer range, it is comforting to make a selection and suppress the costs of its unrealism. (p. 177)

This thesis clearly describes the present situation. One key phrase is "external observers." For example, Jepsen (1989) speculates that, in adolescence, most career decisions are made in response to a social context. He argues that adolescents are greatly influenced by various reference groups, such as parents, teachers, and friends. These groups send overt and/or subtle messages regarding their expectations. Adolescents respond to these expectations, sometimes referred to as peer or parental pressure, in overt and covert ways. In short, they say and do one thing but think another. They do what conforms to social expectations—in this case, they go to college and express intent to enter the professions—even though they covertly or privately know it is the wrong decision.

Gelatt (1989) suggests that this is all normal under the circumstances. In what must be identified as a classic positive spin, he calls this situation "positive uncertainty," a healthy response to an unknown future caused by ambiguous and conflicting information. In Gelatt's model, the one way to win mentality is natural. It may well be understandable, given that no viable alternatives are provided, but it is also terribly costly for all except underenrolled 4-year colleges and universities. It is especially costly to those in the academic middle, where the losers in the one way to win game greatly outnumber winners, even among those few who actually persist in their quest for a baccalaureate degree. Thus the first goal of efforts to create alternatives for those in the academic middle is to replace "positive uncertainty" with "tentative certainty" among high school youth through systematic career guidance. The key element in this program is the ICP.

STUDENT OUTCOME OBJECTIVES FOR CAREER DEVELOPMENT/GUIDANCE PROGRAMS

In order for students to opt for other ways to win, they must have a career reason to do so. Developing such a motive is the objective of career development/guidance programs. Even with the comprehensive content and goals provided for career guidance programs by the American School Counselors Association and by the National Career Development Guidelines Revisions Project, often these programs suffer from a lack of clear direction as to what student outcomes are desired. To be specific, we recommend three (Gray, 2000).

1. By the 10th grade, all students will have participated in activities designed to help them identify several tentative but related career interests that can guide them to prepare for after high school.

2. In the 11th and 12th grades, all students will participate in activities that allow them to verify or reject these choices, using the results to develop postsecondary plans.

3. All students will graduate with a postsecondary plan that has a high probability of success and that will enable them to realize their hopes and dreams.

Systematic career development/guidance programs are composed of a sequential series of activities aimed at developing a student's career maturity. Ideally, such efforts start in the primary grades, but certainly no later than the middle school level. The goal is that by the 10th grade, students will have identified several related career interests. It will be quite natural for teens in the 10th grade to have several—even many—career interests. The point is that by the 10th grade, they should be related. A student who is considering building construction or automated machining is on the right track, whereas a student who is still stuck on professional basketball or tattoo artistry is not.

The 10th grade is important because it is a decision-making point in the high school curriculum. Students should choose their high school academic courses for the junior and senior years based on their postsecondary plan, and that plan, in turn, should be based on tentative career choices. Thus career development/guidance activities for K–10 students should be focused on fostering tentative career choices by the 10th grade.

The 11th and 12th grades are the years when students should be helped to verify and narrow the related career interests they have identified by the 10th grade. Job shadowing, internships, volunteer work, and part-time employment are all excellent ways to help students verify tentative interests. Doing so is critical. Having a tentative career direction is an absolute prerequisite for success in postsecondary planning and postsecondary pursuits. This choice may change in college, but if the original choice was well thought out, the change will likely be to a related field. Thus the goal is to have all graduates ready to implement a plan that has a high probability of success. For many, that plan will be other ways to win.

There are many ways to organize schools. Three specific initiatives develop the three student outcome goals listed previously. These three elements of career guidance will be discussed in detail: the ICP, graduation portfolios, and career majors or pathways.

THE INDIVIDUAL CAREER PLAN

An ICP is a process that leads to a product (the plan) that assists students and parents in relating each student's career interests and postsecondary higher education aspirations to individual aptitudes and achievements. The specific objective is to make a plan of action that the student will follow after graduation. The plan provides concrete postsecondary plans and tentative career goals, identifies the steps (e.g., courses to be taken in high school) that are required, and reinforces the commitment and responsibility of each student to take charge of his or her career. Inherent in the ICP is the importance of requiring students to consider emerging trends in the organization and availability of work options and to anticipate change and the need to prepare for it.

Students, their parents, and school personnel develop this written document jointly. It becomes a part of the student's permanent record file. Thus, although ICP development is a joint venture and the postsecondary plan ultimately reflects decisions made by students and parents, the school is responsible for managing the process and for providing students and parents with objective data that enable them to periodically evaluate the feasibility of the plan. This critical issue is discussed later in the chapter.

Because there are a number of ICP models, ultimately each high school faculty member will have to select one or develop his or her own. One such model, called "Get a Life" Personal Planning Portfolio, was developed by the American School Counselor Association with a grant from the NOICC. The program is systematic; it recommends certain activities at certain specific points in the K–12 years for each student. The resultant portfolio becomes part of a student's permanent record and follows him or her from one level of schooling to another. The Personal Planning Portfolio is divided into two strategic parts. The first, the personal file, contains individual reflections about tentative career plans that are gained from career guidance activities that the school system provides to all students. The second, the competency file, contains objective data that the school system provides regarding a student's academic achievements and abilities. The school expands the competency file at least once each year—usually at the end of the year—on the basis of the student's academic achievements and experiences.

The portfolio would first be developed in the 7th or 8th grade so that it could serve as a basis for high school first-year course selection. The ICP method has been the most effective in those school districts where it is a requirement for high school freshman-year course selection. In these early years, most plans will call for preparation for the transition to a 4-year college and plans to pursue professional work. In the 7th, 8th, and even 9th grades, this level of unreality is tolerable and perhaps even desirable. Clearly, though, the goal is to have students and parents, by the end of the 10th grade or, at the latest, the 11th grade, facing the reality that for most students—in our estimate, 70%—the one way to win paradigm of a 4-year college degree and a career in the professions is not very realistic.

Once again, the goal of this model and of all others is to move students from a state of career immaturity or naive optimism to a state of career maturity or tentative certainty. This transition is achieved by structuring situations that juxtapose tentative postsecondary plans with objective data regarding academic ability and achievement. Thus it is important that the ICP strategy chosen or developed include periodic wake-up calls or objective feedback to students and parents that facilitates the most realistic evaluation of postsecondary plans and career aspirations. Parents are told they will be getting information from the school that should be used to continuously review the ICP.

Unfortunately, since the 1960s, high school educators have grown skeptical of activities designed to give parents anything but good news. This attitude is understandable because, increasingly, parents either lay total blame on the school or ignore the message. Tired of hearing from parents and others about the one youth who went to college and graduated despite his counselor's assessment that he was not "college material," counselors also have taken a passive role. This attitude must change. Presenting the type of data described in this section to parents as part of an ICP process will help high school educators become more willing to deliver wake-up calls. After all, these data are part of an ongoing process that includes delivery of an important message: postsecondary plans are your (parents' and students') decision; our (educators') role is to provide the best education possible to achieve these plans but also to provide you with objective data regarding your probability of academic success. Our responsibility is to help you make the best decisions possible.

Such thoughtful confrontation between plans and academic achievement is critical to the creation of other ways to win because it ensures that the alternative emphasis within the college prep program of study recommended in the next chapter will be considered seriously. The critical players in this thoughtful confrontation are, of course, individual students, but parents also play an important role. In fact, the successful creation of other ways to win relies on reaching out to parents to challenge the one way to win myth and to provide them with advice and counsel regarding their children's higher education plans.

GRADUATION PORTFOLIOS

A similar program to promote career maturity is the graduation portfolio. As a prerequisite for graduating, seniors are required to create a portfolio of their interests, abilities, achievements, and tentative career plans. In some states, a graduation portfolio is required. Unlike the typical high school transcripts that list courses and grades, the portfolio is evidence of what students actually like to do and are able to do based on evidence that they have done it. Required in the portfolio is evidence of activity during the junior and senior years to verify tentative career interests, and a statement regarding what the student has concluded from these experiences.

Of the three programs discussed, the graduation portfolio is probably the easiest to manage and the least expensive to fund. It is a good first step for high schools that wish to begin a program and a good final step in the ICP program just discussed.

CAREER PATHWAYS, CAREER MAJORS, AND CAREER ACADEMIES

A more comprehensive and ambitious effort to develop career maturity among teens involves adding career majors or pathways to the high school program of study. Typical pathways or majors include health/human services, business/marketing, science/natural resources, engineering/technical, and arts/humanities. Some states have designated specific career pathways for all schools within their borders. Each student is required to choose a career major or pathway on entering high school. Making this choice is the focus of a comprehensive career development program in the preceding grades. In larger high schools with more scheduling and course options, different academic programs of study are developed for each occupational level within each major. In smaller high schools, the number of majors is typically four (for example, engineering/industrial, health/science and human services, business technology, and arts/humanities). In these smaller high schools, developing different academic programs of study may not be realistic. Instead, they use programs such as tech prep to provide a focused academic sequence for those interested in preparing for 2-year technical education. Career majors become the focus of career verification efforts in the junior and senior years.

The most comprehensive model of education reform designed to promote academic and career maturity and specific occupation skills is the career academy. There are now about 2,500 of them in the United States. A career academy is an entirely self-contained academic unit focused on providing students the occupational and academic skills related to a specific career cluster such as health or information technology. Often they are as much the result of efforts to provide a smaller learning environment as efforts for career maturity and preparation. Career academies are found primarily in urban centers or large districts that have multiple high schools, providing the opportunity to designate one or more a career magnet. Thus a career academy may be a public school devoted to teaching about one career cluster. However, it is possible to establish a career academy within a large high school in much the same way large high schools have established various houses or schools within a school. In the career academy approach, the occupation cluster becomes the context for academic as well as skill building. Often career academies are sponsored directly by related industry. Research regarding the outcome of career academies is very positive, particularly for males who earn more than 18% more than noncareer academy participants (Kemple & Scott-Clayton, 2004).

Perhaps the true importance of the ICP, graduation portfolio, and career major/pathway/academy efforts is the message they send to students and parents, namely, that career maturity and career focus are critical to success. The objective of these efforts is not to vocationalize the curriculum or take decision making out of the hands of families, but to promote postsecondary success by helping teens and parents make better decisions.

Underlying career guidance, ICPs, and career pathway efforts is career information. Neither students nor parents can choose what they do not know about. Information is power if it is accurate, relevant, and timely to choices that need to be made. However, if one has very limited and biased information, it reduces the likelihood that choices made will be free or informed or will reflect the comprehensive exploration and reality testing that is included in the meaning of the term career maturity.

CAREER INDECISION AND TEEN ANXIETY

All teens, if they think that they have a chance to succeed, want to be a "somebody," to have a decent job and life. Most have at least thought about the details regarding how they can make this happen. Many, however, find it too threatening, too confusing, or too uncertain and just give up. Many teens are worried to the point of immobility by the fear that making a career choice is a once in a lifetime decision and, once made, it cannot be changed or one will ruin one's life forever. They view its importance right up there with choosing a spouse. From the first author's experience teaching a first-year seminar in a large university that is not easy to get into, it is clear that this fear is as much a factor among the academically blessed as among those from the academic middle. Talking them down from this fear is central to any career development efforts. The following message has worked among college freshmen; it should work among high school teens as well.

The goal of career exploration is not to choose a job but to make beginning plans regarding a career. This is not a once and for all time irrevocable decision but the first decision. The likelihood that you will end up in a career you choose now is probably fifty-fifty at the most. But if you work hard to make the best decision you can make now, based on what you know about yourself now and career opportunities now, if you change you mind, the next decision will be an even better, more refined, related decision. Meanwhile, not making any decision does not improve your chances of making the one-time right decision; it actually decreases the time it will take for you to get focused and choose a career.

SECTION II

Providing Feedback to Parents

It is unlikely that even the most sophisticated career guidance program will successfully create a modest level of career maturity among high school seniors or interest them in more realistic post-secondary educational alternatives unless it is accompanied by a parallel effort to provide counseling through objective feedback to parents on labor market realities, college costs, and their child's academic credentials. The parents' role in promoting the one way to win mentality was documented in Chapter 2 (see Figure 2.1). The forces behind the parental one way to win push are complex. They include the reality that (a) college attendance has replaced high school graduation as the final visible sign of parental effectiveness and (b) society seems to agree that once their adolescent is in college, parents have provided the most important opportunity in the society for their child and have done all they can. Parents have their children's best interests in mind when they promote 4-year college attendance because they see it as the only way to win. To quote Secretary of Labor Robert Reich,

> A widening economic gap between better-educated and less skilled workers is creating an "anxious class" of Americans worried about the kind of future their children will face. These people . . . are justifiably uneasy about their own standing and fearful about their children's futures. (Naylor, 1994, p. A4)

Reich's "anxious class" probably includes parents of students in the academic middle. These parents may themselves be in jobs threatened by downsizing or technological elimination. Faced with such uncertainty, they would certainly hope to protect their children from a similar fate in the future. They read that college graduates currently earn 83% more than high school graduates over their lifetimes and conclude that a 4-year college degree is the only hope, the only way to win. Although this logic is flawed, parents can be very reluctant to endorse alternatives, or as summarized by Paul Barton (1994) of the Policy Information Center, "Parents generally fear what appears to them to be any form of tracking away from the college route" (p. 3), a point we return to in Chapters 9 and 10.

Thus working effectively with parents rests on effective communication of the economic axioms of career planning and provision of objective data regarding outlooks for academically average students. At the same time, it means being mindful that, for many parents, anything less than a 4-year degree for their child will be very difficult to accept. In this context, when and how feedback and counseling regarding their child's developing academic credentials are provided becomes very important. Such information needs to be highly structured and the same for all parents of all high school students. Separate efforts, distinct from programs for the academically blessed, will not work.

DELIVERING THE WAKE-UP CALL TO PARENTS

Parental involvement is widely viewed as a key factor in the school achievement and career development of children. Therefore, public school educators expend considerable energy promoting parental involvement and parent groups at the elementary and middle school levels. These efforts typically diminish, however, once students get to high school. It is difficult to decide whether this withering of parental involvement is because of the belief by high school educators that parental interaction is not traditional at this level or because, over the years, parents become less inclined to be involved at the high school level and thus stop trying. There are some exceptions, however, such as the Connecticut Regional Vocational High Schools, wherein secondary schools have very active and effective parent associations. These and other success stories around the United States prove that it is possible to get high school parents more involved than is currently the practice.

Our argument is that such parental involvement is not only possible but also essential to successful efforts to get those in the academic middle to consider alternatives. Parents are intimately involved in the present pressure on youth to go to a 4-year college. If students are to be receptive to alternatives, their parents must be too. The following five-step program is recommended.

A FIVE-STEP PARENTAL INVOLVEMENT PROGRAM

In the following five-step, or five-part, parental involvement program, the intent is to increase the involvement of all parents in the selection of secondary-level courses and programs of study, as well as in the formulation of postsecondary plans. Although the objective is to improve communication with parents of students in the academic middle, the program is for all parents. An emphasis is placed on "structure." It is recommended that a strategy to involve parents be highly structured: parents should understand the purpose of the program—better academic and postsecondary planning for their children—and know when the critical decision points in high school program course selection are and how to use data provided by the school to evaluate their child's ICP.

The program begins with talking to elementary school parents.

Step 1: Orientation For
Parents of Grade School Children

While "the rubber hits the road" regarding career decisions in the high school years, the process should begin much earlier via efforts to get parents to consider the big picture early. The goal of these efforts is to make parents understand that for their kids, career maturity is as important as mastering algebra. Lack of either predicts failure. Later in this chapter, five points to make with parents are recommended. Elementary school parent group meetings are the right place to begin delivery of these messages. Attendance is always good, and because the hard decisions are years away, they are more open to the message. Of course, they will all have the one way to win route in mind for their kids, and at this time, the objective is not to change it. The goal is to make them understand the realities of the future their children will face and the importance of career as well as academic maturity.

Step 2: Have an Eighth Grade Parent Meeting

The best time to involve parents in the tentative formulation of secondary and postsecondary plans for their children is when they are getting ready to start high school. This time is strategic and the best opportunity to get their attention and involvement. Most high schools have an orientation meeting for parents, but this is a one-shot effort, not concerned with anything other than orientation. Unless a student is exceptional in either a positive or negative sense, parents hear or receive nothing further from the high school except during report card periods. This point is particularly true of the parents of academically average youth; they are less apt to initiate meetings with teachers.

We recommend a parental involvement program that is considerably more extensive. This program would be explained during an eighth grade meeting; other activities would include presenting the five points that should be considered before decisions are made about a 4-year college education (as outlined in Chapter 7). The major purpose of this meeting would be to acquaint parents with the school's expectations of them and to hear what they expect of the school. Specifically, school administrators would expect the parents to be active participants in the development of their child's tentative career plan and to be part of and an extension of the school's career guidance program. As such, parents should expect (a) to be called together periodically during the next four years and (b) to periodically be given objective data that enable them to test, with their children, the continued reality of the earlier developed career plan. In addition, parents would be expected to help expose their children to different types of jobs and postsecondary opportunities and to be willing to consider alternatives in which their child may express an interest.

Two points need to be stressed when providing parents with information about their child's academic progress in relation to the ICP. The first point is the issue of providing objective data. There is quite a difference between a guidance counselor's (a) telling a parent that his or her daughter is not "college material" and pointing out that her cumulative average and SAT test score do not compare favorably with those of successful college students and (b) telling parents about educational alternatives that may meet the adolescent's goals more effectively. Announcing that a child is not college material can have a personal pejorative connotation. The second method relays the same information but does so more objectively. Parents— particularly parents of those in the academic middle, the anxious class—can be expected to hold high hopes that their children will obtain 4-year degrees. They will respond best to objective data and positive alternatives.

The second point is that clearly defining the roles for parents and schools will facilitate the delivery of objective data and thus make high school educators more willing to provide it and parents more open to accept it. The school's purpose is to provide parents with feedback regarding the appropriateness of their child's tentative career plan, the program of study they have chosen, and the courses they are selecting. The school will help parents evaluate these data if they wish. This critical message should be delivered to eighth grade parents: "We want you to be involved in the formulation of your child's tentative career plan. We will at specific times provide you with data to test the continued reality of this plan. We will help you evaluate this information if you wish, but we are not here to make the decision for you. It is your choice." After all, because parents make the decision, they will have to live with it; but they have a right to expect the school to provide the guidance and data needed to make a sound one.

The basis for this strategy is a "compact" between parents and school. Prior to the 1970s, high school teachers and guidance counselors took a very directive role in student programs of study and course-taking decisions. In the late 1970s and the 1980s, the pendulum swung the other way: the shopping mall high school emerged, students and parents made all decisions, and the schools stopped providing specific course-planning direction. Youth, in many schools, thus received little to no satisfactory guidance. A compromise could resolve this situation. A compact between the school and the parents would require the provision of highly structured guidance through objective data and counseling; the presence of these elements would help parents and students make informed decisions.

Step 3: Involve Parents in the Career Plan

We argued earlier that creating other ways to win begins with more effective systematic career guidance. The focal point of this effort was an ICP for each student. This plan may best be formulated before a student enters high school, but some formal review process or development of this plan for each student should occur in the first semester of the freshman year, if it has not already occurred. This plan should represent a joint effort or decisions by each student and his or her parents. If nothing else, parents should approve the plan. This process may sound bureaucratic, but human nature being what it is, people tend to take something they sign a little more seriously. Any number of other things can be done to involve parents, such as sending them periodic reminders about their child's plan. Whatever efforts are expended, the objective is to get parents to take responsibility for systematic collaboration with their children in this planning and to get them to confront the facts.

Step 4: Provide Objective
Feedback at Strategic Times

Parents need to be involved not only in the development of their child's ICP but also in the periodic reality testing of this plan as their child's academic credentials evolve during four years of high school. National survey data reveal that currently first tentative career plans of 80% or more of students will include pursuit of a degree from a 4-year college or university. Other national data also show that, on average, only about 30% of high school students will graduate with credentials that suggest this path is a good idea. The objective of the fourth step in the parent involvement plan is to provide data that give parents and students the opportunity to test the reality of the 4-year degree plan and that permit them to alter plans, if necessary.

The types of feedback that can be provided to parents include test results; course grades in strategic courses, such as math, science, and foreign languages; and PSAT, SAT, and ACT test results. The key is to relate the data to the child's tentative career plan. A report card performs one function, but a report card with a note from a school staff member suggesting that a child's performance is inconsistent with his or her tentative career plan is a much better wake-up call. This type of feedback is most effective when delivered at key points in a student's high school career, particularly at the end of the sophomore and junior years. In some cases, key pieces of objective data, such as PSAT scores or SAT scores, arrive in the spring of the junior year—an excellent time for a review of ICPs.

Step 5: Provide Opportunities for Individual Assistance

The final step in the plan to involve parents in the secondary and postsecondary planning process is simple: provide parents with the option of individual advising from guidance staff or teachers. Every piece of correspondence and every meeting with parents should end with instructions for contacting the school for "individual attention." Of course, this proviso also means that counselors must be available at night and on Saturdays on a rotating basis, because today, the parent who does not work during the school day is the exception. It would be nice to think that the response will be so overwhelming that not enough staff will be on hand to handle the requests. Realistically, however, this probably will not happen. Nonetheless, the option should always be present, and as efforts to create other ways to win begin to pay off, responses will increase, and guidance staff can begin to do more of what they were trained to do in the first place.

SIX POINTS TO MAKE WITH PARENTS

When working with parents, it is important to continually stress the following six points.

Point 1. The school's role is to help you make the best decision for your child, not to make the decision for you.

It is critical to continually stress with parents that your role is neither to make decisions for them nor to tell them what their child should or should not be doing after high school. Many parents get very defensive, if not suspicious, when the schools begin suggesting that their hopes and dreams for their teen are not realistic. On the other hand, every parent hopes to make the best decision for his or her child. Parents are more receptive to the message, "The decisions are yours; our responsibility is to provide you with help and information to make the best decision." Many will choose to ignore both the information and the offers for help, choosing instead hope and prayer that all will work. Many, however, will respond positively to this message. As an aside, this message is important to stress with staff as well. Often educators interpret career development programs as ultimately telling teens what they should do. Not so! The goal is to help them make more informed decisions.

Point 2. Commit to having a Plan A, but also a Plan B.

The major challenge in working with parents is to get them to at least consider alternatives to the one way to win mantra. This is not easy. In fact, it is not even worth trying. What is worth trying and does work is to suggest that they commit themselves to having least a Plan B. Plan A is the one way to win plan. Plan B is an alternative to at least consider now, if and when in the future Plan A no longer seems like a great idea. In this way, parents can at least think about alternatives without giving up on their dream for their kids.

Point 3. Focus on postsecondary success, not on college admissions.

Parents who graduated from college during a time when admission was relatively competitive may consider the concern for ability to do college work over successful admission to college to be heresy. At first, they may not understand this message. They may assume, naively, that college acceptance implies that the admitted can do college-level work. The reader should know better by now. Although getting into a college of choice may not be guaranteed, getting into "a college" is guaranteed. The real issue, then, is not admissions, but graduation. A related point to make is what predicts success in postsecondary education. Yes, academic skills are important, but having a career goal is as important. In fact, as argued previously in this chapter, it is now more important.

Point 4. Know the odds and know the costs.

Perhaps the message that parents and students need most to hear is also the most difficult to deliver; namely, among those who try baccalaureate education, losers outnumber winners. Only about one half graduate in less than six years. Among those who do, one third to one half end up in jobs they could have gotten without a college degree. Because no one wants to deliver the bad news, it is easier to look the other way. But students and parents deserve to know. Another point that should be kept in mind is that although some surprises are inevitable, odds are that the poorer a student's academic credentials are, the greater the likelihood is that he or she will end up a statistic in the losing column. Parents and students can no longer count on colleges to deliver the bad news through rejection letters. In these times of excess higher education capacity, one can be sure that colleges will be the last to deliver the message. The high schools have to handle this task.

Point 5. If the goal is a better job, then do not confuse education with occupational skills.

When working with parents, particularly if the objective is to motivate the parents of students in the academic middle to consider other ways to win, it is important as well as effective to stress the earlier referenced five points before the decision is made to pursue a 4-year college degree. Thus this message is important for all parents. The ranks of underemployed college graduates include many bright graduates who got baccalaureate degrees but not in a major whose skills equate with demand in the labor force. Remember this point: high earnings are a reward for skills in demand. The demand for workers with skills learned at the baccalaureate degree level is much too low to accommodate the 1.3 million who graduate each year. At best, one in three will be underemployed. The path to economic security requires individuals to obtain skills that are in demand and necessary for many technical high skill/high wage jobs. Many of these skills can be gained both in school-to-career programs and in 2-year postsecondary technical programs. Some parents may counter that a better job is not the most important reason for getting a degree. This is true for some; these individuals need not be concerned with gaining occupational skills. For the rest—national survey data suggest 87%—whose goal is a better job, gaining skills should be important. If such students are determined to go to college, they should ask themselves this question: what majors will result in skills that will keep me from joining the ranks of the underemployed?

Point 6. There are other ways to win—consider all the postsecondary alternatives.

The final message is the other ways to win message. This includes 1- and 2-year postsecondary education at the pre-baccalaureate level, employer/employee-provided training such as apprenticeships, the military, and taking a year off to develop focus and improve academic skills. For a complete discussion of these alternatives, see Gray (2000). Remembering that the cornerstone of postsecondary success is having a career goal, an appropriate way to introduce other ways to win is to use the labor market information provided in this book. The key or path to other ways to win is high skill/high wage nonprofessional or gold-collar employment. The wages are excellent and the opportunities tremendous. Most require postsecondary education but at the pre-baccalaureate level. It is the best postsecondary education investment in America: 1 or 2 years cost less than 4, and often one's employer will pay the cost of continuing to get a 4-year degree.

OTHER WAYS TO WIN

In this chapter, we have outlined the first steps that need to be taken to create other ways to win for those in the academic middle. We argued that the success of any such efforts would require informed decisions by teens and their parents—thus the importance of career development/guidance programs. These programs have three major goals: (1) to assist students in developing related career interests by the 10th grade, (2) to verify these interests in the 11th and 12th grades, and (3) to use this information to develop postsecondary plans. Parents are an important part of this decision-making process by teens; thus, how to approach them and with what message were also discussed in the chapter. The most important point to make is that these decisions are theirs and their teenager's to make. Our role is helping them make the best decision.

If the goal is postsecondary success and presently few succeed, logic suggests the need to reexamine the high school program of study, or at least the one that teens from the academic middle take. That is the topic of Chapter 9.

CHAPTER NINE

Step 2: Structuring the High School Program of Study

> In the United States, the abrupt cut-off that comes after high school graduation leaves a great many adolescents floundering, vaguely hoping for the best.
>
> —*E. Herr and S. Cramer*[1]

A second step in creating other ways to win for high school students from the academic middle is to reengineer the high school program of study. When the first edition of *Other Ways to Win* was published in the 1990s, there was little talk in education policy circles about improving the American high school program of study. But by 2004, it had become the "hot topic" of would-be educational reformers in state capitals and Washington, DC, as well as philanthropic groups and policy think tanks that feed on them.

Unfortunately, most of the recommendations for reform of the American high school are predicated of the one way to win philosophy; namely, that all teens should be educated as if they were going to the university whether they plan to or not. Common was the idea that high school should be all about academics. In short, the proposals all seem to boil down to "all kids should be in the college prep academic program." Programs such as high school career and technical education (CTE) are viewed as inferior or a digression from academic content and thus eliminated. The Bush administration's budget proposal for 2006, for example, proposed eliminating federal funds for CTE and using the money instead for more academic programs and more testing.

There is a problem with such proposals. They leave more than half of all teens with no real reason to go to school. With a national dropout rate of 33% and with 30% of high school graduates going to work directly after high school, not college, it is hard not to conclude that most proposals about education reform provide little or nothing for more than half the kids. One of the main reasons teens stop coming to high school in the first place is that they have had nothing but academic courses for 9 or 10 years and they do not find them useful, interesting, or relevant, nor are they very good at learning such content.

Meanwhile, it is hard to understand how 12 years of academic study alone will help kids who plan to go to work, not college. Do these kids need more academic skills? Yes they do. But they also need occupational skills that will provide them the advantage to compete for careers that provide family-sustaining income, and academic courses alone will not give them a competitive edge. If the school feels responsible for preparing some teens for college, then it is also responsible for providing for those who go to work and, by so doing, reducing the number of teens who drop out as well. Therefore we argue that at the high school level, creating other ways to win, thus leaving no child behind, requires alternative pathways of study within the high school program. The academic program alone cannot be of value to all teens; some of them need a different content and delivery system.

The intent is not to minimize the importance of academic course work. The intent is to suggest that the standard college preparatory program alone is not effective for many students in the academic middle. Alternate programs of study such as tech prep or CTE are to some students what advanced placement (AP) and honors programs are to others. In these cases, the academic programs that exist, typically called college prep, do not meet their needs. This is not surprising. This curriculum was never designed for all those who now are enrolled or are forced by testing requirements to take it. The current idea being promoted by the mass media and by some policy makers that an academic curriculum alone will effectively prepare all students is both naive and condescending. At the high school level, students need alternatives.

SECTION I

Structuring the High School Program of Study

Prior to the 1970s, the academic program in U.S. high schools was a highly structured sequence of courses offering limited course selection options. Since the 1970s, this structure has largely faded away. The reasons for this ebb are many and varied, including the development of a "supermarket" array of options and a matching philosophy toward high school course offerings. This trend has been accompanied by a corresponding liberalization (some say decline) of admission standards at all but roughly 250 competitive colleges and universities.

In the past, completion of a college prep program of study was required for a student to be recommended by his or her high school for college admission and necessitated four years of specific college prep English, three years of college prep math, two years of college prep laboratory science, and two years of the same foreign language. This requirement is no longer applicable. Now, the typical high school program selection book begins with, "The following courses are 'recommended,'" and then offers an amazing array of courses. Some of these are advanced, some regular, some remedial, some politically correct, and some designed to attract more students to a particular academic department. Importantly, even within content areas such as English or math, little or no effort is made to articulate or ensure sequential skill development among the many course offerings.

Our point is that reengineering the college prep program of study does not mean dismantling a highly structured program of study, but instead requires putting some structure into a highly unstructured activity. Also, it should be noted that high school educators have already bifurcated or created different emphases within the college preparatory program of study. Virtually all high schools have an honors program for the academically blessed, with very specific, demanding, and competitive courses. Meanwhile, those who need structure the most—the academically average students— dabble here and there in a highly unstructured, undemanding, and noncompetitive environment.

It is proposed that the precedent of developing a unique emphasis within the academic program, namely, AP and honors, be expanded for those teens who seek other ways to win in such options as pre-baccalaureate technical education, the military, or full-time employment.

CREATING ALTERNATIVE PROGRAM PATHWAYS TO SUCCESS

Building on the example of the honors emphasis that currently exists within most high school college prep programs of study, we propose that the curriculum be reengineered to add other emphases for students who aspire to different types of higher education. The guiding belief is that creating other ways to win requires alternative emphases within the high school program of study. These different emphases are organized around different transitional alternatives students may choose: application to highly competitive colleges and universities, general baccalaureate education, postsecondary pre-baccalaureate technical education, the military, or full-time employment, including apprenticeships. Each emphasis includes challenging academic course work at levels appropriate for the transitional goal of the student. The transitional emphasis is chosen at the end of the 10th grade.

OBJECTIVES OF HIGH SCHOOL PROGRAM STUDY REFORM

Developing "other ways to win" is best served when the high school program of study has three broad objectives:

Developing core academic skills
Developing career maturity
Preparation for post–high school transition

All three of these objectives are necessary to ensure success. Academic skills alone are not sufficient; post–high school failure is not limited at all to the academic underachievers. Even among the most academically blessed, lack of direction leads to failure in higher education or underemployment later in life. Meanwhile, no one curriculum can prepare all teens for the various transitional paths students will take upon graduation, including baccalaureate

Figure 9.1   The Proposed High School Program Design

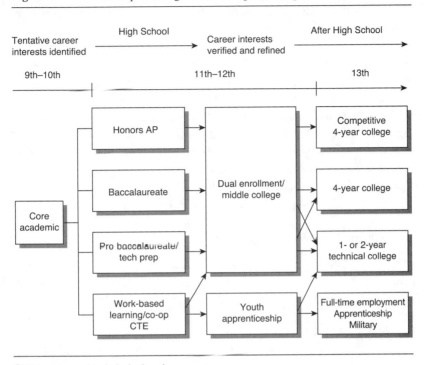

CTE = career and technical education.

education, preprofessional technical education, military service, formal apprenticeships/on-the-job training programs, and other forms of full-time employment.

A schematic design is provided in Figure 9.1. The proposed design has three phases: (1) a common core of academic courses for all students in the 9th and 10th grades, (2) four different transitional emphases in the 11th and 12th grades, and (3) transitional postsecondary placement services in the 12th grade, including dual enrollment/ middle college. Activities to promote career maturity occur during all three phases.

Phase 1: Core Academics: Grades 9 and 10

The core academic component is best viewed as a common academic curriculum approach recommended by numerous educational reform reports and the No Child Left Behind (NCLB) legislation. All 9th graders take a specific set of prescribed academic courses that will vary depending on the level of academic achievement of each student when entering high school but for all should include English (with an emphasis on reading for comprehension and writing), traditional math (pre-algebra, algebra, geometry, or more advanced courses for those able to take them), science (including laboratory biology), and for those who aspire to baccalaureate education, a foreign language. This freshman and sophomore year experience not only forms the academic basis for the last two years of high school but, equally important, also provides objective academic performance data that students and parents can use to make decisions about the emphases to complete in the 10th and 11th grades.

Develop Tentative Career Choices

The second goal of Phase 1 is to help students develop several related career interests by the time they must choose a transitional emphasis in Phase 2. In schools that have career pathways or career major programs, helping students reach this level of career maturity is the objective. Likewise, the individual career plan is designed to provide a structure that helps students make individual career interest decisions as a prerequisite for Phase 2. At the end of the 10th grade, students are asked to select one of four transitional options. This decision should be based on an evaluation of tentative career interests and academic record to date.

Phase 2: Four Transitional Emphasis Alternatives: Grades 11 and 12

In the 11th grade, students would select one of four transitional emphases. At least two of the four already exist in most high schools. One is honors/AP. Another exists by default—the largely unstructured, relatively undemanding college prep course taken by those who are not qualified for the honors/AP program. We call this second emphasis the "baccalaureate emphasis." Two other emphases should be added officially, meaning that they are identified in the high school course selection booklet and have a prescribed set of academic and technical/occupational courses.

The first is a pre-baccalaureate or tech prep emphasis design that will prepare students academically and technically for success in

1- or 2-year postsecondary education programs that lead to high skill/high wage careers. The second is a school-to-career option that prepares teens for formal on-the-job training and other forms of full-time employment after graduation. Within this emphasis, there can be two options. The first is a work-based learning/cooperative education model; the second is a more traditional school-based CTE model. High schools that do not have a technical education facility would opt for the work-based co-op model. Each of these emphases is described later. Importantly, whereas the honors and baccalaureate emphases are composed exclusively of academic courses, the other two emphases include technical skill instruction and/or work-based learning in the 11th and 12th grades.

Academic course work continues to be emphasized in Phase 2. During the last two years of high school, all students, for example, should be required to take math every year. This does not necessarily mean a higher level of math; some schools have had great success with senior year math that reviews algebra and geometry. The object should be to have as many students as possible master traditional math at the Algebra 2 level. Likewise, reading and writing for comprehension and communication should continue to be a priority. The point to be made however, and where this proposal differs from NCLB advocacy, is that while academic courses are emphasized, they are not stressed to the point of excluding other programs of study that prepare students for the transition from high school to whatever path they have decided on.

Verify Career Choices

While teens are progressing through the program of study in their chosen transitional major, they will also need structured assistance to verify the tentative career choices. As discussed in Chapter 8, these activities can include job shadowing, internships, externships, paid employment, volunteer work, interviewing for information, guest lecturers, and so forth. Verification of career interests is critical during these years, as it is the number one piece of information used to develop postsecondary plans for after high school.

Phase 3: Transitional Placement Services: Dual Enrollment/Middle College

The final component of a redesigned high school program of study is the provision of placement services to all students. Thus services for those going to 2-year technical colleges, work-based learning programs, or regular employment will be identical to those already provided for students applying to competitive colleges. This placement effort should be viewed as the culminating activity within the systematic career guidance program recommended, as well as the implementation of the ICP recommended in Chapter 8. Although placement is now traditionally viewed as a guidance function, a look at the ratio of counselors to students reveals that this point of view is impractical. Thus placement of the graduating class must be the responsibility of the entire staff. Everyone on the faculty knows something about a service or option that could assist in placement. Everyone must pitch in.

As will be discussed later in this chapter, transitional placement has taken a rather dramatic turn in the past five years, namely, the senior year of high school becoming the first year of college via programs such as dual enrollment and the middle college concept. It is proposed that such transitional models be developed for all high school students.

In summary, these three components are offered to reengineer the college prep program of study. This proposal is admittedly a departure from the current shopping mall philosophy that exists in many high schools. In fact, it is quite directive. In the first two years of high school, students are given little latitude. The only latitude will be in the different courses for students who enter the ninth grade with more advanced math, science, and foreign language skills and in social studies and other electives.

Student performance in the first two years, as well as their tentative career choices, will be used in conferences with parents about the selection of an emphasis for the last two years of high school. Each high school administration must decide how directive it wishes to be regarding the election and completion of an emphasis. Many may worry about parents' reactions to a more directive, prescriptive approach to high school course selection.

Parental Acceptance

After years of allowing students to select courses without regard for need, high school educators may be leery of parents' reactions to a more structured program of study. Recent studies suggest, however, that the public is actually looking for such a program. In recent polls, parents indicated they believed that high schools should be more prescriptive; many thought that students who had not mastered basic skills should not graduate.

Students agree, indicating they did not get adequate help selecting courses in high school.

SECTION II

Transitional Emphases for the Non-Baccalaureate Students

We propose the addition of two new transitional emphases to the existing two (honors and baccalaureate) that officially or unofficially exist within the traditional academic program of study. The intent of both is to prepare students from the academic middle for transitions into settings in which they can learn skills that are prerequisites to competing for high skill/high wage jobs that do not require a baccalaureate degree. One is a postsecondary technical education emphasis (pre-baccalaureate) designed to prepare students for success in 1- and 2-year technical postsecondary education programs. The second (school to career) is an emphasis designed for students seeking full-time employment after high school. This emphasis has two options: work-based learning and vocational technical education.

The Pre-Baccalaureate Emphasis (Tech Prep)

The pre-baccalaureate emphasis is an old idea whose time has come. It is a variation or refinement of the 2-plus-2 concept: 2 years of high school education that lead to 2 additional years of postsecondary education. The goal is to motivate and prepare high school juniors and seniors to successfully pursue 1- and 2-year programs of postsecondary technical education. These programs are cooperative efforts of high schools and postsecondary technical education providers. A schematic of tech prep programs is presented in Table 9.1.

Typically, tech prep programs are organized around specific occupational clusters or majors. For example, a health-occupations cluster or major would be designed to prepare students for a transition to a variety of postsecondary 1- and 2-year technical programs in the health field. The key element is the articulation agreement.

Table 9.1   Pre-Baccalaureate (Tech Prep) Emphasis

High school 11th and 12th grades	Transition	Postsecondary technical education
Focused academics, CTE courses	Formal articulation/ dual college enrollment	1- and 2-year college technical education

CTE = career and technical education.

The Articulation Agreement

The most important element in the tech prep transition program is the dual enrollment articulation agreement that formally links high schools with postsecondary technical education providers. These agreements form the basis both for organizing the junior and senior year academic and technical education component and for identifying the "perks," or benefits, to be accrued by students who participate in the program. The agreements specify three things: (1) what academic and technical competencies students are expected to have mastered in high school in order to be admitted into and successful in the specified postsecondary program or programs, (2) how these competencies will be assessed by the postsecondary provider, and (3) what benefits will accrue to graduates who have these competencies.

For example, an articulation agreement related to an associate degree in architectural engineering would specify math and science competencies; adequate computer skills, including familiarity with computer-assisted drafting; and other academic requirements that form the academic focus of the junior and senior year academic and technical program of study. The agreement would then state how these competencies would be assessed. Often, this assessment is accomplished through course grades. A better approach, however, is some type of more formal assessment, such as portfolio or performance skill assessment that leads to a clear message to students and parents regarding readiness to pursue this postsecondary option. Finally, the agreement specifies the benefits to be gained by students after participating in this transitional emphasis. This last item is the key to everything.

Motivating Students to Participate in Tech Prep

Although much has been written about the merits of tech prep programs, little has been said about students' reasons for taking them. But high school educators know that this is the key issue. Why would students and parents choose this program over the baccalaureate emphasis within the college prep program? Improved systematic career guidance that includes an ICP, programs of postsecondary planning and counseling for parents, and objective data regarding each student's academic performance will go a long way toward motivating students, particularly those in the academic middle, to elect this option. Additional incentives will also help.

Incentives for students to participate in a pre-baccalaureate emphasis take three basic dual enrollment forms: (1) advanced standing, (2) advanced standing with time shortened, and (3) preferred admissions. The first allows students to enter the postsecondary technical program with advanced standing; certain courses normally required are waived. These waived courses are often in the technical area—thus the importance to provide opportunities for students to take CTE course work in their junior and senior years. This advanced standing leaves open the second incentive, shortened time, which means that the postsecondary program of study will take less time and fewer tuition dollars to complete. Postsecondary providers are not always willing to negotiate such time-shortened options. Students still benefit, however, from the opportunity to take more advanced courses or additional electives for the price of a standard certificate or degree.

Another powerful incentive emerges when admissions to relevant postsecondary programs are competitive. Programs in certain 2-year technical health occupations that typically turn students away are a good example. In these cases, students who complete the technical education emphasis and meet the expected competencies are given admission preference to specific postsecondary institutions and curricula. A final incentive is an arrangement in which those who meet certain academic and technical education standards in their junior year and the first semester of their senior year are allowed to begin their certificate or associate degree program as college students during their last semester in high school. Obviously, this option is not possible in many local high schools, but when possible, it is a very powerful motivator and is popular with parents.

Regardless of the incentive outlined in the articulation agreement, the essential point is to be able to demonstrate to parents and students clear advantages to participating in these pre-baccalaureate or tech prep transition emphases. This is why so much importance is attached to a written, formal articulation agreement. Experience with tech prep transitional programs across the United States has shown that the credibility of such a program increases dramatically with both students and parents when it is viewed as jointly sponsored by the high school and one or more postsecondary institutions. In some cases, the specific incentive will be preferred admission; in others, it is the promise of a degree for less money or a better degree for the same amount of money. Of course, these emphases have one other benefit: some likelihood of academic success.

The Transitional Academic Program

Whereas the linchpin of tech prep programs is the articulation agreement, the heart of these programs is the focused academic course work that takes place in the junior and senior years. The content and skill levels for this curriculum are dictated by the articulation agreement. Recommendations for these courses are discussed in Chapter 10. It should be emphasized that most of this course work will not require the addition of many new courses but rather the redesigning of courses that already exist. Remember that because these students are already in the college prep program of study, they will be taking math and science in their junior year and—as recommended in Chapter 10—should be taking math and science in their senior year as well. The obvious need here is for a refocusing of the courses already being offered. One possible exception is science courses. Typically, few high school students take physics or advanced biology, but all students in these technical emphases will need one or the other. The problem is that these students do not need the same physics or biology courses that will be needed by students preparing for a 4-year engineering or biology degree. In cases like these, new courses will need to be developed.

The School-to-Career Emphasis

The school-to-career emphasis is for those students whose postsecondary plan includes full-time employment after high school graduation. Follow-up data suggest that many of these students will also become part-time students as well. The core academic program in the 9th and 10th grades should have given them the requisite level of academic skills to prepare for high skill/high wage employment that does not require postsecondary education.

Table 9.2   School-to-Career Emphasis

High school 11th & 12th grades	Transition	Postsecondary
Option 1: work-based learning		
Focused academics		Full-time employment
Job shadowing	Dual employment	Employer-sponsored OJT
School-sponsored/ monitored OJT		Apprenticeships
		Military service

Option 2: career and technical
    education
		1- or 2-year technical
		    college

Focused academics	Capstone work-based
	    learning/dual
	    college enrollment
		Full-time employment

School-based technical
    training
	Dual employment	Employer-sponsored
		    OJT

		Apprenticeships
		Military service

OJT = on-the-job training.

There are two designs, or options, that can be used in the school-to-career transitional emphasis: work-based learning and school-based CTE. The objective of both options is to provide students with occupationally specific skills that lead to labor market advantage when they apply for jobs after high school.

Option 1: School-Sponsored Work-Based Learning/Co-op

In this option, the occupational specific skill instruction takes place on the job in the workplace under the supervision of the school. The student's status is that of high school student, not part-time employee—thus the term school-sponsored work-based learning. It is similar to the school-to-work and the youth apprenticeship programs of the 1990s. As illustrated in Table 9.2, students in this option receive focused academic courses in the first two years of high school just like everyone else. However, they also take a course or courses in job-readiness skills that stress safety, appropriate work habits, and ethics. Equally important, students participate in a series of job-shadowing experiences to facilitate the choice of work-based learning at specific sites in the last two years of high school.

As a basis for the work-based learning, the school works with cooperating employers to assist them in the development of work-based learning sites and experience. Unlike cooperative education programs of the past, the school takes a more active role in developing and monitoring the work-based learning to ensure that students are exposed to a variety of job experiences and thus receive skills training.

During the junior and senior years, school-to-career students in this option become part-time paid employees as well as full-time students. The work-based instruction often takes place during the school day, but provisions are made to continue academic instruction in communications and applied math and science.

There are two significant advantages to this option. First, for schools that do not have a modern career and technology program or have a program that is over-enrolled, the work-based option provides a very realistic way to provide excellent job preparation. Second, for the students, the advantage is part-time employment that phases nicely into full-time employment their senior year. If they are at all successful, their work-based learning site becomes their full-time job when they graduate. Often, their work experience during the high school years leads to an advancement in pay or credit in an apprenticeship program when they graduate. In many cases, employers encourage a student to pursue postsecondary education part time, and they pay for it.

The school-to-career emphasis has two unique features: (1) During their final years in high school, students will begin to participate in a work-site learning program on the job; and (2) after they graduate, they continue that program as full-time employees. Participants may also attend 1- or 2-year postsecondary technical education institutions on a part-time basis, often at employer expense. Prior to the work-based learning in the 11th or 12th grades, most employers require that students have relevant introductory technical training, including relevant safety instruction. Both of these are typically provided via high school vocational education programs, as is discussed in the following pages. To accomplish this work-based learning, schools will have to develop various "connecting activities," such as the formulation of school/industry compacts to locate work-based learning sites or provision of assistance to on-the-job trainers in such areas as instructional techniques. Many high school staff are already certified in cooperative education; they can lead these efforts. In fact, this emphasis can be conceptualized as a type of cooperative education program (not to be confused with cooperative or group learning techniques) for a different student cohort.

There are numerous examples of effective school-to-career programs. The Pro-Tech Program in Boston is one such example. In the final two years of high school, students spend a good part of the school week in Boston health care facilities in work-based learning experiences. If they are successful in the program, they transition to full-time employment at these sites after graduation and continue their training as part of the facility's ongoing staff development effort. In addition, many attend community college part time. The essential feature of this and similar programs is that, in the final two years of high school, students retain the status of full-time high school student, but much of their education takes place on the job. Thus after they graduate, the transition to full-time employment is almost seamless.

Apprenticeships. Arguably the best school-to-career opportunity that can be arranged by a school is the transition to a registered apprenticeship program. Registered apprenticeships (endorsed and regulated by either the federal or state departments of labor) are run by both employers and workers' groups and, almost without exception, are in high skill/high wage occupations. An important and often misunderstood element in the success of such programs is that they require a relatively high level of academic ability, including reading for comprehension, computational skills, and problem solving by using science principles. This reality led a RAND study of the apprenticeship to conclude that the most promising prospects for these programs were students who "enter postsecondary education directly after high school but never obtain a degree" (Finegold, 1993, p. 5). This is exactly the group we have argued would benefit from the creation of other ways to win.

Unfortunately, the availability of registered apprenticeship programs varies dramatically across the United States. As a result, this option for school-to-career programs may not be available in all communities. Where they do exist, they are one of the best roads to high skill/high wage work.

Military Service. It is speculated that the most common way present technicians received their training was in the military. Recent conflicts have aptly demonstrated that the military is probably the most high-tech bottom-to-top organization in the world. It has always been a provider of opportunity via its training. Educators who question the military as a good alternative need to rethink their prejudices, as it is one of the best routes to high skill/high wage technical employment, and the training is free. Of course, military service brings the risk of being in a war or combat situation. In fact, however, because of the technological nature of the military and the large number of support roles required in such a military organization, only about one in eight or nine persons in military service is likely to be in a direct combat role.

Option 2: Career and Technical Education

The CTE option is a revitalized version of traditional vocational education. It is superior in teaching prerequisite job skills in high skill/high wage occupations that do require postsecondary education as well as the academics that are embedded in the occupational content and are necessary for career success and lifelong learning. Importantly, now over 60% of CTE students who take three or more courses in a single occupational area in this curriculum become upwardly mobile and go on to college, most to pre-baccalaureate technical education. In the CTE model, the instruction is still school based; the curriculum is totally under the supervision of educators. The option is best linked, however, with a work-based "capstone" learning experience in the senior year.

MOTIVATING STUDENTS TO PARTICIPATE IN THE SCHOOL-TO-CAREER OPTION

Why would students even consider the school-to-career option? At first, it seems highly unlikely. Remember, however, that a percentage of academically average students, even when they take a college prep program, go to work rather than to college after graduation. They may do so after realistically considering their motivation, academic skills, and the costs involved in attending college. It is difficult to pinpoint exactly when these students make the decision not to go to college, but the High School Follow-Up Study described in

Chapter 5 found that students from the academic middle who went to work instead of to college were already working 20 hours per week while in high school. Thus it is highly likely that they will begin developing strong connections to the workplace about the same time they could legally work, which for most is also about the time they start their junior year. Viewed from this perspective, it seems very likely that during their junior year—certainly by the beginning of their senior year—some college prep students have already, no doubt quietly, opted for employment, not college. Although these students may be unwilling to enroll in a concentrated vocational education program and thus lose face, they would be interested in and certainly would benefit from a school-to-career option within college prep.

Also, it is important to remember that many employers who offer these formal training programs also provide tuition reimbursement for relevant postsecondary education courses that lead to a degree. Thus a student can participate in a paid formal training program and go to college part-time at no net expense; this would be a strong incentive for some students and parents.

It is also good to keep in mind that many students decide early, for a variety of reasons, to continue their education part time while working full time. Typically, however, they end up working in dead-end jobs for low wages. The school-to-career option offers a decidedly better opportunity for this group of students in that it allows them to go to school part time but also to begin a high skill/high wage career, instead of earning minimum wage.

Finally, as is discussed in Section II of this chapter, for some students of all abilities, the school-to-career option is the only reason they stay in school. Many teens, regardless of academic ability, find traditional academic courses meaningless and foreign. CTE and school-sponsored work-based education keep them from dropping out.

SECTION III

Transitional Placement Services for All Students

The third and final phase of a redesigned college prep program of study is a commitment and (re)organization of staff to provide transitional postsecondary placement services for all students, not just for those applying to competitive colleges. This assistance for all students clearly does not happen now. In fact, all too often, many of those in the academic middle never talk with a guidance counselor during their entire four years in high school. In all fairness, high school guidance counselors give help to all who ask. The problem is that, in most cases, neither teens in the middle nor their parents ask for it. Thus in too many cases, counselors with huge client loads take an "I am here if you need me" approach. The academically blessed—those who need help the least—show up for services; the unblessed do not. This dichotomy should no longer be acceptable. Creating other ways to win requires a commitment to providing structured postsecondary placement services for all students, regardless of program of study or postsecondary goals.

The transitional placement commitment begins with a caseload philosophy. This means that the faculty views the entire senior class as needing directive placement assistance and organizes to provide these services. Schools can be organized in a variety of ways to do this, but in most cases, guidance counselors cannot do it all. Another approach, then, is the placement team approach. The senior class is divided into groups, and teams of faculty/administrators/paraprofessionals—anyone else working in the building—are formed. Each team is assigned responsibility for a student group. In such an effort, a guidance counselor can be assigned to each group to provide postsecondary planning expertise. The placement team's job is to provide significant individual attention and individual help in making a successful transition from school to postsecondary education or career.

A comprehensive postsecondary placement effort by high schools that aggressively seeks out all students and offers help is very important in the creation of other ways to win for those in the academic middle. Many of these students do not get as much direction from home or have the range of role models available as do their more academically blessed peers; thus they flounder. Instituting a systematic career guidance program that centers on ICPs for all students will help, but a large dose of individual attention for each student by a member of the high school faculty, particularly during the senior year, would do a world of good to ensure that those in the invisible middle make a successful transition from high school.

Dual Enrollment/Middle College

In general, the American high school has proven to be the waterloo of education reform: impervious to change, tradition bound, and diverted from its academic mission by numerous distractions such as high school athletics. But high schools have changed remarkably in one area: the senior year has become, for many, the first year of college. Be it called "middle college" or "dual enrollment," the concept is the same: high school seniors take course work for college credits while still officially high school students. Sometimes these courses are taught at the high school, sometimes at the college campus. Many states have enacted legislation to promote such programs. Colleges view them as a form of early admissions and filling seats. Meanwhile, high schools, under pressure to do something to make the senior year more rigorous, are all too happy to cooperate. Needless to say, such dual enrollment approaches are growing quickly.

Dual enrollment–type arrangements have existed for a long time, but only for the academically blessed. What is being proposed and in fact what is happening across the nation is that such arrangements are becoming more common for all students, including those from the academic middle. It is proposed here that such an arrangement be developed for all students, including those who go directly from high school to work. For those going on to postsecondary pre-baccalaureate education, dual enrollment will likely involve taking technical courses, either at a CTE center or at local community/technical colleges, for transferable college credit.

For those who plan to go to work after graduation, the concept behind dual enrollment, namely, starting the transition from high school to higher education while still a student in high school, takes the form of entering employment related to their CTE program of study either part time or even full time in their senior year. The importance of such flexibility cannot be overstressed. Unlike in college, where the first semester starts on a set date that is almost always after high school graduation, the opposite situation exists for full-time employment. Opportunities develop throughout the year: employers cannot wait until June. Work-bound seniors, therefore, need the flexibility to take advantage of good opportunities when they occur.

SECTION IV

The Role of High School Career
and Technical Education

The focus of creating other ways to win has been on reengineering the academic program of study. The rationale for this focus is that this program includes many of the academically average youth who will go off to college but would be better off at least considering 1- and 2-year technical education programs. But what about CTE? Is CTE obsolete? Not at all! In fact, whether leaving no child behind or creating other ways to win, CTE is critical. When joined with challenging academics, it is arguably the most important program of study for more than half of all high school students.

To begin, let us not lose sight of the reality that one-third of teens who enroll in the ninth grade fail to graduate. Research by Plank (2001) and others demonstrates that CTE is the most effective program of study in preventing students from dropping out. While taking any number of CTE courses increases high school student retention, a combination of 60% academic courses to 40% CTE courses is the best high school program of study to keep at-risk kids from dropping out.

Then there are those who have special needs and federally mandated individual education plans. They and their parents also hope for ways to win. Research by Harvey (2002) suggests that special needs students who enroll in CTE are more likely to stay in school, be employed when they graduate, and be employed in the higher paying craft occupations.

Importantly, around the country, a consistent 30% of high school graduates go to work. While some are special education students, most are not. They also hope for ways to win. And while academics are important for these students, academic course work alone will qualify them for only low skill/low wage employment. To compete for better paying jobs, occupational skills are needed—thus the need for CTE linked with academics.

Today, many of the students who in the past would have taken CTE now dabble in the college prep program but do not go on to higher education; instead, they seek regular employment. As revealed by the high school follow-up study conducted for this book, most of these students earn minimum wage in retail and food service;

they were not prepared to compete for entry-level high skill/high wage work because they had no skills. If they had taken a transitional emphasis within the college prep program of study that included some technical education, they would have had basic occupational skills to be competitive for some types of high skill/ high wage employment when they decided not to continue their education.

There is one final group of students who without CTE would not be served well in high school. These are the college bound who go not to universities but into pre-baccalaureate technical education programs in technical colleges, community colleges, and proprietary schools. Just as those who go to universities need course work specific to this pursuit, such as foreign languages, so too do these students. The majority of them find these courses in CTE. Today, 60% of CTE students go to college, and of this group, two-thirds go into 1- and 2-year technical programs. Probably most important to this group of students, CTE provides the technical specific instruction required as part of the tech prep curriculum.

For a majority of students, CTE offerings will provide the background technical skills needed to increase the probability of success in postsecondary technical education and even baccalaureate-level education. A case in point involves high school business education courses. Some students will continue to take the three-year business education sequence of skills courses in preparation for entry into the workforce after graduation. Even greater numbers will take business education courses, because they provide essential skills such as keyboarding and word processing for all those who are college bound, and accounting and spreadsheet courses that are important for those with aspirations toward employment in business or engineering. Another example is high school vocational education drafting programs: some students will take this vocational sequence in preparation for full-time employment as drafters (because many are still hired directly from high school). Most in this curriculum, however, will actually be preparing themselves for certain types of postsecondary education, such as engineering and architecture, wherein computer-assisted drafting skills will have to be mastered. A final example is high school health occupations: some students will take the full course sequence in preparation for full-time employment as paraprofessionals in the health field. Other students with aspirations toward a postsecondary education in the health fields will take health occupation single-semester courses designed to prepare them for pre-baccalaureate or baccalaureate education.

In essence, then, the creation of other ways to win does not diminish, but in fact increases, the value of a strong high school vocational technical education component. Such a program does three important things. First, it provides a relevant program of study for those who are work bound. Second, it provides an important source of technical skill training that is a prerequisite to successful 2-year technical education programs and that provides a fallback for those in the academic middle who take the baccalaureate option but go directly to work after graduation. Third, many vocational technical programs provide important opportunities to learn specialized skills needed by the 2- and 4-year college bound. Thus a viable vocational education integrated into the comprehensive high school curriculum is a necessary element in creating other ways to win. In high schools that do not have access to vocational education, other appropriate alternatives can often be developed within technology education and home economics and the community.

OTHER WAYS TO WIN

In this chapter, we have argued that because most high school students take a college prep/academic curriculum, creating other ways to win requires that this curriculum be redesigned to be more effective for the diverse student cohort now enrolled in it. Building on the reality that this program of study has already been bifurcated into honors and non-honors, we recommended that two additional emphases be added. One (tech prep) prepares students for 2-year technical education; the other (school to career) prepares them for full-time employment and provides work-based formal training and part-time postsecondary education. The goal of these emphases is to effectively educate those enrolled so that they will be academically successful in whatever postsecondary pursuit they choose. In many cases, new courses will not be needed, but it is clear that teaching and scheduling them in the same old way will not work. Furthermore, the educational modalities by which academically average youth learn best are often different from those most effective with the learning styles of the academically blessed. This situation is discussed in Chapter 10. We also argue in Chapter 10 that if these students are to become more involved in the new options, high school faculty and administrators must stop treating them as second-class students.

NOTE

1. Herr, E., & Cramer, S. (1996). *Career guidance and counseling through the life span* (5th ed.). New York: HarperCollins.

CHAPTER TEN

Step 3: Ensuring Equal Status and Focused Academics

The strength of the Wolf is in the Pack.

—Rudyard Kipling (1865–1936), The Law of the Jungle

Those in the academic middle often feel about high school the way second- and third-string athletes feel about filling out the roster, serving as the competition in practice, or riding the bench: technically, they are part of the team and must dutifully show up for practice, but their real involvement is minimal and subservient. Their major role is to be spectators in uniform. They get little or no attention from the coaches and often are treated as unwelcome baggage.

This same role is played by the majority of high school students who make up the academic middle. They are enrolled, come to school, and attend class most of the time, but they are there in body only. Their real engagement in the curriculum is nil. They are passive to the point of being almost invisible. Some people would argue that this "invisibility" is their fault, but considering the amount of attention they receive from high school staff (typically none), who can be surprised at their passiveness? The way they act mirrors the way they are treated. When they do manage to get someone's attention in school, the treatment they get differs considerably from that given to their more gifted peers. The academically blessed are treated by teachers as future peers; the less blessed are treated as future subordinates and, in many ways, inferior. This culture must change if high schools are to become more effective for those from the academic middle.

Often, relatively little effort is made in the high school classroom to reach those students who populate the academic middle. Just having to teach these students is considered by some to be "hardship duty"; status among high school teachers comes from teaching honors and advanced placement (AP) courses. Even though a majority of those in the academic middle now take so-called college prep courses, these courses are still taught in the same modalities as when only the academically blessed took them. The attitude seems to be, "OK, if you want to take these courses, we cannot stop you, but if you don't learn, it's your fault, not mine." Likewise, few teachers make much of an effort to motivate these students whom they now find taking their college prep classes. Both of these situations must change if high schools are to become more effective for those from the academic middle.

In the previous chapter, we outlined a plan that would redesign the college prep curriculum to better meet the postsecondary transitional needs of those who now enroll. In this chapter, we discuss three other fundamental aspects of this reform: (1) the need to change the culture of high schools to increase academic expectations for students who make up the academic middle, as well as the amount of time, energy, and personal attention they receive from the faculty, a process we call "ending Taylorism"; (2) the need to modify the overall educational modalities by which these students are taught in order to increase learning; and (3) the need to make renewed efforts to motivate and challenge this generally uninvolved cohort.

Section I

Putting an End to Taylorism

It is very unlikely that academically average students will be more engaged in the high school curriculum unless they feel more a part, a more valued part, of school itself. To use an analogy, although multitudes may dutifully show up at church on Sunday, only those who feel like a real part of things show up at the potluck suppers and other church functions; those who feel like an unwelcome or unimportant part of the congregation will generally stay uninvolved. Those in the academic middle share this feeling. Thus, if the goal is to transform these youth from spectators of the academic process to active participants, they will need to feel important. At present, they are treated as unimportant and inferior. If educators want to make them distinctive, they must be treated as distinctive.

As part of the high school Follow-Up Study done for this book, we sought to determine the degree of alienation of those in the academic middle. Scant actual evidence of alienation was found, but when these youth were asked whether "some students were treated better by the faculty than others," 84% said yes. Interestingly enough, this double standard was not missed by the more academically blessed either; 75% of the most academically successful students also observed that some students were treated better than others.

Most readers can simply recall their own high school experience to verify the dual standards or differing treatment of students, depending on their status among staff. Some students, the academically blessed, and certain athletes could roam the halls at will, unquestioned, whereas the mere sight of others in the hall was enough for a teacher to call the office. Nothing has changed; high school still has a double standard. This dual standard is not necessarily the result of a widespread pejorative attitude toward those in the middle, although undoubtedly some of this exists among some staff. Instead, it stems from an ideology held by teachers about children and the role of the school. It is most reminiscent of a set of beliefs called Taylorism (with a little bit of social Darwinism thrown in).

DEFINING TAYLORISM

Although students may be taught in school that the United States is founded on the principle that all are created equal, they learn in school, particularly in high school, that apparently some of their peers are more equal than others. In every high school in the United States, there is a predictable "in crowd"—those anointed and honored by teachers, school administrators, school boards, and school policies. Predictably, they are mostly the academically blessed, although some with special athletic prowess or well-connected parents may join the ranks. The point is that most high school educators take this situation as perfectly natural and even desirable because of 90-plus years of Taylorist influence on the schools.

Although Frederick Taylor (1856–1915), the father of scientific management, was a proponent of close cooperation between workers and managers, his theories of organizing for efficiency were interpreted differently. In brief, managers were to assume "all burden of gathering the traditional knowledge which in the past had been possessed by the workmen" (Taylor, 1911, p. 83). Thus, in the Taylorist model, the importance of managers increased dramatically and suggested that only those of high intellect were capable of assuming this role. Meanwhile, the level of intellect needed by the worker diminished significantly; in fact, the Taylorist model suggested that the fewer decisions the workers had to make, the better. The important thing was that they learn to do as they were told. The bottom line, from the Taylorist frame of reference, was that the academically blessed were destined to be the captains of industry and thus infinitely more important to the nation than the less academically blessed, who were destined to be subordinates.

TAYLORIST INFLUENCES ON HIGH SCHOOLS

The division of labor implied by scientific management quickly became a fundamental paradigm that structured the expectations that educators had for the increasingly diverse student population at the turn of the century, especially for students in high school. As argued by economists Samuel Bowles and Herbert Gintis, the success of capitalism came to be viewed as dependent on a "minimal participation in decision-making by the majority of workers and protecting (the power, prerogatives, and privilege of) a single minority of managers" (quoted in Cole, 1988, p. 2). The role of the school as a social institution came to be viewed as teacher of this social order. This is not to say that high school teachers, most of whom were first-generation college graduates, set out deliberately to train those in the middle to be drones. Still, that is exactly what they did, seduced by the belief that they were justifiably rewarding merit. The typical attitude among high school educators and the public was that the privileged status that some students enjoyed was simply a reward for their hard work; the conventional wisdom was that these students were the most meritorious because they worked the hardest. Thus any special privileges or attention they may have received in return was deserved. This same rationale buttresses current discriminatory policies, such as weighted grading.

CHALLENGING THE TAYLORIST RATIONALE

The rationale of merit that justifies Taylorist practices in high schools has many flaws. One is that most of the more academically successful students succeed, not because they work harder, but because they were born academically blessed. Powell, Farrar, and Cohen (1985), for example, found that in private high schools where performance pressure was evenly applied, the brightest students reported working the least. Parents of the most successful high school students often seem a bit bewildered about their children's performance because the youngsters do not seem to work very hard at their studies; typically, they do not—they are simply academically talented. The hardest-working students in any high school are probably the average students who, through hard work, overachieve and graduate with respectable academic credentials. Thus policies that discriminate against the academically average teen are misguided.

A second flaw is the attitude that somehow the academically blessed are more important to the prosperity of the United States. Modern economic realities suggest that the opposite may be true. Lester Thurow (1992) of the Massachusetts Institute of Technology, for example, suggests that the real problem is not the education of the academically blessed but rather the education of the rest. In nation after nation, it has become clear that it is not possible to compete successfully in a global economy with only an educated elite. Workers at all levels must be equipped to change with change and to have the literacy and numeracy skills required of emerging occupations. Perhaps the key point in the "total quality management" philosophy of Deming is the equal importance of all workers and the need for collaboration; the Taylorist view of the manager as a source of all information and the savior of the common worker is old-fashioned. The new economic order requires all workers to be a part of the team, but it is difficult to figure how the workforce of the future is to learn this value and these interpersonal skills when the first major organization they belong to—namely, their school—is run in the opposite fashion.

The basic irony of this treatment of students in the academic middle is that, as Thurow suggests, these students may be more important to the nation's economy than most college graduates. For example, it is largely the students in the academic middle, the non-college graduates, who find themselves as the backbone of the technical, skilled, clerical, retailing, distribution, and transportation systems of the nation. As any administrator knows, it is the clerical support staff of the organization, most of whom are high school or 1-year business school graduates, whose skills, insights, and loyalty literally make the organization function. So it is with the vast array of individuals who hold jobs in craft, precision manufacturing, and customized repair occupations that make the economy function. These vital elements of the national and, indeed, international infra-structure rely on a constant infusion and availability of youth from the academic middle, most of whom enter the labor force with a high school diploma or a pre-baccalaureate technical degree/certificate, not a 4-year college degree. Given their importance in an era of short-ages of skilled workers, their effective education and their being treated as a precious national asset should be a national, state, and local priority (Herr, 1995).

For those who seek to create other ways to win for those in the academic middle, ending Taylorism is not only an egalitarian issue but also an educational imperative, because it is closely linked to self-esteem, curriculum engagement, and the overall motivation of these students. When graduating high school seniors are asked to describe themselves, the academically blessed exhibit considerably higher self-concepts than those in the academic middle. More dis-turbing, the academically blessed not only have good things to say about themselves but often have pejorative things to say about the less blessed. In fact, there seems to be a dual problem: Students in the academic middle generally have a rather low opinion of themselves, whereas the academically blessed graduate with serious delusions of grandeur. It seems that Taylorist assumptions do not serve either group very well.

STRATEGIES FOR ENDING TAYLORISM

It will be difficult to motivate those in the academic middle unless Taylorist attitudes and practices are eliminated in the schools, particularly high schools. Such efforts may also infuse some much-needed humility into the academically blessed. The following strategies are recommended.

Challenge the Culture: The Equity Audit

Taylorist attitudes have been around for five generations. They will not go away unless challenged in the same way people question attitudes about race, gender, and the environment. One does not change attitudes, however, by putting educators on the defensive. Change theory would suggest that a better approach is to let them discover they may unconsciously have been doing the wrong thing. One way to reach this discovery is through a faculty-led "equity audit." The intent of this internal audit is to simply document time, services, and preferential policies that have different effects on different groups of students. For example, divide the senior class into three academic groups by using the criteria suggested in Chapter 4. Then document for each group such things as average class size, services provided by the school guidance office, participation in special trips, seminars, etc. The results will be obvious: 30% of the students will be getting 50%–70% of the institutional resources and attention. The question then is this: is it OK to be doing this? And if not, what should be done about it?

Challenge Discriminatory Policies and Practices

Just about every high school in the United States contains policies and practices that discriminate in favor of the academically blessed at the expense of those in the academic middle. Although the word discriminate may seem strong, the U.S. Department of Education's Office of Civil Rights does not regard it as too harsh. It has made segregation of students within schools a target of its enforcement efforts. The Lawyers Committee for Civil Rights Under Law worked to make ability grouping a central issue in the Wilmington, Delaware, segregation case, and similar action led the San Jose, California, school district to drop its ability grouping system. In Amherst, Massachusetts, in response to a challenge from parents of average youth, most of whom were minorities, a review panel recommended to the school board that the district drop the "use of weighted grades, class ranks, and courses labeled 'basic,' 'standard,' and 'advanced'" (Schmidt, 1994).

Is it too early to say that these cases are a signal of changing attitudes toward policies and practices that favor the academically blessed? It may be, but it also is a sign that high schools functioning in this way are vulnerable in the courts (see Weiner & Oakes, 1996). The advent of state-mandated standardized high stakes testing of "all" students at the high school level might actually serve to diminish these practices, but one wonders.

Although some of these practices, such as AP and honors courses, may be justified because some students are not well served by the low level of rigor in the standard academic program, giving extra weight to grades in these courses is not; John Dewey would call it "cruel and illiberal." Policies and practices such as these send the wrong messages to all children: to the blessed, it leads to delusions of grandeur; to the less blessed, the message is they are second-rate. In these times of litigation, it may be only a matter of time before weighted grading goes the same way as single-gender gym classes. In reality, the practice is somewhat comical because it leads to mathematical impossibilities: in high schools with weighted grading systems, it is not uncommon for a student to graduate with a grade point average (GPA) of greater than 4.0 (A); this fact explains why most competitive colleges first evaluate a student's high school records by recalculating or unweighting his or her GPA so that it can be realistically compared with those of others who apply. The point is that schools committed to creating other ways to win for those in the academic middle should debate these policies. These debates should include a representative group of parents and the public, not just the advocates of the academically blessed.

Stop the Obsessive Rank-Ordering of Students Against Each Other

Even at the worst of high schools, it can be predicted that the senior class will be ranked from top to bottom in terms of academic performance. High schools seem obsessed with rank-ordering students. The grading system of most teachers is designed first and foremost to rank-order the class. If you do not think so, imagine what would happen if a teacher gave all students an A; even if they all mastered the material, the teacher would be risking serious condemnation by peers and administrators as being too easy.

When one is challenging the obsession with rank-ordering students, it is effective to point out the implied philosophy behind this practice, namely, that for some to look good, the rest must look bad. The logical extension is that for some to look really good, a lot have to look bad. When teachers announce that they rank on a curve (and most do, whether they admit it or not), they need to understand what is implied: the objective of the evaluation is to rank-order the class, not to evaluate learning. To understand this issue better, let's consider the case of the President's Physical Fitness Award and the attitude of teachers toward this evaluation. Interestingly, although teachers and parents would consider it outrageous if everyone received an A in English, they would think it was great if everyone achieved sufficient physical fitness standards to receive the President's Award. What is the difference? First, the award is based on a set of very objective criteria, such as the ability to jump so far, run so fast, and so forth. Second, because it is an objective standard, the competition is against the standard, not against other students, and therefore there is no need to rank-order students against one another. The goal is to make all learning fit this paradigm, whereby the goal is to achieve the standard, not to do better than other students in the class. This is a far cry from current practice. The point is that if for some to win big, the rest—namely, those in the academic middle—must lose, why should they try?

Seek a Way to Integrate Students of Differing Academic Ability

Most high schools begin the day with something called homeroom period. Homeroom is truly a unique phenomenon because it is probably the only circumstance, other than lining up alphabetically for graduation, in which the school does something that results in bringing high school students together on an egalitarian basis, independent of course selection, intellectual ability, athletic prowess, family income, or even race. More needs to be done to promote this intermingling among students of differing academic characteristics. Particularly detrimental is the segregation of students according to program of study; such division amounts to segregating students by ability. Although perhaps not by design, the realities of scheduling classes are that the academically blessed often end up in the same classes. Likewise, those in the academic middle spend their high school careers interacting with others in the academic middle. Arguably, this practice does not serve either group well, but it is particularly harmful to those in the academic middle and perhaps explains why these students go unchallenged, unmotivated, and unengaged and why some teachers hate to teach them.

A commitment to those in the academic middle calls for doing things to end their isolation. Finding ways to ensure interaction among students of all academic abilities should become an obsession. One tactic is the institution of a portfolio requirement in which the portfolio team must include a mix of students from varying curricula to jointly plan and complete selected learning tasks or projects. Another is to resist ability grouping and to do whatever is possible to correct what occurs naturally because of the master schedule. For example, one alternative is not to put all students enrolled in calculus in the same social science class.

Create a "One Team" Culture

The final strategy is perhaps the most important. Although most high school mission statements suggest an interest in all students, they are, in fact, elitists; that is the culture. This condition needs to be changed. Kipling reminds us that the strength of the wolf lies in the pack; schools should embrace this philosophy as well. The desperate need is to convey this message to students on a daily basis: all are equally valued, no one is better than anyone else, arrogance is frowned upon, humility is valued, and harassment will not be tolerated. The goal is to go from having an in-group to having one group. This conversion will not happen unless the principal, teachers, and guidance counselors are committed to creating such an environment.

Section II

Modifying Instructional Modalities and Practices

In the first section of this chapter, we argued that creating other ways to win for those in the academic middle begins with changing the treatment of these students. Only when these adolescents feel equal, not inferior, can educators expect them to exert equal efforts. The next step is to ensure that instructional modalities and practices used in college prep courses populated with academically average students match their learning styles.

The following eight strategies are offered as ways to improve the instructional effectiveness of the high school program of study to make it more effective for all students.

Emphasize Contextual, or Applied, Learning

The dominant instructional modality in most high school college prep classes is the "student/copying machine" model of instructional effectiveness. Teachers lecture, students copy down in their notebooks what the teachers say, and on tests students are asked to reproduce their notes. Although cognitive learning researchers suggest that this is the least effective instructional modality for all students, the academically blessed, perhaps because they are blessed, master the student/copying machine game early in their high school careers and become quite good at it. When the content itself becomes more and more abstract or detached from the real world, their performance, in comparison with that of students in the academic middle, becomes even better because those in the academic middle learn best when the instructional modality and the material itself are "applied" (see, Bottoms, Pressons, & Johnson, 1992).

The dilemma for those in the academic middle who now enroll in college prep courses is that they are taught primarily in modalities not appropriate for their learning styles. For example, national studies of high school classroom instruction find that only 18% of teachers spend more than 10% of class time putting the course content into a real-world context (U.S. Department of Education, 1994). High schools committed to creating other ways to win for average youth need to address this instructional modality mismatch.

Contextual or applied learning strategies may be worth considering for all students. Research by the Southern Education Board revealed a fascinating inconsistency: although vocational education students' scores on the National Assessment of Educational Progress test were lower than the scores of students in the college prep curriculum, the gap was significantly closer in problem solving than in math knowledge. Thus vocational education students did much better on the problem-solving items than would have been predicted on the basis of their performance in math courses. This finding leads to speculation (Bottoms et al., 1992) that, when math is taught in a real-world context, as occurs in vocational education, students learn to apply the knowledge and are better problem solvers, a worthy goal for all students, even those heading off to Ivy League colleges. John Dewey (1900) wrote that "education through vocation . . . combines within itself more of the factors conducive to learning than any other method" (pp. 82–83).

In applied learning modalities, the content is grounded in the real world; the learner is active, not passive; and the emphasis is on problem solving, knowledge, and skills that are needed by problem solvers. Although the student/copying machine instructional modality is measured in terms of what students know, the contextual modality is more interested in what students can do. One such example is the City Watch program at Ridge Tech in Cambridge, Massachusetts, where the entire ninth grade curriculum is taught within the context of an exploration of the students' community. Mathematics, for example, is taught by using the local community as the content to be numerated, measured, and otherwise described in mathematical terms.

Such dramatically different approaches are not necessary, however. What is necessary is a commitment by teachers to face the fact that their earlier instructional methods may not be effective for the growing number of academically average youth who now take college prep classes. Unfortunately, more than a few teachers take the "blame the learner" approach; that is, if students do not learn from a teacher's instructional method, the trouble must reside in them and not in the teacher. After all, the better students seem to be doing just fine. This point of view may be one good reason for the fact that the fastest growing groups of courses in higher education are remedial. Facing the challenge of academically preparing those in the middle to be successful in 2-year technical education requires a change to contextual learning modalities.

Emphasize Reading for Comprehension

When one looks closely at enrollments in remedial courses in higher education—those that are required but do not count toward a degree—we see that an interesting trend has developed. The percentage of students who must take math has actually gone down a bit, but the percentage of students who must take remedial reading has gone up. Remember that almost one-fifth of semi-competitive students in the follow-up study reported being required to take remedial English; in other words, they were found to be deficient in reading for comprehension. The point is that if educators assume that the majority of those in the academic middle will continue on to higher education, preferably in 2-year technical programs, the goal is to ensure that they do not have to take remedial courses. This point translates into an important reality: high schools need to face the fact that many students graduate with poor reading skills.

Over the years, the college prep English classes have changed little. In some cases, the literature selections have been modernized, and more emphasis has been placed on writing. In times past, English teachers who taught college prep courses could be assured that their students were good readers. Today, this assumption is false. Contemporary adolescents as a group do not spend as much time reading for pleasure as those of the past; they watch television instead. Those who seek to create other ways to win, which includes ensuring the success of students who select these alternatives, must face the fact that the instructional objectives of high school English now must include improving student ability to read.

Emphasize Math and Science for All Seniors

It seems to be almost a certainty that youths who graduate from the academic middle and head off to college end up having to take remedial English and remedial math. We have just addressed the reading issue; now, what can be done about math and science? This question is complicated by the finding in our Follow-Up Study that many academically average students who ended up in remedial math and science courses had taken above-average levels of math. In many cases, those who had to take remedial math courses had taken three years of college math in high school. The trouble was that very few had taken a math course during their senior year. Thus these students entered college not having taken any math for nearly a year and a half. No wonder they ended up in remedial courses. The same pattern was found for science. Those students who most need to take math and science in their senior year, those in the academic middle who head off to higher education, are the least likely to be found in these courses in the 12th grade.

In light of these findings, it is recommended that every effort be made to encourage all students to take math during their senior year in high school. For those whose tentative career choice is a post-secondary program that will require science—all paraprofessional health careers—taking science in the 12th grade is likewise important. One way to accomplish this goal is to adopt local graduation policies that require four years of math and science to graduate, a practice that has been in place in the Connecticut Regional Vocational High School system for years.

Teach Keyboarding and Computer Software Skills

One cannot be successful in higher education without gaining the ability to use a standard keyboard effectively and to use standard software packages, especially word-processing, spreadsheet, and tele-communications software that now provide access to everything from the card catalog of the campus library to the worldwide Internet. Likewise, computer skills are as important today to those who aspire to high skill/high wage work as physical strength was to the craftsperson of the past. In the modern workplace, computer skills have replaced manual dexterity and strength. Preparing students from the academic middle to be successful in pursuing pre-baccalaureate education that leads to technical high wage work, therefore, requires adequate preparation in both keyboarding and software manipulation.

Despite all the hype in the press about how much time teens spend on the Internet and playing video games, evidence from the Follow-Up Study conducted for this book suggests that most high school graduates, regardless of their academic credentials, may be graduating with inadequate computer skills that are related to success in the workplace or higher education. Teens may be video game whizzes but dunces when it comes to word-processing or spread-sheet applications. Even among those graduating with academically competitive credentials, only 48% indicated entering college with adequate computer skills. As might be expected, even fewer (38%) of those in the academic middle reported having adequate computer skills. Importantly, among this group, very few had taken a computer-intensive course in high school, and more than half had not taken a beginning typing course that would provide them with keyboarding fundamentals. But remember that more than half of those graduating with academically noncompetitive credentials now enter college, where computer skills are a necessity; those who lack such skills are at an immediate disadvantage.

Experiment With Portfolios and Cooperative Learning

A portfolio is defined here as a collection of evidence or products that demonstrates a student's ability, as opposed to his or her knowledge. This emphasis on application is important for all students but is particularly successful with academically average students. Although some states, most notably Vermont, have experimented with portfolios as a replacement for more traditional high school assessment techniques, such dramatic departures from present practice probably will not occur. Instead, it is recommended that a portfolio requirement be added to current graduation requirements. Doing so sends a message to all students—even to teachers who need to get the message—that, in schools, both knowledge and ability are valued. This message has the potential to be a strong motivator of academically average youth.

Portfolios have another potential benefit: to increase the interaction of students and thus end isolation based on students' course selections. Portfolio policies can be developed to encourage collaborative or cooperative efforts that reach across program lines. The key words are collaborative/cooperative efforts and peer learning, new words for students' collaborative work in groups.

Consider Block or Intensive Master Scheduling

A block or intensive master schedule typically replaces the standard seven-period high school day with a four-period day plus lunch. Instead of being the typical 55 minutes, each period is now 90 minutes. The result is that courses normally taught over 180 days can be completed in one semester. Thus a student interested in math could take eight math courses in high school. Unlike the typical high school schedule in which students take five or six courses each semester, in this plan students typically take only three major courses. This latter point is the reason for our recommendation of block scheduling.

Whereas the academically blessed can take five or six major courses each year, less able students often cannot handle so many different courses and different demands. They do much better when they are able to concentrate on three. This has been the experience at Hatboro Horsham High School in Pennsylvania, which uses block scheduling. Teachers reported that, whereas the achievement of the best students remained high, the achievement of those in the academic middle increased significantly. Block or intensive scheduling has many other advantages as well, including significantly greater flexibility for creativity in the development of additional emphases within the college prep program of study (as recommended in Chapter 9). The major advantage, however, is that average youth are allowed to concentrate their efforts on fewer subjects during a semester.

Provide Dual Enrollment/Transition
Programs for All Students

As elaborated previously, the senior year for some students, the academically blessed in particular, has become the first year of college. Sometimes called dual enrollment, other times middle college, the result is that for some, the transition from high school starts before they graduate. This is a very powerful incentive for all teens, not just the academically blessed. Dual enrollment programs with community/technical college occupational programs have proven to be especially effective with some teens in the academic middle, including some who probably would have dropped out of school. As outlined in Chapter 9, such programs should be designed for the 30% or more of most high school graduating classes who go to work, not college. If anything, these teens face a much greater transition challenge than the college bound because good jobs do not wait until high school graduation the way the first day of college does.

Provide Alternative Curriculum
Emphasis Within the Program of Study

Finally, it is recommended once again that those seeking to create other ways to win remember that one curriculum or course sequence will not effectively prepare all teens for success after high school. Nor will a shopping mall curriculum that is a collection of courses that has no logical sequence. Just as those who seek to gain admission to the medallion colleges need AP and honors programs, those who wish to go to work need, for example, career and technical education. A suggested format is provided in Chapter 9.

SECTION III

Motivating the Academic Middle

When asked to describe those in the academic middle, high school teachers typically have some difficulty—in itself, a testimony to the invisibility of these students. The most-cited characteristic is their lack of motivation. Probed further, teachers view these students as generally taking the easiest route in order to do as little as possible. Although some are very interested in certain aspects of the high school experience, in general, they are not very interested in their course work. The accuracy of this perception is not debated here. In fact, research conducted as part of the background for this book confirmed that, compared with their more academically blessed and successful peers, this group of students is largely not engaged in the curriculum; when it comes to academics, many may as well be taking correspondence courses. The issue, then, is not whether they are unmotivated, but how to motivate them.

STRATEGIES FOR MOTIVATING THE MAJORITY

There is little doubt that the majority of those in the academic middle can be motivated. In fact, most are motivated to do many things with great enthusiasm and energy; the problem is that the list does not include schoolwork. How does one motivate these youth, then? Some suggested strategies follow.

Develop Career Motives for Learning

Unlike the academically blessed, who perform even the most irrelevant academic schoolwork out of a sense of duty or foreknowledge of their future success, those in the academic middle are not so motivated. Academic work is often difficult for them, and they have received little reward for their efforts; thus they will not make an extra effort unless they believe it can make a difference. The most important connection to help them make is that it will make a difference when they graduate. Thus we recommend that teachers of college prep courses populated by those in the academic middle make concrete efforts to relate classroom activity to probable future course work in higher education, which currently is the career goal of most in this group. This strategy has the potential for greater success if a good job has been done in developing the students' ICPs (see Chapter 8). Vocational educators have found, for example, that even the most recalcitrant and limited students can be motivated to learn basic academic skills when they see the need for them in the type of work they plan to pursue.

Have High Expectations for All Students

Throughout this book, the limited expectations of teachers for those in the academic middle have been both documented and discussed. In our view, these limited expectations ultimately limit motivation. Human nature is such that, lacking intrinsic motivation of the type developed in the first strategy mentioned previously (develop career motives for learning), most will do only what is demanded. The motivational force of such demands should not be overlooked.

At present, little is asked of students from the academic middle even when they take college prep courses. In fact, it is not uncommon for students to drop vocational education courses because they demand more work than college prep courses taken by average students. The most direct result is that when these students graduate, they end up in remedial courses that are very expensive and that predict fairly accurately that a student will not graduate from college. A more productive strategy both for students and parents is to demand more from these students: to ask them to seek personal excellence in what they do, rather than simply getting by. Most students will respond to this external motivation. Not everyone will, of course. High expectations will mean that students who in the past got C's— given as gifts by teachers to keep the peace when they should have gotten D's or even F's—will now receive the grades they deserve. This experience will cause some degree of discontent among some parents, but not only is it the ethical thing to do, it is also in the best interests of those whom it will make the most unhappy. Better a D or an F in high school that leads to plans other than pursuing a 4-year college degree than $40,000 in financial aid debt and no degree, which occurs in all too many cases.

Improve Academic Self-Concepts by Catching Students Doing Things Right

This strategy is borrowed from the book *The One Minute Manager* (Blanchard & Johnson, 1982). Those in the academic middle need more old-fashioned attention and recognition from their teachers. A key to academic motivation is a positive self-concept about one's ability. Those in the academic middle typically have a low academic self-concept and are in the college prep program because they can see no other way to win. Little wonder that these students have negative academic concepts. During their first eight years of school, teachers gave them negative feedback by catching them doing something wrong. Contrast this with the feedback received by the more academically blessed. They have had eight years of teachers catching them doing things right.

A useful example of catching people doing things right is the one used by Blanchard in the film *The One Minute Manager*, in which he asks the viewer to remember how parents act when they are trying to teach children to walk. In short, they watch for even the smallest sign of success and then praise the children. Contrast this approach with another alternative, namely, punishing a child for attempts that are anything less than perfect steps. This sort of treatment would cause most of us to still be crawling around. But the latter approach may all too often be that applied to academically average youth throughout high school. In particular, teachers should begin by positively reinforcing effort and then work on achievement by catching students making small improvements and praising these efforts.

OTHER WAYS TO WIN

In this chapter, we began by arguing that if the goal is to ensure postsecondary success for all high school graduates, then high schools must (a) stop treating all but a few students as second-class citizens and (b) take a hard look at the instructional modalities and practices within the academic/college prep curriculum now taken by most students. Specific strategies were offered to achieve both. These steps, plus the implementation of a systematic career guidance plan that includes an ICP for each student and a redesign of the college prep curriculum to include additional emphases aimed at alternative postsecondary alternatives, were recommended as ways to create other ways to win for graduating high school students, particularly those from the academic middle. All of these efforts are necessary because, as discussed in Part II of this book, the number of students who pursue a 4-year college degree in the hope that it will lead to a job in the professional ranks but end up not realizing this goal and the costs, financial and psychological, to individuals and the nation from this mass failure are staggering. But despite the costs, one is left with a nagging question: Will such changes ever take place, and will the plight of academically average youth in U.S. high schools ever become part of the mainstream of the American educational reform debate? That question is the topic of Chapter 11.

CHAPTER ELEVEN

Other Ways to Win and Success for All

> The term community should be defined not only as a region to be served but also as a climate to be created.
>
> —*The Forgotten Half*[1]

It is perhaps wise to begin this concluding chapter by again summarizing the argument for creating other ways to win that was presented in Chapter 1. And again, it is important to make the point that this is not an anti–higher education/college-bashing book. "Do not go to college" is not the message of this book for teens and parents. Instead, the intent is to document that there are alternatives to baccalaureate education that make a lot more sense for some teens. The following five points summarize this argument.

The one way to win paradigm, the message that the best hope for future economic security lies in getting a 4-year college degree that guarantees a high-paying career in the professional ranks, is not just false; it is destructive to many kids, particularly those in the academic middle of their high school class. Those who preach the one way to win mantra may have good intentions, but the result is setting the majority of teens up for failure. They either fail to graduate or, if they do graduate, fail to find commensurate employment and end up in jobs they themselves report have limited prospects and do not require a baccalaureate degree.

There are other ways to win, ways that do not require a 4-year college degree, ways that result in salaries comparable to those earned by university graduates and ways that actually provide more net opportunity, particularly for those in the academic middle.

All students should go on to some form of post–high school education/training but only (a) when and (b) if they can benefit from the experience. Postsecondary training includes 4-year baccalaureate education, but also pre-baccalaureate technical education at the certificate, diploma, and associate degree level, as well as other occupational training opportunities, such as formal apprenticeship programs, and the military.

The go-to-college message here is a qualified one. First, many teens are not ready right after high school to leave home and go to college, and many are not adequately prepared or occupationally focused to succeed. Second, some teens simply are not intellectually or emotionally equipped to do legitimate college-level academic work at the baccalaureate or any other level and never will be. Present educational policy seems to deny they exist. Yet we all know that not only do they exist but also exist in significant numbers, and they deserve some attention from their school and their country.

High schools have as much responsibility to teens who are at risk of dropping out of high school and those who want to go immediately to work after graduation as they do to the 4-year college bound. Those who have a pejorative attitude toward teens who do something other than pursue a 4-year college degree should rethink this prejudice; it is just plain wrong, it is unethical, and it is destructive. These kids (a) are the majority and (b) are just as deserving as the academically blessed.

The traditional academic program of study alone is not likely to serve well those in the academic middle who, after graduation, go directly to work or on to pre-baccalaureate technical education or some other form of postsecondary occupational education. If anything, academic courses alone will increase the dropout rate in most schools. Leaving no child behind in today's high schools requires alternatives for teens with different ambitions and talents, alternative transitional pathways that prepare teens for other ways to win.

THE AMERICAN HIGH SCHOOL

Creating alternatives for graduating high school seniors should be a constant educational concern. Currently, this is not the case. Events at a meeting of a local school's strategic planning committee observed by one of the authors exemplify this situation. The purpose of the meeting was to develop questions for a follow-up benchmarking survey of recent high school graduates, much like the Follow-Up Study referred to in this book.

The leader of the group opened the meeting by asking a rather straightforward question: what did members of the group want to know about their graduates that could be asked on a questionnaire? Everyone took a posture of involved thought: Some looked at the ceiling thoughtfully; others rummaged through the handouts for the meeting. Clearly, no one wanted to speak up first. All were waiting for or deferring to those with power in the group to set the tone and direction of the meeting. They did not have to wait long. The superintendent of schools cleared his throat and gave the group his most wise posture; clearly, he was ready to deliver a question of immense significance. Everyone waited expectantly. "I wonder," said the superintendent, who then paused briefly to build the suspense, "what happens to our kids who take calculus in high school?"

From then on, the rest of the meeting was predictable. Attention focused solely on the academically blessed. One member asked a question that pertained to students who went to work after graduation. Although everyone noted that this question was a concern, it clearly was not too great a concern, as the topic was quickly dropped. No one ever raised a concern about those in the middle group. This group had no advocates at this meeting, nor do they almost anywhere else.

This scenario is played out in various ways day after day in U.S. schools. According to the National Center for Education Statistics (NCES) (2000c), only 16% of all graduates take calculus in high school. Only about 40% complete a rigorous academic program of high-level math, science, and language courses. But this minority receives a disproportionate share of the resources, most of the attention, and virtually all of the recognition from high schools. And while No Child Left Behind (NCLB)–mandated state testing may have led to attention given to the less academically blessed, in all too many cases, it has led only to many of these teens being viewed as failures who make the rest of the school look bad when test results come in.

The purpose of this book is to bring to center stage the plight of the less blessed, those in the academic middle. Instead of asking about the academically blessed, we investigated the situations of the others. Research suggests that for every student who graduates with academic credentials suggesting readiness to do legitimate college-level academics, two do not. Thus it has been argued that the relevant question is not what happens to the one in three who heads to a college of his or her choice; data suggest these teens are mostly doing just fine. The relevant question is this: what happens to the other two in that ratio? In this case, data suggest that all is not well.

One of our particular concerns is those in the academic middle of U.S. high schools—the "unspecial," meaning those who are neither special needs students protected by legislation and taught in small classes by specially trained staff nor the academically gifted who are rewarded with the best teachers in equally small classes. Data suggest that, by and large, those in the academic middle of U.S. high schools are seriously adrift. They face a very uncertain future and get little help in preparing for it. The only message provided to them and their parents by the schools and seemingly everyone else is that there is only one way to win: trying to get a 4-year college degree in the hope that it will lead to a job in the professional ranks. As documented in this book, most who follow this advice fail.

Challenging the One Way to Win Paradigm

The one way to win paradigm is largely a myth—the belief that future economic security can only be gained from obtaining a 4-year degree that will lead to a job in the professions—is, like all myths, mostly fiction with a dash of truth. Since the early 1980s, this widely held myth has been accepted almost without question by nearly everyone. Data from national surveys of graduating high school seniors demonstrate the wide acceptance of the myth. In such surveys, 94.7% report that they are planning to continue their education, 83.9% at the 4-year baccalaureate level. When asked to name the occupation they expect to be in at age 30, 49.3% of males and 68.8% of females cite "professional." Virtually all high school youth have the same career plan, the path recommended by the one way to win myth.

The one way to win message pressed on youth regardless of academic ability or interests comes from all sectors of society, especially since the NCLB legislation, but most notably, the message comes from parents and educators. According to an NCES study,

82.9% of high school sophomores reported that their mothers were recommending college, compared with 64.8% just 10 years before. Although parents may not be objective when it comes to their children's future, one might expect high school teachers and guidance counselors to be more so, particularly in advising academically marginal students to pursue interests other than a baccalaureate degree program. But data suggest the opposite. Between 1982 and 1992, the percentage of high school sophomores who said their teachers and counselors were recommending college doubled from 32.3% to more than 65%.

No doubt, both parents and high school faculty have students' best interests in mind. Their advice is based on a belief that today there is only one way to win. Unfortunately, they are misled and are giving well-intended but nonetheless poor advice to those in the academic middle. Although their intent is to ensure that adolescents will be winners in life, the advice they give often ensures the opposite for those in the academic middle. Instead, it ensures that they become a part of the college dropout or underemployment statistics.

The first hint that the one way to win advice may not be suitable for all is that among those who pursue a 4-year college degree, at best only half ever graduate. A close look at the academic credentials of high school graduates reveals the reason. The implicit assumption of those who indiscriminately provide one way to win advice to today's youth—that everyone is academically qualified to do college-level academic work—is not true. Viewed from a national perspective, only about 40% of those graduating from U.S. high schools have the credentials that predict readiness to do legitimate college-level work (see Figure 4.1). Thus, when a national average of 60%–70% go directly on to higher education, it is clear that many who are admitted are simply unprepared, and there is little or no evidence that state-mandated testing that began in earnest across the nation long before NCLB has improved the situation at all.

Most of those who begin a 4-year college program academically unprepared spend their freshman year in college taking remedial courses. Although most colleges do not willingly publicize the percentage of incoming freshmen taking remedial courses, available data suggest that it is not uncommon today to find 50% of freshmen at some 4-year degree–granting institutions having to take one or more remedial courses. Although colleges do their best to put a positive spin on these courses, the fact is that they are the first predictor that the majority who take them will not graduate. Most ultimately cool out or fade away. The result is predictable: nationally, of those who start a 4-year degree program, at best only half have graduated not four, not five, but six years later. And which are most likely to drop out—the academically blessed or the academic middle? Although admittedly too many of the academically blessed drop out, particularly in their freshman year, the likelihood is that most graduate in four years. Those from the middle, however, are the most likely never to graduate and probably should have considered other postsecondary alternatives, such as a 1- or 2-year technical program or a school-to-career option.

The second flaw in the one way to win advice is the scarcity of college-level jobs for those who do graduate. In the 1960s, only one in five 4-year college graduates failed to find college-level work. In the 1990s, it was one in three; in the professions, such as accounting or teaching, it was one in two. Again, the important point to ponder is this: who is at greatest risk of not finding college-level work even after graduating? Is it the academically blessed who graduate from the most prestigious colleges with the best-connected alumni, or those from the academic middle who squeak through in five or six years and graduate from second-tier colleges? In the 1980s, big-name corporations, for example, recruited at more than 40 campuses; now they recruit at only a few prestigious and competitive colleges and universities. The likelihood that those from the academic middle will ever graduate from any of these institutions is next to none. Thus those in the academic middle are the most at risk of being frustrated in realizing professional jobs in major corporations, even if they graduate from college. Such findings lead to the conclusion that the one way to win paradigm, though good advice for the academically blessed, is largely a myth for those from the academic middle. For those in this group who follow such advice, losers—those who drop out or end up underemployed and frustrated—will outnumber winners.

The third fault with the one way to win myth is its cost, which, in both unmet expectations and monetary terms, is huge. The number of underemployed college graduates who hold jobs they could have gotten after high school or who are returning to a 2-year technical postsecondary program to acquire occupational skills to get a decent job increases each year. Unfortunately, many of these young adults who cannot find college-level work have student loan debts to pay off. The dilemma is this: fewer families can afford this cost of education. The growth in the student loan debt is evidence of families' growing inability to pay. This situation, accompanied by a national debt of approximately $4 trillion, leads us to wonder how much longer the United States will be able to provide such loans to so many persons without stricter criteria about recipients' abilities to do college-level work.

Finally, there is the unmeasured human cost to youth who early in life sense that the only valued thing to do after high school graduation—pursue a 4-year college degree—is clearly beyond their ability or what they can imagine as possible and thus give up. The need is for alternatives, for other ways to win that can be effectively communicated to them and valued as ways to develop all our human resources. The one way to win myth makes it all too easy for policy makers, teachers, and just about everyone else to ignore the needs of half of all kids in high school. The preoccupation with college makes it easy to forget that now one-third of youth drop out of high school, and of those who graduate, 30% go directly to work. The idea that more academic rigor and more testing will help these Americans is nothing but nonsense.

THERE ARE OTHER WAYS TO WIN

There are alternatives, other ways to win, other routes to financial security and rewarding careers that should be particularly relevant to those in the academic middle, those most at risk of losing if they pursue the one way to win myth. This argument is developed in detail in Chapter 7. Suffice it to say that if the goal is an economically and personally rewarding career, the goal should not be education per se but rather gaining the requisite skills necessary to compete for high skill/high wage work. The advice that such work can only be obtained with a baccalaureate degree is not true. Many high skill/high wage occupations in technical fields do not require a baccalaureate degree. Just as high skill/high wage professional work requires prerequisite skills, so too do these occupations require specific occupational skills. Unlike professional work, however, for which requisite skills are certified by baccalaureate or graduate school degrees, the skills required to obtain technician-level employment can be learned either in 1- and 2-year postsecondary technical programs or in school-to-career programs that include formal work-based preparation.

How well do these jobs pay? According to U.S. Department of Labor data, they pay very well. For example, individuals who successfully pursue high skill/high wage occupations, particularly in the occupational group identified as craft, precision metal, and specialized repair, as well as certain technical occupations in health and engineering, will earn more than all college graduates except for those baccalaureate degree holders who successfully pursue careers in the managerial or professional ranks. Meanwhile, unlike the more glamorous managerial and professional occupations, the demand for skilled workers in these fields greatly exceeds the supply.

Thus there is another way to win, namely, obtaining the prerequisite skills for competing for high skill/high wage work that does not require a BA degree. The challenge is to reform the schools to motivate those in the academic middle to pursue these alternative ways to win, redesign the high school curriculum to increase their propensity for success, and do it so well that parents will want their children to be involved. But will such efforts work?

Will Efforts to Create Alternatives Succeed?

Although veteran high school educators, especially those who teach college prep courses to academically average students, will readily admit a need for alternatives, their encounters with parents, school boards, elected officials, and so forth may well leave them skeptical about the viability of efforts to change the situation. As one counselor interviewed for this book put it, "Whenever I mention 2-year education to parents, I see their eyes glaze over. They have their minds set on a 4-year college." This counselor expresses a reality that cannot be denied.

The present mind-set in favor of 4-year college education will negate efforts to create alternatives for those in the academic middle of U.S. high schools. But at the same time, it has been documented that providing only the 4-year alternative ensures that more than half who try it will fail and that the cost of this failure is terribly high. Thus, although the obstacles may be formidable, the need to create other ways to win is great. A design for creating these alternatives is presented in Chapters 8, 9, and 10. The recommendations are designed to meet the need to create openness to alternatives, as well as an academic program to ensure that those who choose these alternatives are successful.

REACHING OUT TO PARENTS

Parents are arguably the most critical variable in determining success of efforts to create alternatives for those in the academic middle. Survey research found that 82.9% of high school sophomores mention at least their mother as the individual recommending college. The unavoidable conclusion is that involving parents of academically average youth in secondary course selection and postsecondary planning is critical. These parents must be given objective data about probabilities of their child's success in different postsecondary alternatives and the financial costs involved. In Chapter 8, a number of strategies are suggested for involving parents. Parents must be involved in the ICP process, especially the points at the end of the 9th, 10th, and 11th grades when a student's plans can be matched with his or her academic record.

At first, the majority of parents can be expected to resist anything but a 4-year college degree for their children. Aside from genuine concern about the economic future of their children, many parents are sometimes under intense social pressure to have their children attend a 4-year college. But conditions are changing. Very few individuals can afford to send their children to college without borrowing money or taking out a second mortgage. Meanwhile, they are well aware from personal or friends' experience that many who graduate from college do not find the expected high-paying job waiting for them. The net result is that more parents are willing to consider alternatives, particularly if their child is not a great student.

CAREER DEVELOPMENT AND
GUIDANCE FOR ALL STUDENTS

The successful creation of other ways to win for those from the academic middle requires a systematic program of career development/guidance. This plan requires the involvement of both students and parents in its formulation and in structured "thoughtful confrontation" of career aspirations and academic achievement. Although the evidence for the need to create other ways to win for high school students from the academic middle is overwhelming, this in no way ensures the success of efforts. It is quite possible that much effort will be invested in redesigning the college prep program of study to include new emphases for those in the academic middle, only to have no one elect to take them.

Career development and guidance are equally critical in helping students and parents make postsecondary plans. Whereas most teens indicate that they plan to go college in order to "get a good-paying job," a career choice should be the foundation for making postsecondary plans. Most important, the focus or commitment that comes from having a career motive for pursuing higher education is now the most powerful factor predicting whether a student will graduate and find commensurate employment.

Career development/guidance programs should have three goals. First, by the 10th grade, the student should have identified one or more related career interests as the basis for course selection in grades 11 and 12. In the junior and senior years of high school, students should have the opportunity to verify these tentative choices as a basis for making postsecondary plans. Finally, all students should graduate with a postsecondary plan that has a high probability of success so that their hopes and dreams will be realized when they do.

Although career guidance is important for all students, it is important to understand the role it plays in ensuring the success of efforts to create other ways to win. The target groups of students in our discussion, those from the academic middle, are the most likely to exhibit the signs of career immaturity. They do not know what to do, so they take what they see as the only alternative and passively prepare to go to 4-year colleges. They will continue to select this option unless an effort is made to develop a process in which they are forced to confront the realities of their plans and are provided with alternatives. They may still choose to pursue the one way to win myth. In fact, at first, most of them will; but over time, their involvement in a systematic career guidance program structured to provide them with data about the reality of their plans will lead them more and more to choose the two new options recommended to be included within a broad college preparatory curriculum.

CREATING MULTIPLE PATHWAYS TO SUCCESS

Creating other ways to win calls for doing things differently in U.S. high schools, particularly in the so-called college prep curriculum now elected by more and more academically average youth. Faced with the political reality that they cannot bar these youth from taking college prep courses and that failing most of them is also not an option, high school educators will have two choices. First, they can pretend that these teens are, in fact, preparing for college and let them slide through unchallenged and unprepared. Second, they can reform the college prep program of study to make it more instructionally effective for average students. Ethically, there is no choice. Doing nothing means continuing the downward spiral of these youth, leading to their enrollment in remedial courses at 4-year colleges and later dropping out after having collected significant levels of student loan debt. It is time to redesign the college prep program of study.

Specific recommendations to reform college prep are offered in Chapters 9 and 10. The redesign proposal centers on adding different emphases within the academic/college prep program of study and moving away from the shopping mall approach to a significantly more structured, sequential, and articulated curriculum.

In Chapter 9, we argued that virtually every high school in the United States has already bifurcated its college prep curriculum into two emphases—the highly structured and demanding honors/advanced placement emphasis and a mostly unstructured, undemanding, unarticulated potpourri of college prep courses. We recommended two additional emphases. One prepares students to make the transition to, and to be successful in, 1- or 2-year postsecondary technical education programs that lead to high skill/high wage work. We call this the "pre-baccalaureate technical postsecondary emphasis." The other is a school-to-career option. The goal of this emphasis is to prepare students to make the transition to, and to be successful in, one of a variety of employer-sponsored employer/worker group training programs in high skill/high wage occupations that now require academic skills commensurate with those taught in the college prep academic program.

It is important to assert here that these recommendations to add different emphases within the academic/college preparatory curriculum are not intended to make the education of the academically average student less rigorous or inferior. The intent is to make it different in the junior and senior years in order to prepare students to successfully pursue different postsecondary alternatives.

The redesign proposal calls for a departure from the take-what-you-want philosophy of student course selection that has predominated since the 1970s. We advocate the structuring of these emphases, meaning that students will follow a well-planned sequence of articulated courses, and at the completion of one of the emphases by each student, the high school will be expected to recommend him or her to higher education institutions. The message to students and parents is this: complete one of the four emphases if you expect the school to recommend you for any form of higher education.

This message may sound like too strong an assertion, especially to those who started their educational careers in the 1970s, during the advent of the shopping mall high school. Many may think that parents would not support a directive approach. National survey data suggest the opposite. The authors of a study conducted by the Public Agenda Foundation (Walsch, 1994) concluded that educators might be out of sync with parents on a variety of issues, including the degree of structure in the curriculum. Those in the sample were asked whether they believed that setting up clear guidelines on what students should learn and what teachers should teach in every major subject so that students and teacher know what is expected would improve academic achievement. Both the general public and parents overwhelmingly agreed, including 92% of parents of African-American students. The public wants structure! We believe that parents of high school students would welcome clearly defined programs of academic courses that lead directly to alternative types of postsecondary education or other options.

In Chapter 10, we suggested strategies designed to make instruction within these four emphases more effective for academically average youth. Many of these strategies, such as emphasizing reading for understanding and mastery of computer software skills (e.g., word processing), are applicable to all. Other proposals, such as ensuring that all students take math and science in their senior year, are clearly aimed at those in the academic middle, who are the least likely to be found in these classes during their last year in high school. Their absence often results in the need to enroll in remedial courses in college.

One significant obstacle to effective educational redesign for those in the academic middle is the fact that they have been largely written off by some veteran high school teachers as unmotivated and lazy. Thus in Chapter 10, we present strategies to motivate those from the academic middle. Although a number of approaches to motivating these students exist, they all begin with changing the treatment of these students in high school. Currently, those in the academic middle are largely relegated to second- or spectator-class status. Thus, why should anyone be surprised by their lack of motivation? Efforts to create other ways to win will work only if this aspect of the high school culture can be changed.

CHALLENGING THE HIGH SCHOOL CULTURE

The creation of alternatives for average youth will not occur without a groundswell of concern about this group from teachers, administrators, and school boards and without a willingness to try to change Taylorist attitudes. Creating other ways to win in U.S. high schools will require much work and the courage to stimulate much more thoughtful confrontation by parents and students regarding the reality of postsecondary plans. None of this will happen or will be effective without a change in attitude among high school educators about the relative importance of average youth. The policies and cultures of most high schools favor the intellectually blessed.

Taylorism is alive and well in U.S. high schools. As long as it prevails, average youth will remain invisible and unmotivated.

Clearly, in the distribution of school resources, those in the middle do not receive their fair share. As reported earlier, even the courts are taking note of discriminatory practices such as weighted grading systems, disproportionate class sizes, and disproportionate allocation of resources and guidance services. These inequities have been tolerated for years because of the Taylorist attitude that the academically blessed are more important to society and therefore deserve special treatment. This is an old, unfair idea that needs to be challenged. It represents a form of intellectual bigotry that should not be tolerated.

Another aspect of challenging the culture is taking an honest look at the college prep program of study and recognizing its deficiencies. It needs to be redesigned. We see promising signs that high school educators sense this need. The rather quick spread of tech prep efforts across the United States can be interpreted as evidence that high school administrators, counselors, and teachers are well aware that the academic complexion of those who now take the college prep curriculum has changed and that something needs to be done.

One final element of the high school culture that needs to be challenged is the widespread belief in the one way to win myth by a majority of teachers and counselors. Data reported earlier indicate that the number of high school students who say their teachers and counselors advised them to go to college has doubled in the past 10 years. Considering the absence of evidence that the number of students who are academically prepared to do college work has doubled, we must assume that most teachers and counselors have bought the one way to win myth. They also have been convinced that getting a 4-year degree is the only hope for attaining success in society and therefore appear to be advising all but a very few students to give it a try.

We hope this book provides the reader with an understanding of the myth of one way to win. Educators who advise students on postsecondary plans have an obligation to know what they are talking about. According to the facts, there are other ways to win in which the propensity for success both in postsecondary education and future economic security is a lot higher for those in the academic middle. Those who seek to create other ways to win must challenge the prejudice that school staff have in favor of the 4-year baccalaureate degree. Educators must understand that, for the majority of youth in their schools, pursuit of a 4-year degree is a very risky proposition.

Doing What's Right

This book was written to draw attention to students in the academic middle of U.S. high schools. We sought to expose the false complacency that emanates from the belief that if only most youth would enroll in the college prep program of study and go to 4-year colleges in record numbers, then all would be well. On the contrary, data reveal that, for the majority, all is not well: Of those who go to college unprepared, most fail either literally or fail to meet their aspirations to obtain professional jobs, and they often suffer great financial and personal costs in the process. But even if no costs were involved, educators have a professional obligation to treat all students equally.

Clearly, those in the academic middle are not receiving their fair share of high school educational resources. Those from the academic middle have a right to equal attention, resources, and—when deserved—recognition. Their successes and failures are just as important to the larger society, to the community, and to their families as those of the academically blessed, and they should be just as important to their high school as well. And once again, let us not forget that one-third of entering high school ninth graders drop out of high school.

This chapter began with an account of a school district planning meeting. The dialogue at this meeting began with questions, not about the majority, but about how the few who took calculus were doing in college. This little scenario illustrates the preoccupation of public schools with the academically blessed and is played out in differing ways day after day, week after week, in U.S. high schools. It would have been significant if someone had said, "I think our real concern should be the students who did not take calculus." These students should take the center stage in the educational debate. These students need advocates. Maybe you will be one. Maybe the next time attention turns to the academically blessed, you will voice some interest and/or concern about the rest. After all, it is the right thing to do. It is the right thing to do for the adolescents involved and for attaining the appropriate balance of human resource development for the 21st century.

NOTE

1. W. T. Grant Foundation: Commission on Work, Family, and Citizenship. (1998, January). *The forgotten half: Non-college youth in America*. Washington, DC: Author.

References

Adelman, C. (1999). *Answers in the tool box: Academic intensity, attendance patterns and bachelors degree attainment*. Washington, DC: U.S. Department of Education.

American Council on Education. (2004). *The American freshman national norms for fall 2004*. Washington, DC: Author.

Anderson, E. (1990). *Street wise: Race, class, and change in urban communities*. Chicago: University of Chicago Press.

Anderson, L. (1983, December). Policy implications of research on school time. *The School Administrator*, 25–28.

Barton, P. (1994, April). *Indicators of the school-to-work transition*. Princeton, NJ: Educational Testing Service, Policy Information Center.

Blanchard, K., & Johnson, S. (1982). *The one minute manager*. New York: Morrow.

Boesel, D., & Fredland, E. (1999). *College for all? Is there too much emphasis on getting a four-year degree?* Washington, DC: National Library of Education Research and Improvement, U.S. Department of Education.

Bottoms, G., Pressons, A., & Johnson, M. (1992). *Making high school work*. Atlanta, GA: SREB.

Boyer, E. L., Altbach, P. G., & Whitelaw, M. J. (1994). *The academic profession: An international perspective*. Princeton, NJ: Carnegie Foundation for the Advantagement of Teaching.

Brooks, D. (2000). *Bobos in paradise*. New York: Simon & Schuster.

Campbell, C., & Dahir, C. (1997). *Sharing the vision: The national standards for school counseling programs*. Alexandria, VA: American School Counselor Association.

Carnevale, A., & Desrochers, M. (2001). *Help wanted, credentials required: Community colleges in the knowledge economy*. Annapolis, MD: Community College Press.

Carnevale, A., Gainer, L., & Villet, J. (1990). *Training in America*. San Francisco: Jossey-Bass.

Chew, C. (1993). *Tech-prep and counseling: A resource guide*. Madison: University of Wisconsin, Center on Education and Work.

Clark, B. (1962). The "cooling out" function in higher education. *The American Journal of Sociology, 65,* 576–596.

Cole, M. (1988). *Bowles and Gintis revisited.* New York: Faler Press.

College Board. (2004). *Trends in college pricing 2004.* Princeton, NJ: Author.

Dewey, J. (1900, April). Psychology of occupation [Monograph No. 3]. *Elementary School Record.*

Dykeman, C., Wood, C., Ingram M., Pehrsson, D., Mandsager, N., & Herr, E. (2003). The structure of school career development interventions: Implications for school counselors. *Professional School Counseling, 6*(4), 272–278.

Eck, A. (1993, October 4). Job-related education and training: Their impact on earnings. *Monthly Labor Review, 116,* 21–38.

Engle, S. (2004). *College completion declining, taking longer.* Los Angeles: Higher Education Research Institute. Retrieved August 12, 2005, from www.gseis.ucla.edu/heri/darcu_pr.html

Finegold, D. (1993, March). *Making apprenticeships work* (RAND Issues Paper). Santa Monica, CA: Institute on Education and Training at RAND.

Fussell, P. (1983). *Class: A guide through the American status system.* New York: Simon & Schuster.

Garten, J. (2002, June 17). When everything is made in China. *Business Week,* p. 20.

Gelatt, H. B. (1989). Positive uncertainty: A new decision-making framework for counseling. *Journal of Counseling Psychology, 36*(2), 252–256.

General Accounting Office. (1991). *Characteristics of defaulted borrowers in the Stafford student loan program* (Publication No. HRD-91-82BR). Washington, DC: Author.

Gray, K. (1980). *Support for industrial education by the national association of manufacturers: 1895–1917.* Unpublished doctoral dissertation, Virginia Polytechnic Institute, Blacksburg.

Gray, K. (1993, January). Why we will loose: Taylorism in the America's high schools. *Phi Delta Kappan, 72*(5), 370–374.

Gray, K. (2000). *Getting real: Helping teens find their future.* Thousand Oaks, CA: Corwin.

Gray, K., & Wang, D. (1989). An analysis of the firm size variable in youth employment using the NLS-Y data base. *Journal of Vocational Education Research, 14*(4), 35–49.

Gray, K., & Xiaoli, S. (1999). *A benchmarking study of the Class of 1998.* Unpublished research manuscript, Pennsylvania State University, University Park.

Greene, J. (2002, April). *High school graduation rates in the United States.* Manhattan Institute for Policy Research. Retrieved August 11, 2005, from www.manhattan-institute.org/html/cr_baeo.htm

Gross, K. (2004, December 3). For student loan borrowers, good credit where it's due. *The Chronicle of Higher Education,* p. B16

Haney, W., Madaus, G., Wheelock, A., Miao, J., & Gruia, I. (2004). *The education pipeline in the United States 1970–2000* (The National Board on Educational Testing and Public Policy Report). Retrieved August 9, 2005, from http://www.bc.edu/research/nbetpp/statements/nbr3.pdf

Harvey, M. (2002). Comparison of post-secondary transitional outcomes between students with and without disabilities. *Career Development for Exceptional Individuals, 25*, 99–122.

Hecker, D. (2001, November). Occupational employment projections to 2010. *Monthly Labor Review, 124*(11), 57–84.

Hecker, D. (2004, February). Occupational employment projections to 2012. *Monthly Labor Review, 127*(2), 80–105.

Herr, E. (1995). *Counseling employment bound youth.* Greensboro: University of North Carolina at Greensboro, CAPS Publication.

Herr, E., Cramer, S., & Niles, S. G. (2004). *Career guidance and counseling through the life span: Systematic approaches* (6th ed.). Boston: Allyn & Bacon.

Hilton, M. (1991). Shared training: Learning from Germany. *Monthly Labor Review, 114*(3), 33–37.

Holland, J. L. (1985). *Making vocational choices: A theory of vocational personalities and work environments* (2nd ed.). Englewood Cliffs, NJ: Prentice Hall.

Hossler, D., & Stage, F. (1992). Family and high school experience influences on the postsecondary educational plans of ninth-grade students. *American Educational Research Journal, 29*(2), 425–451.

Hoyt, K. B. (1994). A proposal for making transition from schooling to employment an important component of educational reform. In A. Pautler (Ed.), *High school to employment transition: Contemporary issues* (pp. 189–200). Ann Arbor, MI: Prakken Publications.

Jepsen, D. (1989). Adolescent career decision processes as coping responses for the social environment. In R. Hanson (Ed.), *Career development: Preparing for the 21st century* (Chapter 6). Knoxville: University of Tennessee.

Kemple, J., & Scott-Clayton, J. (2004). *Career academies: Impact on labor market outcomes and educational attainment.* New York: MDRC Publications. Retrieved August 9, 2005, from www.mdrc.org

Lovett, C. (2005, January 21). The perils of pursuing prestige. *The Chronicle of Higher Education*, p. B20.

McCormick, A., & Knepper, P. (1996). *A descriptive summary of bachelor's degree recipients one year later* (NCES Publication No. 96-158). Washington, DC: U.S. Department of Education.

Merriam-Webster's collegiate dictionary (11th ed.). (2004). Springfield, MA: Merriam-Webster.

Mohammed, A. (1998). *Participation in vocational education and under-employment among U.S. high school graduates.* Unpublished doctoral dissertation, Pennsylvania State University, University Park.

Monastersky, R. (2004, July 9). Is there a science crisis? Maybe not. *The Chronicle of Higher Education.* Retrieved August 18, 2005, from http://chronicle.com/weekly/v50/i44/44a01001.htm

Mosisa, A. (2002, May). The role of foreign-born workers in the U.S. economy. *Monthly Labor Review, 125*(5), 3–14.

National Center for Education Statistics (NCES). (1988). *National educational longitudinal study of 1988* (NCES Publication No. 92-084). Washington, DC: U.S. Department of Education.

National Center for Education Statistics. (1992). *Digest of educational statistics* (NCES Publication No. 93-299). Washington, DC: U.S. Department of Education.

National Center for Education Statistics. (1998). *Condition of education 1998* (NCES Publication No. 98-013). Washington, DC: U.S. Department of Education.

National Center for Education Statistics. (2000a). *College quality and the earnings of recent college graduates,* NCES 2000-043. By R. A. Fitzgerald. Washington, DC: U.S. Department of Education. Retrieved August 18, 2005 from http://nces.ed.gov/pubs2000/2000043.pdf

National Center for Education Statistics. (2000b). *Remedial education at degree granting institutions.* Table 4. NCES 2004010.

National Center for Education Statistics. (2000c). The nation's report card, math report card. Retrieved August 21, 2005, from http://nces.ed.gov/nationsreportcard/pdf/main2000/2001517b.pdf

National Center for Educational Statistics (2001). *The 1998 high school transcript study tabulations: Comparative data on credits earned and demographics for 1998, 1994, 1990, 1987, and 1982 high school graduates.* NCES 2001-498. Retrieved December 31, 2005, from http://nces.ed.gov/pubs2001/2001498_1.pdf

National Center for Education Statistics. (2005). *College persistence on rise (1994–2000),* NCES 2005-156. Washington, DC: U.S. Department of Education.

Naylor, R., Jr. (1994, September 1). Education gap widens to form anxious class. *Patriot News,* p. A4.

Noel, L., & Levitz, R. (Eds.). (1985). *Increasing student retention.* San Francisco: Jossey-Bass.

Oakes, J. (1985). *Keeping track: How schools structure inequality.* New Haven, CT: Yale University Press.

Office of Education Research and Development. (1991). *National longitudinal study of 1988 second follow-up.* Washington, DC: U.S. Department of Education.

Passmore, D., Wall, J., & Harvey, M. (1996). *Community cost of technical skills deficits: A Pennsylvania case study.* Occasional paper, Pennsylvania State University, University Park, Workforce Education and Development Program.

Pennsylvania Economy League. (1996). *Building a world-class technical workforce.* Philadelphia: Author.

Plank, S. (2001). *Career and technical education in the balance: An analysis of high school persistence, academic achievement, and postsecondary destinations.* Columbus: Ohio State University, National Center for Dissemination.

Powell, A., Farrar, E., & Cohen, D. (1985). *The shopping mall high school* (National Association of Secondary School Principals and the Commission on Educational Issues of the National Association of Independent Schools). Boston: Houghton Mifflin.

Rothstein, R. (1997). *Where the money goes* Washington, DC: Economic Policy Institute.

Roueche, J., & Roueche, S. (1999). *High stakes, high performance: Making remedial education work.* Washington, DC: Community College Press.

Roy, R. (1992, June 7). One science myth down, many to go. *Centre Daily Times* (State College, PA), p. A-5.

Samuelson, R. (1991, June 24). The school reform fraud. *Newsweek*, p. 44.

Schmidt, P. (1994, October 5). Amherst schools urged to drop ability grouping. *Education Week*, p. 1.

Schmidt, P. (1999, July 2). A state transforms colleges with performance funding. *The Chronicle of Higher Education*, pp. A26–A27.

Sedlak, L. (1986). *Selling students short.* New York: Teachers College Press.

Silvestri, G. (1997, November). Occupational employment projections to 2006. *Monthly Labor Review*, *120*, 58–83.

Stern, M. (1992, June 29). Employer survey. *Adult and Continuing Education Today*, *22*, 25.

Sternberg, L., & Tuchscherer, J. (1992, May). Women in non-traditional careers: Setting them up to succeed. *Vocational Education Journal*, pp. 33–35.

Taylor, F. (1911). *The principles of scientific management.* New York: Harper & Row.

Terrell, K. (1992). Female-male earnings differentials and occupational structure. *International Labor Organization*, *131*(4–5), 387–405.

Thurow, L. (1992). *Head to head: The coming economic battle among Japan, Europe and America.* New York: William Morrow.

Thurow, L. (1996). *The future of capitalism.* New York: William Morrow.

Thurow, L. (2003). *Fortune favors the bold: What we must do to build a new and lasting global prosperity.* New York: HarperCollins.

Uchitelle, L. (2005, January 13). College degree still pays but it's leveling off. *The New York Times*, p. 1, section C.

U.S. Department of Education. (1994). *National assessment of vocational education: Interim report*. Washington, DC: Author.

Vocational Training News. (2004, December). *Education stresses college prep track for all students,* p. 1. West Palm Beach, FL: LRP Publications.

Walsch, M. (1994, October 12). School experts found out of sync with public. *Education Week*, p. 6.

Weiner, K., & Oakes, J. (1996). Liability grouping: New susceptibility of school tracking systems to legal challenges. *Harvard Educational Review, 66*(3), 451–470.

Index

CORWIN
PRESS

The Corwin Press logo—a raven striding across an open book—represents the union of courage and learning. Corwin Press is committed to improving education for all learners by publishing books and other professional development resources for those serving the field of PreK–12 education. By providing practical, hands-on materials, Corwin Press continues to carry out the promise of its motto: **"Helping Educators Do Their Work Better."**